Yoga inVision 2

subtle body
right hand clutching
stub kundalini

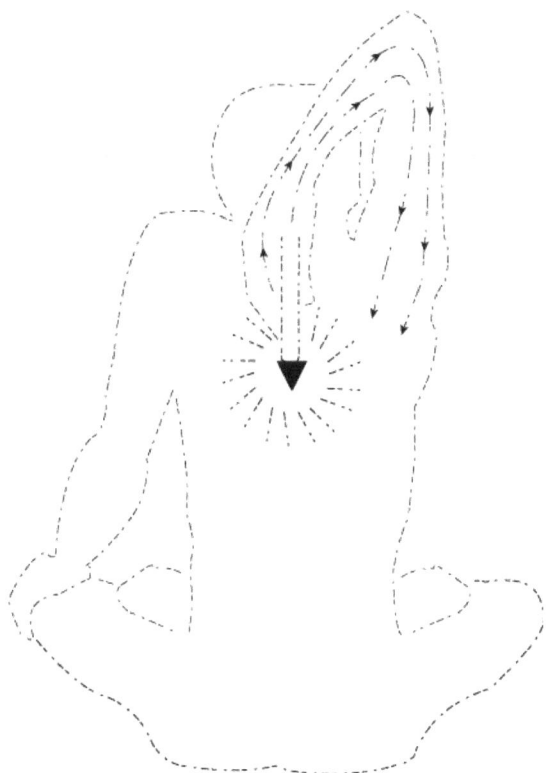

I0140433

Michael Beloved

Shiva Art: Sir Paul Castagna
Illustrations: Author
Correspondence:
Michael Beloved
19311 SW 30th Street
Miramar FL 33029
USA
Email: axisnexus@gmail.com
              michaelbelovedbooks@gmail.com

Paperback ISBN: 9781942887096
ebook ISBN 9781942887119
LCCN: 2017911175

Table of Contents

INTRODUCTION

This is the second in the series of Yoga inVision transcendent experiences reports.

Over the years, I noticed that small details which were important at one stage, lose their significance at a higher stage, when those small developments are integrated in the larger scope of yoga.

By making these notation, I show what a yoga progression could be and thus encouraged readers who were in doubt about the validly of the numerous experiences had by a practicing yogin.

Everyone will have to start where he or she is, and work the way up to the higher stages. It may be painstaking for some and rapid for others. By keeping notes of the practice, one may from time to time, review the progress and gain confidence to continue.

Even though many of my experiences are standard and may match exactly what was described by ancient yogis, many of them are irregular and do not match established conventions. This is because my destiny is to a degree unique. Yours is too. Hence you may have totally different experiences. Still the similarity should be progression.

Part 1

Shiva

He gave some gayatri locations used by some technique yogins. Using these, the limited spirit, being tiny, faces the deities from the back of the body. They are in the front of the body looking to the back. This is a diagram of the causal cove and the locations of each deity.

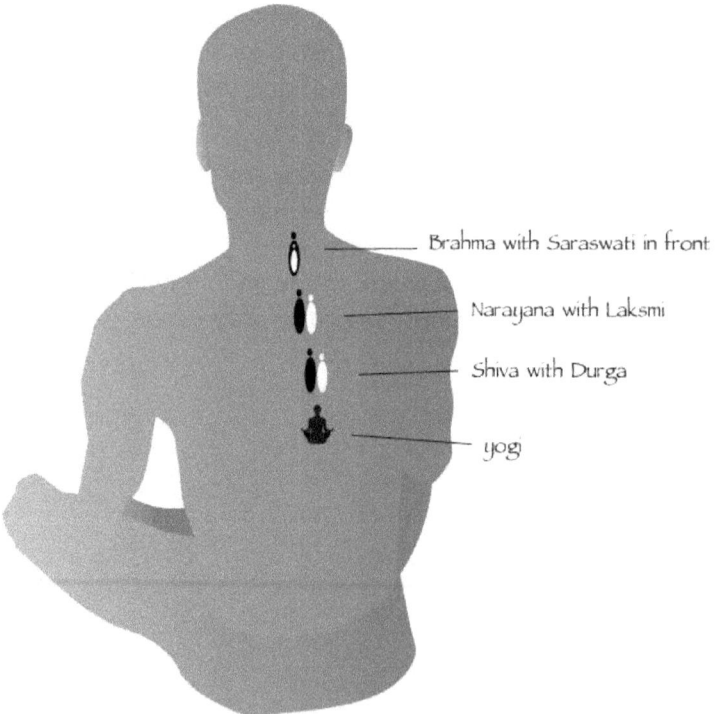

Brahma with Saraswati in front

Narayana with Laksmi

Shiva with Durga

yogi

Agastya

He introduced the idea of Pranavayu, a female deity. Generally it is felt that Pranavayu is a male supernatural being. A beginner feels this way since usually beginners use male bodies and aspire to transcend if not eliminate their attraction to female forms. Subsequently they display bias towards females. From that they derive a feeling that Pranavayu is a male entity. Agastya revealed her as a female with the nurturing power which is usually exhibited by human women. It is through this nurture energy that beginners continue doing pranayama breath-infusion of various sorts and make advancement, otherwise they would not succeed.

Shiva

He gave a technique for concentrating subtle energy from an intellect pull-down.

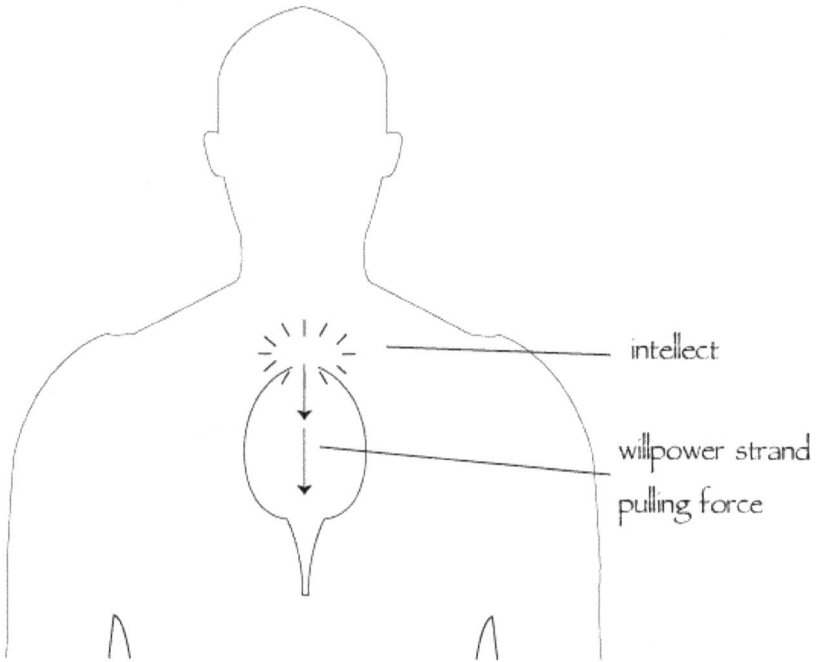

intellect

willpower strand

pulling force

September 26, 1999

Krishna

He said, "Sexual indulgence leads to mandatory responsibility, voluntarily or involuntarily, forced or willing.

"In all directions, it is set. In all places, it approaches, even through vegetation and scenery. The material creation is pervaded with that energy as a cloth is created on and reinforced by threads. Though regarded as its symbol and utility, women are not its cause.

"Brahmanirvana, which I discussed in the discourse with Arjuna, cannot be achieved generally. The sexual energy is on-going, continuous and automatically emanating from the mundane force, which by its very nature, non-deliberate as it is, expresses it. One particular spirit may get out or achieve some type of brahmanirvana but overall, things remain the same in the mundane environment. An ascetic, as soon as he observes the connection between sexual indulgence and responsibility, should by all means, through alertness, decrease the contacts by a systematic curtailment of flirtations and by rampant avoidance of sexually-charged potencies.

"Even the Mahavishnu is said to be involved with Goddess Durga by a flirtatious glance, and thus the responsibility for producing, managing and terminating the material world is endured by him. Understand this. Protect yourself from the sexually-charged potencies.

"Sexual power may command you. Wherefrom has it got that authority. The wonder of it! Such a great soul as you and such a demand by that conglomeration of persons and energies for your attentive care!"

Remark:

Most sexual indulgence or flirtation is based on connections of the past lives. There are many millions of these connections. As such it is foolish to feel that one must complete any or all urges. They are on-going. One will never exhaust them. Any such involvements are intertwining and set the stage for future contacts. Material nature keeps all imprints as a basis for reactivation in the future.

Relations from the past which are not yet manifested, remain dormant like seeds which are kept in a dirt-free dry place. Those seeds will sprout if thrown on moist ground. Thus, if one moves into a social setting in which one encounters someone who is a potential sexual partner, one will be exposed to the responsibility of such a relationship. However one may not see the full scope. One may only see the initial pleasant or intense enjoyment, which is merely the release of the pressure of the past imprint. Based on that limited perception, one may encourage rather than discourage the formation of the relationship. In social affairs, there is an underlying sexual urge to be fulfilled. We can be sure about that. Thus there should be no rush for sexual fulfillments.

October 4, 1999

Yogeshwarananda

He said, "Bring the intellect downward into the subtle energy in the spinal area of the subtle body. This is a preliminary practice for transferring to a higher plane."

Remark:

This technique is done after one energized his subtle system by doing postures and breath-infusion. If however one tries to do this, before he achieves that, he may get some slight result but it would not be consistent. It would not be part of an on-going progression. For full success, one needs to have practiced asana postures and pranayama breath enrichment.

October 5, 1999

Yogeshwarananda

A higher level transfer

This was the same practice as in the previous entry. On this day, Yogeshwarananda said that some yogis consider this action of moving the intellect to meet the subtle energy as synonymous to Shiva moving near to Goddess Durga. Sometimes they say that Shiva came close to or is unified with Shakti.

October 6, 1999

Yogeshwarananda / Agastya

This technique is similar to the ones on the previous day, pulling the intellect down into charged subtle energy, except that the intellect was pulled down to the location where the subtle energy was stirred. There is frontal kundalini, back kundalini, central body kundalini and also two side

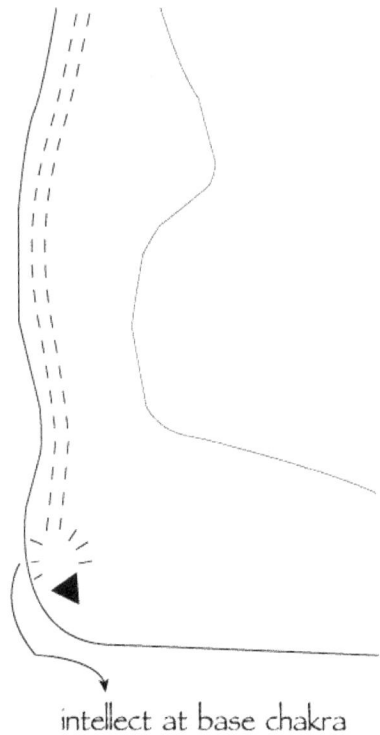

intellect at base chakra

kundalinis. Generally it is taught by yogis to beginners, that there is only one kundalini which travels through the spine. This is known as prana-apana (positive-negative) kundalini. However the same type of vital force occurs in other parts of the body and can be awakened by various types of breath-infusion.

In spinal kundalini (back kundalini), the base chakra releases its stored energy. In front kundalini, the sex chakra fires itself through the sex organ center and then travels up the groin and solar plexus. However there are other kundalini passages and sources in the body. The idea is that once the kundalini is stirred in any part of the body, unpolluted subtle energy begins to move polluted subtle energy and the two energies participate in a polarity exchange which causes light or fire in the subtle body.

October 6, 1999

Ganesh

He instructed that I do a pull-down. This means pulling down the intellect into the pain that is felt when one does any yoga posture and stretches. When one stretches there is pain. Some do not understand the value of this. In technique yoga, we take the intellect to the pain. In that way it is trained to explore and to be concerned inside the psyche, instead of its habit of chasing objects outside, and not being concerned with itself, taking a keen interest in everything else, and forgetting self-advancement.

In some creations, the Ganesh deity, promotes yoga as his main teaching but in this one it is rare for this particular Ganesh to give yoga instructions. Agastya Muni, his uncle, told me that this particular Ganesh mastered the yoga disciplines in previous time cycles.

October 10, 1999

Shiva

Round round current

This is a technique to track pranic energy which travels around the inner edge of the body from front to back. It is a connection of front and back kundalini, travelling through the head. This is not done in an imaginative way. One should do this after an intense breath-infusion session, when by providence, front and back kundalini are aroused simultaneously.

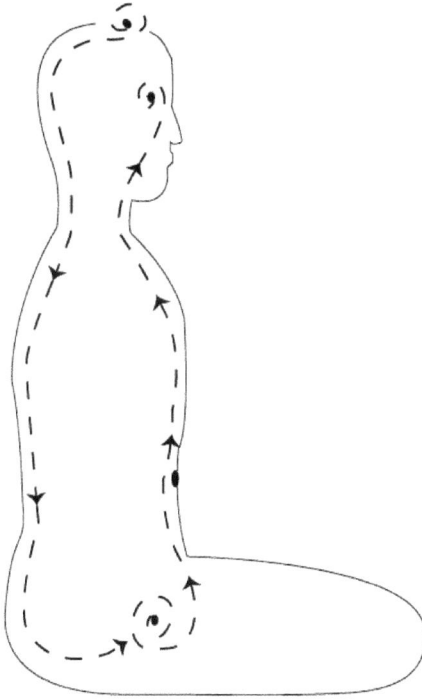

Babaji

On this day, he supervised the activation of front kundalini. The front system is more or less, based on strong celibacy, because its power springs from the sex kanda, which is a small bulb in the subtle form, in the lower groin area. While back kundalini springs from the bottom or anal chakra, it can be activated even if one still participates in sexual indulgence and has wrong eating habits but front kundalini usually does not manifest if these vices function.

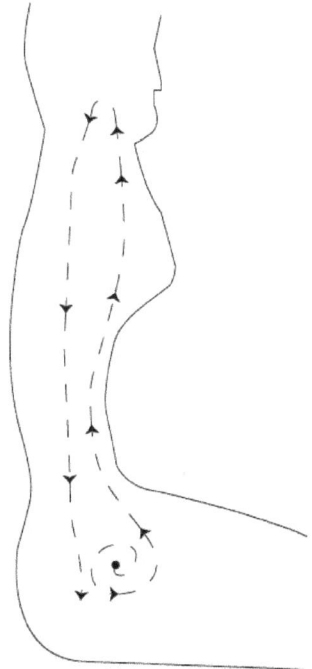

Babaji Mahasaya

Front kundalini kriya

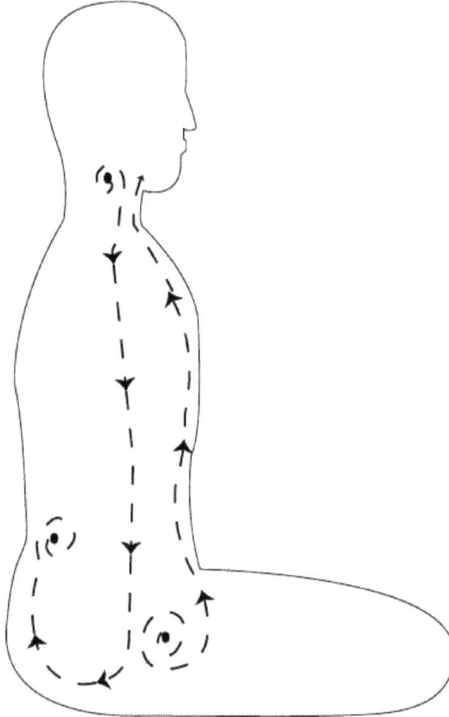

One may try to arouse, to meditate or to visualize kundalini, but one should know for sure, that from my experience, it is only activated permanently when one gives up sexual focus and stops all night and late-afternoon eating for some time. One has to master the nauli stomach pump exercises and be obedient and loyal to Hatha Yoga Devi, the female deity who is the personification of hatha yoga. She is the mother of the hatha yogis. If one disrespects or neglects her, one cannot activate front kundalini permanently.

Without its activation, the lower groin, lower and higher abdomen will not be under the control of yoga, and as such part of the psyche will elude purification.

October 17, 1999

Shiva

He said, "The same energy is important. Develop and catch it within."

Remark:

This is the energy used in communication with a deity form. This energy is also used on the causal level by the great yogins who reside there. This energy is a specific energy in the psyche and should be identified. Early in the morning, when I do call-prayers to the great yogins and to Brahma, Vishnu and Shiva, I use this special energy.

The energy has three parts. One part is the contribution of energy made by the one who calls. The other part is a matching power from the universal reserves of energy. And the last part is from the deity.

October 20, 1999

Balarama

He asked, "Where is my pet cow? How cruel to steal a pet?"

Remark:

This was a cow given to me by Balarama to be kept for his brother's girlfriend. Once in another dimension, Balarama gave me a white cow to keep for his brother's girl-friend. He wanted me to tend the cow and take it to Radha daily for milking by her. I was to take the cow for grazing on certain pastures. I used to do this. Somehow, I faded away for that place.

Later, much later, I discovered myself on this planet. I again found that cow in a sculptured brass form. I used to keep the form next to Radha-Gopinath deities. This was a set of brass forms.

As destiny would have it, those deities were given to my friend. After this happened, Balarama came and said this. It appears that He was unhappy because the cow went with deities. What can I do now? I lost my way from the original place, where Balarama left me with the cow. I do not know how to transfer from here to there. In the future, I will return there, retrieve that cow and take care of her. Somehow I transited to this weird cross-world with these insane eternal living beings.

October 20, 1999

Agastya

A small transcendence zone

These small transcendence zones usually occur after doing breath-infusion either in the morning, afternoon or at some other time. Rarely do these occur otherwise. Unless the subtle energies are charged, stirred up and activated, one can rarely experience a high level zone. This is why some yogis do many sessions of breath-infusion before entering transcendental states.

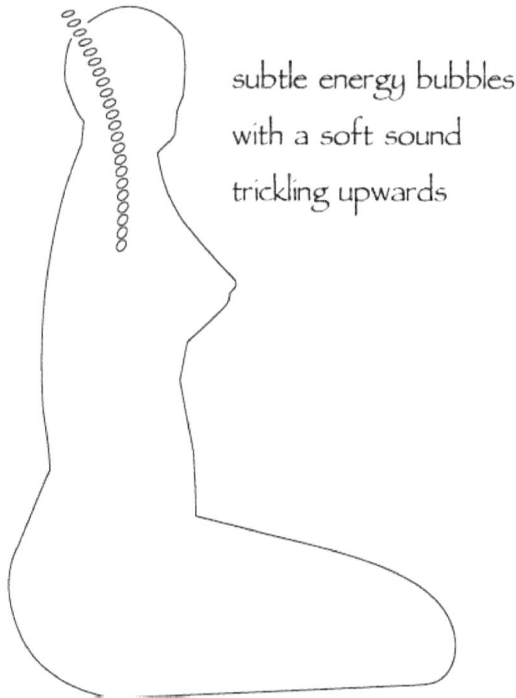

subtle energy bubbles
with a soft sound
trickling upwards

October 22, 1999

Hanuman

He said, "Experience this transcendental zone which is based on accumulated sustained clean subtle energy."

Remark:

This experience was due to his influence. This was a small short duration transcendence. By accumulated sustained, Hanuman meant built-up energy which is not expended in sexual indulgence, flirtations or other social dealings. By clean subtle energy he meant new subtle energy from higher levels which was drawn in while doing breath-infusion. One cannot pull in such energy merely by willing, thinking or contemplating.

brightly-lit energy

darkness energy

October 23, 1999

Shiva

He said, "Maintain the transcendental contact."

Remark:

This is an instruction to connect with the transcendental experience throughout the day. This is not an easy advice to follow. At any time, by a lack of vigilance, the intellect and the general mind space which it inhabits, may resume the normal course of ranging over gross and subtle mundane objects. However I consistently applied the mind with this instruction. It increases daily as a cultivated habit. Each yogin should cultivate the practice and give up useless hopes about being blessed, graced or bestowed with spiritual advancement without practice.

October 24, 1999

Yogeshwarananda

This was a realization which occurred under his influence. I saw within a knee cap while doing a backward stretch. This is mystic vision. It is different to pranavision. In pranavision one sees through pranic energy. But otherwise one may see visually through mystic eyeballs that may manifest anywhere in the body or outside of it. When persons take hallucinogenic drugs, they also experience this pranavision and multiple vision, but unfortunately that is not the proper method. Yoga alone is the correct procedure for developing these insights.

October 24, 1999

Hanuman

A central samadhi

This transcendence zone was in a central area. It occurred after I centered some stirred-up subtle energy which disappeared and left sheer clean enriching energy in its place. The ingested subtle energy disappears as it is mixed with the polluted energy. There was a small explosion in the subtle body. A sheer clean energy manifested and with it a small transcendence zone occurred. In such absorptions there is a loss of distraction. The mind and intellect become internal focused.

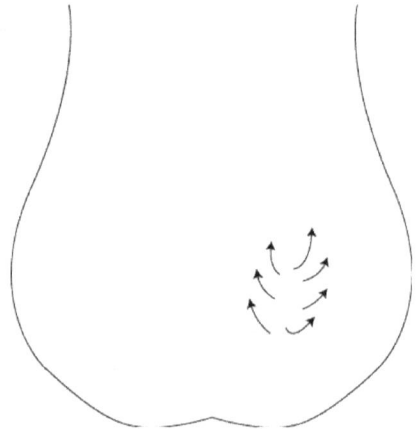

Radha-Kanta

These were deities at a temple in the USA.

Radha said, "Yoga is part of the Bhagavad Gita. Ignore them. Adhere to the Gita. As the yogi told you, the focusing power should be retracted from the external world. Learn how to manifest it elsewhere. Be a free spirit. We came out to tell you to go back in."

Remark:

This was an instruction to counteract the influence of devotees who feel that yoga is useless and is not part of devotion or Bhagavad Gita. I have to be a free spirit. As Radha said, Krishna projected from the spiritual lands into these material provinces, just to tell people like me that we should transit to the spiritual places.

October 25, 1999

Valmiki

Valmiki who became known as the author of the Ramayana was a master of pranayama breath-infusion but that is hardly known. He told me that when the rest of the polluted energy is driven out on a consistent basis by steady exercises and by the sincerity derived from losing interest in the activities which the polluted energy sponsors, most of the cells in both the physical and subtle bodies no longer retain that energy. They lose the attachment to it. He said that if a yogi consistently practices, he will attain longer and longer transcendence states.

October 25, 1999

Valmiki

He said, "Press the throat chakra. When it is time, you will eliminate it."

Remark:

This pertains to the time of death, and being ready to eliminate the gross and subtle eating urge. Some yogis like Yogeshwarananda and Valmiki, went to the causal plane where they is no eating action. They eliminated the need to eat through a gross or subtle body. In fact, recently, after being visited by Yogesh, I saw him living in the causal form only. Sometimes he lives with his causal body with an intellect organ stationed above it. He enters my brahmrandra to give instructions. He does not eat because he has no kundalini force to maintain. Here is the technique Valmiki.

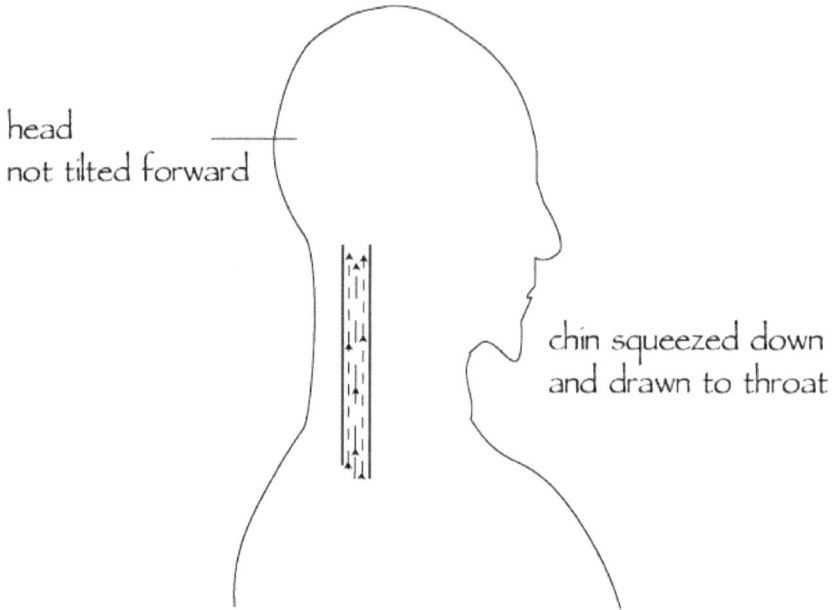

head
not tilted forward

chin squeezed down
and drawn to throat

October 28, 1999

Balarama

He said, "Make the crown chakra shrink to the base."

Remark:

This is a mystic practice to see the chakra system as one energy movement. These practices prepare one for transcendental experience and for getting nearer to the time when one may exist without a kundalini.

October 28, 1999

Yogeshwarananda

He instructed, "Sit between legs with feet at right angles. Have hands on thighs with finger pointing backwards touching the abdomen.

He gave another posture, "Sit between heels, feet not at right angles. Hands in back in prayer fashion, pushing up. Head and neck are strained back. Do breath-infusion. Suck semen up and out of chest area."

Remark:

These psychic actions have to do with drawing semen from the subtle chest area. This is effective after one has drawn semen from the groin to the chest on a consistent basis, and made a cleared passage there. After doing this for some time, years or months, according to what is required in one's individual case, the semen moves up on its own accord. It may remain in the chest area in a small bulb or kanda in the subtle form. From there one should draw it out of the body through the chest and up further to the throat and then at last draw it out of the body through the brahmrandra. This takes time to practice and master by postures, breath-infusion and sincerity of purpose.

October 28, 1999

Mahadeva

He said, "I reside in that purified energy stream."

Remark:

This purified energy stream is subtle semen energy in the subtle body. Its color is crystal clear with a slight white-yellow tinge. Shiva appreciates such energy coming from the subtle sexual function, since such energy only comes in sincere celibates who have out-grown the need for sexual indulgence and who, under the influence of either Narad, Skanda or Shiva, mastered celibacy by postures and breath-infusion. There are many persons who without yoga practice aspire for celibacy. That is different.

On this day I saw Brahma manifest from the causal energy. When he emerged, he appeared to be like a closed lotus. A person should not wait for his next body to do yoga. A person should not feel that yoga is not for him or that he is too old to practice. These considerations are conducted by the mentally-retardative mode. One should do any bit of yoga, regardless of how old or young the body is.

October 29, 1999

A nadi-in-the-back technique

In this technique one keeps the neck bracing the chest with crisscrossed hands, holding the sides of the sole of the feet as shown in the diagram below. Doing this posture with breath-infusion, one can realize some nadis which are in the back of the subtle body.

hands crisscrossed on back

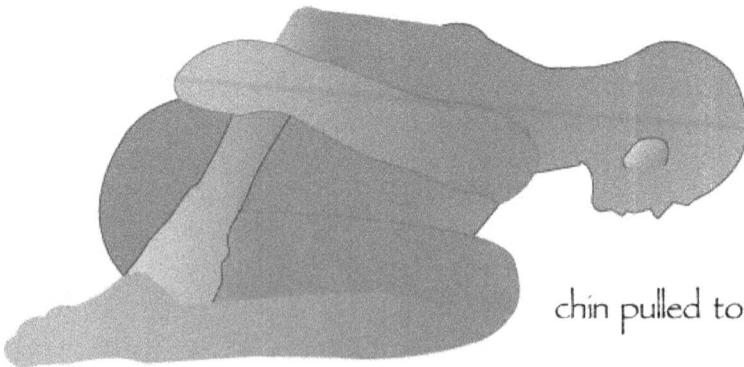

chin pulled to throat

fingers under foot

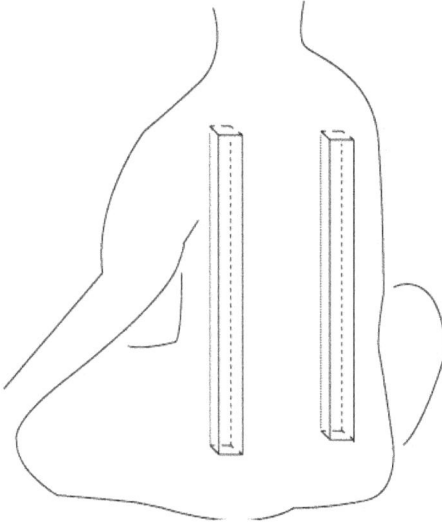

October 29, 1999

Krishna Deity

He said, "Because he gives political power, they will side with that man life after life."

Remark:

This was in reference to some persons who followed a religious leader. The leader gave followers broad political powers, which were mistaken for spiritual authority. Because of a certain innate need within one's psyche, one takes to a certain spiritual authority. Thus one becomes satisfied even without making spiritual advancement.

October 29, 1999

Shiva

He said, "Six months for a firm practice. Six-years for the perfection of it."

Remark:

This refers to the drying-up of the gross and subtle bodies. This means the drying out of the food-need from those forms.

Eventually one has to curb the food-need. It begins by regulating the quantity of food. It progresses to checking the quality of nutritional food and the inclusion of medicinal food which impels the appetite for proper eating at the proper times and curbs one from improper eating at any time. If one curbs the eating, his path for celibacy by postures and breath-infusion, will be clear.

October 30, 1999

Indra

Indra is a supernatural person who controls rainfall by gaging and activating electrical energy which builds up in the atmosphere. This energy is produced from our physical and psychological activities.

He checks me now and again when I attempted to purge out and purify the navel region. After a time I did not see him. He returned on this day to check on my navel area. He was pleased with my progression In relation to cleaning the navel. It is mastered mostly by breath-infusion to blow subtle energy into the navel region and to curb late eating and to eat as early as possible in the morning, so that by the next morning the stomach is empty and the higher intestines have no food matter in them. There are also some subsidiary practices like the stretching of the thigh muscles and tendons.

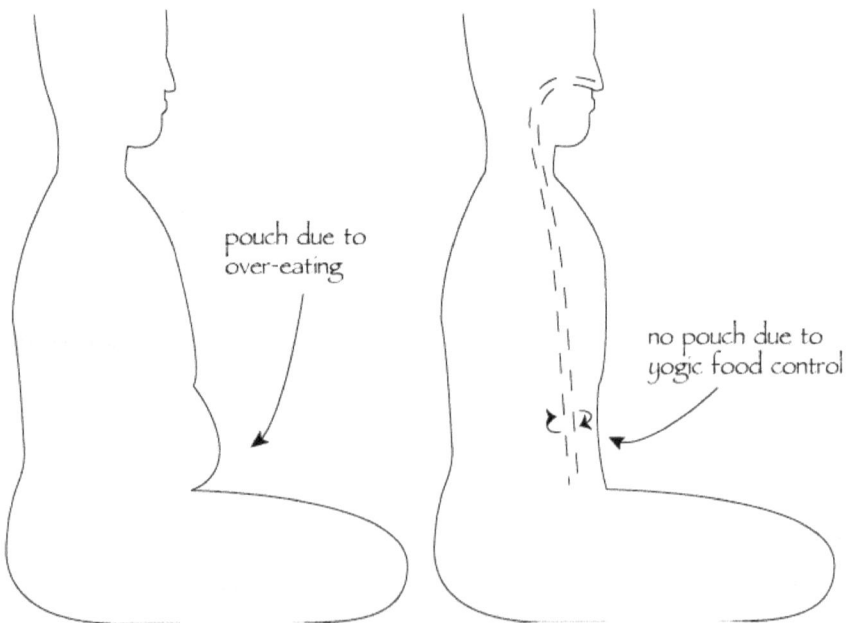

pouch due to over-eating

no pouch due to yogic food control

Shivananda

He said, "Reduce the interests. Remove interest in sexual attraction."

Remark:

This was an instruction to reduce the interests of the gross and subtle bodies.

Some years ago, Swami Shivananda took a keen interest in my attaining celibacy. He wanted me to produce a yoga siddha body, just as I had before in many former lives. I took help from many celibate yogins for celibate practice but in this life, this Swami started me on the course.

Regardless of the type of subtle body used before assuming an embryo, the subtle form changes to confirm to the new physical body, which means that the yogi has to elevate that degraded subtle system which he finds himself to be.

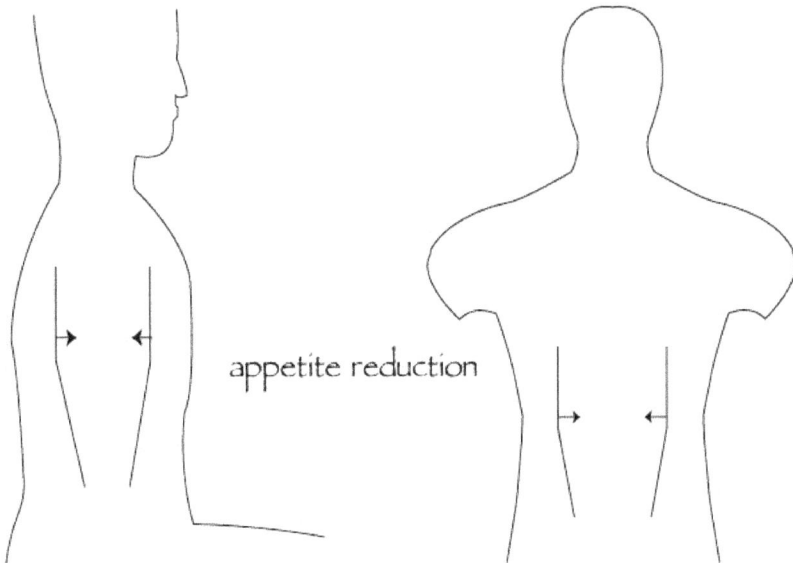

appetite reduction

October 31, 1999

Yogeshwarananda

He said, "Do rooster pose. Do breath-infusion. Move eyes into the center of the turmoil with other allied energies."

Remark:

This is a technique for curbing the optic energy

Yogeshwarananda

He advised, "Do a dot focus."

Remark:

Dot techniques are known as bija psychic actions. Sometimes they are called bindu. To do this one should do an intense session of breath-infusion. Then assume lotus posture. One then moves all upper energies into the base dot hole. After a time the dot hole alone remains as one meditates at the very bottom. It looks and feels like this:

⊙

The way it looks and feels would depend on if one uses pranavision or visual vision, depending on the level of purity of the subtle body and how far one advanced in mystic yoga.

October 31, 1999

Shiva

A continuous transcendental energy.

Remark:

It may be asked, "What is transcendental absorption?"

It is a state of self or psyche absorbing consciousness. In transcendence experience the consciousness is either inwardly occupied or attracted to something in an external but internal world. The consciousness stops moving in its regular way of hunting external objects which are outside the physical body in the physical world. It may pursue objects which are outside the mind but which are not in this physical world. In transcendence zone also, the consciousness stops pursuing memories and images which pertain to anything in this physical world or to the subtle dimension which is directly corresponding to the physical.

In transcendental energy, the senses fold in, so to speak. The sensual energies retreat to the intellect. They stop their demands and lose their hypnotic power. Other senses may develop which can be used to perceive other levels of reality which do not correspond to this physical world.

During a session of breath-infusion, one has to be on the alert for any small-duration or long-going transcendental shifts. If one is careless of this, one will not advance as rapidly. Sooner or later, a yogi realizes that he must be attentive to these transcendental shifts which occur while doing breath-infusion.

He should stop as frequently as these occur, so that he can focus into the transcendental energy. Otherwise if the higher energy concentrations occur without his notice, he will derive little benefit from the practice.

It is a mistake to do breath-infusion and not be attentive to the small collections of transcendental energy. However if one makes such mistakes, the time will come, if one continues the exercises on a daily basis, when one will feel the necessity for focusing on the transcendental energy.

Shiva's idea is that for a continuous transcendental contact, one should focus on the morning transcendence energy gained while doing breath-infusion.

One should focus on this during the day, even if one is employed. This is easier said than done. By practice one sets the stage in one's life for longer duration transcendental energy later. One encourages material nature to set up social conditions in which one may practice transcendence energy continuously.

Shiva told me, "If you keep away from foreign thoughts during the day and focus on the transcendence energy, banishing daydreaming and other types of voluntary or involuntary mind focus, you will increase the practice."

October 31, 1999

Agastya

Stomach pumps in relation to technique yoga

He informed me that if one ate anything after 11 am the stomach pumps cannot be done effectively in the afternoon about 5 or 6 pm. He said that under the influence of non-yogis, of various sorts, a yogi may not follow the correct eating schedule. The progression will be slow.

November 1, 1999

Brahma

He asked, "What was the technique yesterday?"

Remark:

This question was asked in order to remind me that I did not practice the technique that day. This was a reprimand, a grim reminder; that I would not progress rapidly if I did not adhere to the disciplines. Technique yoga has its own system of grace, whereby the grace of the practice causes advancement.

That technique which I did not practice was one of shifting the intellect into the pinhole at the base of the spine.

November 1, 1999

A standing kriya.

This one for males, is done while standing with the thumbs on the back pointing upwards, the other fingers being in the front. One does breath-infusion. One draws energy through the thighs into the groin area, when one is affected by women whose bodies have a deep inset part there. This is a sexual energy retention procedure, which is part of the course of celibacy.

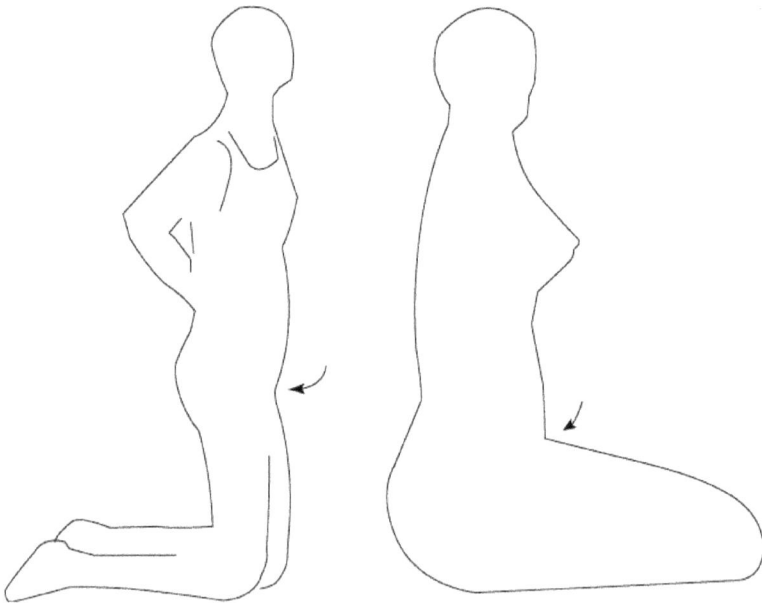

November 1, 1999

A celibate tantric technique

In some astral bodies, able yogis direct the astral semen to the top of the head of their partners. This is done by yogis who have spouses in the astral world, and who are trying to elevate their spouses, by making them be ridden of the need for astral sexual linkages.

It is best that one trains the partner while using a physical body but if one does not complete the training before passing from the physical form, one may complete it in the astral world hereafter. In some cases, a yogin becomes celibate while on earth using a bachelor's body but when he departs he finds himself involved with angelic women or sex-needing yogini women. Then he has to work again for celibacy since his restraint ceases by astral contact.

November 1, 1999

Murlidhara Krishna

He said, "Apply the advice. Be prompt."

Remark:

He spoke of the advice of Shiva about continuing transcendental energy during the day even if I had to work or had to deal with non-yogis. There are many types of non-yogic association. Some persons are interested in religion but they abhor yoga. Some dislike yoga and have no religious interest. The effect of this association is the same, to deter or discourage yoga.

November 2, 1999

Indra / Varuna technique

Indra and Varuna are two supernatural authorities. Indra controls the rainfall. Varuna controls the seas. That is how they are described in Vedic literature. This is a front kundalini current. It looks like this.

Each of the supernatural persons moves in the passage of kundalini energy. One ascends. The other one descends. They sit in large baskets. They use miniature forms. Indra regulates nutrition. Varuna regulates hormones. By controlling rainfall, Indra regulates agriculture, the source of nutrition. By

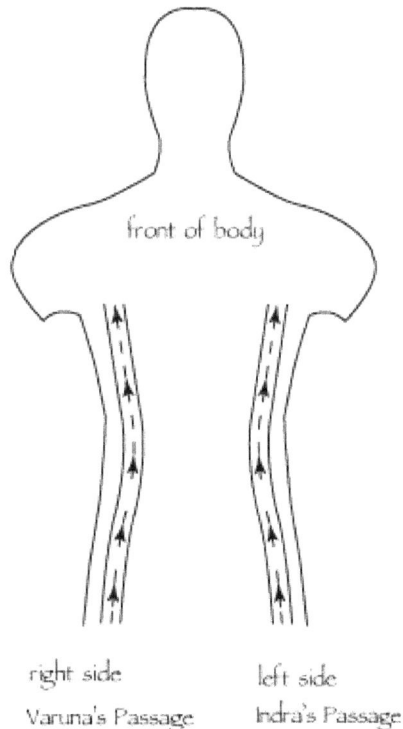

front of body

right side
Varuna's Passage

left side
Indra's Passage

controlling the seas, Varuna regulates the water table under the land.

Water affects the composition of sexual hormones. Even though these supernatural persons, devas, were seen in my psyche, I still respect them just as if I had seen them outside the subtle body. One should not think that because a deity resides in the psyche, one does not have to respect him or that one has merged with him or is identical with him.

Someone else can live in one's psyche, just as someone else can live in one's house. One is not identical with everything nor everyone within the psyche.

November 2, 1999

Narayana

In the causal cove he said, "You cause the boat to rock. You disturb the other passengers. What a bad captain you are!"

Remark:

This deity is a deity in marble, which I received from an Indian lady, who was affectionate to me. Later on, this deity appeared in the causal cove region in a four-handed form as Narayana, the Personality of Godhead. Since I had not kept the day transcendental energy, He complained. The day transcendence is the transcendence zone experienced during the day, as one maintains whatever early morning transcendence experience one experienced while doing breath-infusion.

November 3, 1999

Vasishtha Muni

For my sake, he lit some subtle energy in my body. After that I saw a small flame like the flame of a kerosene lamp. For a while, I saw through subtle energy, then there was darkness. I used the base dot meditation with the intellect brought down to the base, while the other chakras were compressed downwards.

November 3, 1999

An eating-procedure to be done when by subtle influence one is forced to eat physical food.

Remark:

In some cases when alone, one may find that one is being forced to eat, as if a powerful subtle giant stands over one's shoulder and commands one to eat. In such cases, one should simply take the food item into the mouth but not swallow it. Or one may take a tiny piece, chew that and then spit it out, without regret or remorse.

By bad association in this world and in the subtle realm, as well as in the subconscious zone of consciousness, one picks up bad eating habits but they can be abandoned gradually.

Some ancestors have leverage over the psyche. They may have an urge to eat. Their appetite may enter one's body. One should not resent this. One may do as suggested above and they will be satisfied by the action.

November 3, 1999

Murlidhara Krishna

He said, "Look there."

Remark:

When I looked I saw the over-eating deity, rising through a passage in my abdomen. After he came up he went to the tongue and looked out of the body through the mouth. There was a force which induced my body to take an apple. I did not respond to it. Later, about half hour later, I took some hot milk and popcorn. The milk burnt the tongue on the same spot where that deity emerged earlier. I offered that deity my respects.

It should be noted that in normal experience, the movement of this deity is interpreted as appetite or food satisfaction. When he moves up through the abdomen, it is interpreted as appetite when he moves down to the abdomen, it is interpreted as satisfaction. In a higher stage, one experiences that as the movement of subtle energy and feelings. In a yet higher stage, one sees the deity moving up and down directly.

These are some subtle energy check points.

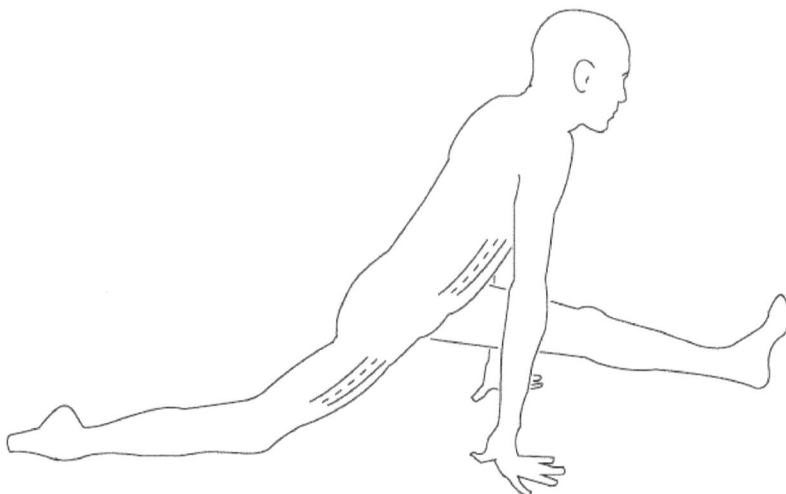

November 4, 1999

Babaji

This is the person whom Paramhansa Yogananda wrote about in his book, *Autobiography of a Yogi*. Babaji helps yogis in this era. He will be staying in this zone for this time cycle, just to help yogis. He is not easy to contact but if one maintains firm technique, being sincere and applying oneself, he will assist one. Sometimes, he appears to beginners, but generally he communicates with advanced yogins.

On this day he said, "Transcendence contact comes easy after the polluted subtle energy is removed. Once the system gets accustomed to subtle energy cleanliness, transcendence energy flows continuously. See this."

He showed a right side tunnel vision in the right astral line of sight. It was like a tube telescope but seeing through any part of the inside of the tubes. He showed a cleaned area, downward from the lower brain.

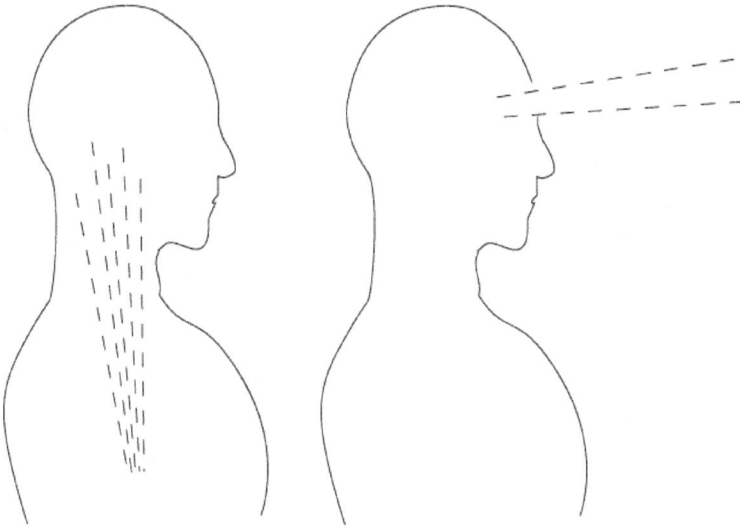

About three hours later, Babaji gave a technique for seeing inside the usual darkness of the subtle body. It was a vision access. This is insight which comes as a result of contentment with the subtle energy darkness. By alignment with Babaji's energy, a yogi who already developed brow chakra focus and who learnt to be satisfied with the feelings inside the subtle body, can begin to see inside that energy. One has to stop craving external sensation and internal turmoil of emotions.

November 5, 1999

On this day I met a female deity who monitors the bliss power of sexual energy. This bliss potency is different to the begetting force. In a sexual indulgence there are three primary forces. One is simply the lust enthusiasm which drives the persons involved to get their bodies and subtle energies linked. The other is the contributory energy which comes from departed entities who are require embryos. Whatever energy they contribute is retrieved if they do not get a body from the would-be parents. While being in the womb of the mother, they use that energy to draw hormones energy to themselves. The other energy is happiness-pleasure energy. Modern people procure this and avoid producing babies.

The female deity took some subtle marrow from each of my thighs. This energy produces sexual pleasure which produces or causes paramour affairs to develop. For celibates it is a detrimental energy, which always threatens to disrupt their aspirations. In the higher stages of yoga, this energy is removed completely but in the lower stages it causes flirtations and various subtle sexual connections.

When I met her in my body, the deity manipulated the energy of another male body. In that case, she held the attention of the other male for the production of a livelihood for his being able to support a family. In my case, she assisted to take exit from the parental duties.

When I saw her, I recently completed months of backward thigh stretches with breath-infusion. This proves that these exercises may yield desired results.

After I saw her, she propped up her left foot, and somehow by mystic power, exposed the bliss energy in her body. This act of hers facilitated a joining for the bliss energy flow in my subtle form, while she talked business to encourage the other yogi to produce a livelihood for his family.

This activity was multi-dimensional. These supernatural people act on the mystic planes. Sometime after, about three hours, it dawned on me that she may be Jara (Juh-raa) the female deity in control of old age. However when I consider this, the bliss controlling Devi said to me, "No. I am the other side, her sister, not her. I am the person of vitality and youth."

November 5, 1999

Yogeshwarananda

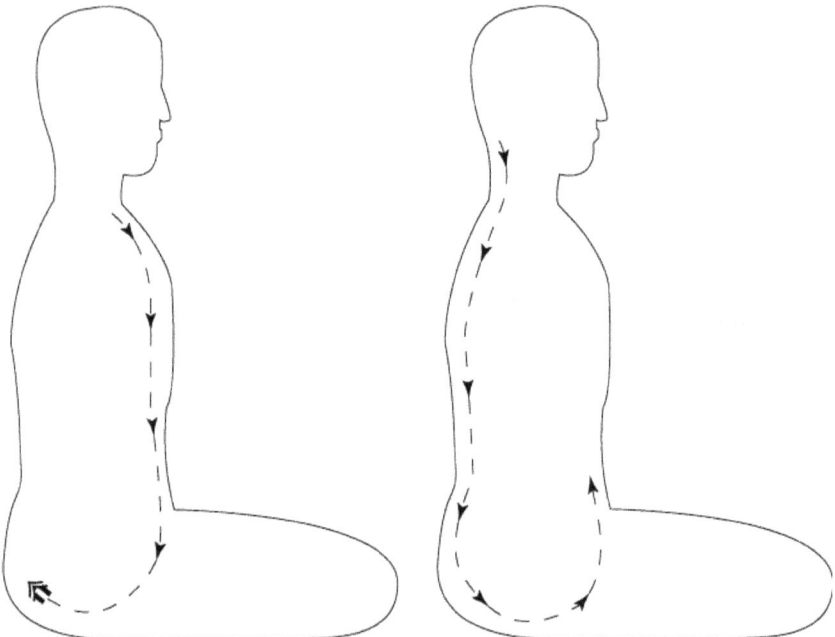

He gave a reverse down-draw.

One does breath-infusion, then after the energy accumulates a charge one does a pull-down-the-back-up-the-front breathing exercise. Then one reverses the process.

After one feels the energy travelling in the directions indicated by the arrows (previous page), one holds the locks at the stomach and lower trunk of the body. One then pulls in the big toes and lets them point firmly into the ground. In the final posture it is best to be on the knees.

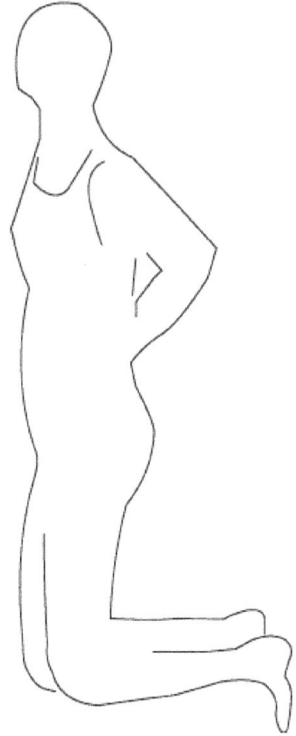

November 6, 1999

Babaji

He said, "For the advanced stages, the teacher enters the subtle body but he will not do so unless it is cleared of pollution. Thus the need for advanced postures and breath-infusion, through which that body is cleansed. Once the teacher enters he can show various parts."

Remark:

In the year 2001 on the date of March 4, I decided to publish what Babaji said on November of 1999. I can say that it is factual. Yogeshwarananda entered my subtle body after it was somewhat cleansed, He showed and continues to reveal much in the line of technique yoga. It is very convenient to have a mahayogin enter one's brahmrandra to teach. He can do so anywhere. He does not have to rely on one's being in a particular physical place. No matter where one's physical body is located, one can take instructions.

November 7, 1999

Babaji

He said, "Get subtle energy purity. After doing breath-infusion transcendental energy will be experienced whenever you sit to meditate."

November 7, 1999

Shiva

He said, "Give some explanation. Show how to move the psychic tools. Slow down the actions so you can describe details."

Remark:

This is an instruction to explain in detail how to move certain psychic instruments like the intellect organ in the subtle head. Normally, a human being considers this subtle organ to be his or her understanding. He or she does not perceive it as merely an organ in the subtle body. Many persons following a spiritual path, and desiring to get out of material existence by one means or another, simply ignore the details since they take recourse to a religious shelter which advocates freedom from material existence without having to sort out subtle objects.

Basically speaking, to grasp the subtle organ, one has to do the following.

- Get in proximity to it.
- Take firm grasp of it.
- Move or attempt to move it from its default location.
- Check to see if it will move when the attempt to relocate is made.
- Go to the place where you desire to transfer it.
- Look back from that place to the place where the organ is usually located.
- Stay positioned in the desired place and pull the organ by mystic force.
- Stay there forcibly. See if the organ will come to you by adhesive power.

One may practice what is described above. Each of the subtle organs maintains a distance from the core self, just as by gravitational power, various planets stay in orbit in reference to powerful bodies like the sun.

November 8, 1999

Babaji

He said, "I see your endeavor. It will take years to accomplish. The intellect usually moves in pursuit of sensation. It works from the brain space position. What you try to accomplish is done in the higher stage. Use some intellect light and gradually. Take it down. Let me go now. I will come tomorrow."

Remark:

I tried to go down to the base chakra from within the psyche. Babaji, produced the light of intellect all over inside. It was very bright. He told me to stay in it and gradually move the intellect as desired. After this he rose out of my psyche. His appearance was one as a bright effulgent being. He put his hand on my subtle head and left.

November 8, 1999

Brahma

He said, "More means responsibility. As the elder bodies pass off, the social responsibilities they carried and represented, stays in the world and is borne by others. Maintain yoga practice. Everything else is incidental."

Remark:

This was advice for me to refrain from social involvement and to side-step responsibilities which may be thrust upon me. As far as possible for success in yoga, I must avoid responsibilities. I may be capable of carrying social burdens but that is beside the point, since an absorption with such duties would consume the time required for yoga development.

November 9, 1999

Babaji / Yogeshwarananda

They gave information of stretching the knees and legs in the bow pose. They advised that I develop the advanced practice of toning the abdomen, back and waist.

November 9, 1999

Babaji

He said, "Go back to the throat. Wait there. Pull. Grasp. Down-draw the top sensuality. Take the energy down to attain transcendental absorption."

Remark:

This has to do with the intellect energy being brought in proximity of the causal form.

November 9, 1999

Brahma

He said, "Accept those energies which are not controlled by you but which are due to contributory powers of others."

Remark:

This was in reference to a meal I took at 5:30 in the afternoon. To facilitate yoga and celibacy, I eat very little after the main meal in the early morning.

However from time to time, someone may invite me to eat. Then according to the force of destiny, I may take a meal. It used to be that these haphazard meals, which are inconsistent with yoga practice, used to disturb my psyche, but after getting advice from Brahma, Shiva and others, these hazards do not vex me.

November 11, 1999

Babaji

He said, "After the chest-abdomen back-stretch, the nadis being clean, the energy passes easily for transcendental experience. Do lotus. Stretch the subtle abdomen to about 3 inches of thickness. It will thin much more than the gross form. It is best to shift energy by special actions, rather than by willpower."

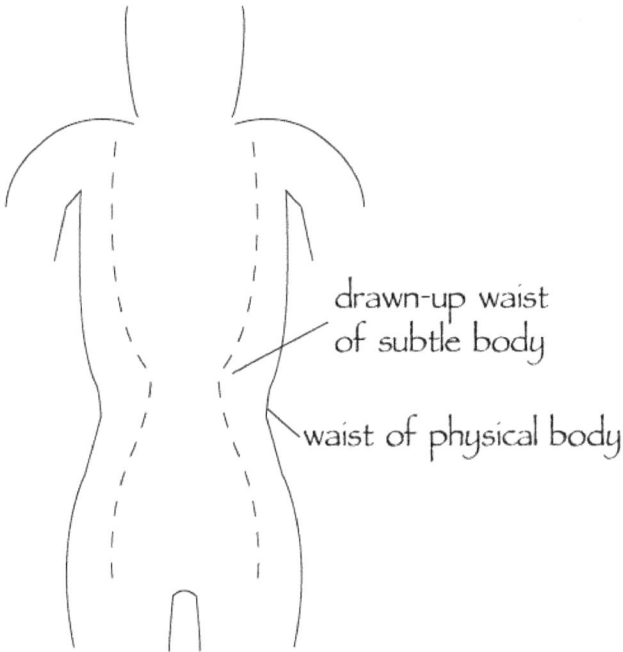

drawn-up waist
of subtle body

waist of physical body

Part 2

Babaji

He said, "Generally, when the intellect goes down, there is light. When the core-self goes down alone, there is darkness. The core-self is dark in this case. Even though it impels energy into subtle energy by its presence, it is unable to illuminate subtle energy. Carry the intellect into the sexual apparatus to see how it functions for or against celibacy.

"The supernatural beings, devas, do not harass someone who pulls out with his entire baggage, but they do trouble others. This is how they sort the non-siddhas from the siddhas. It is not by religious affiliation."

He showed a technique for passing intellect in the back, between the spine and the skin.

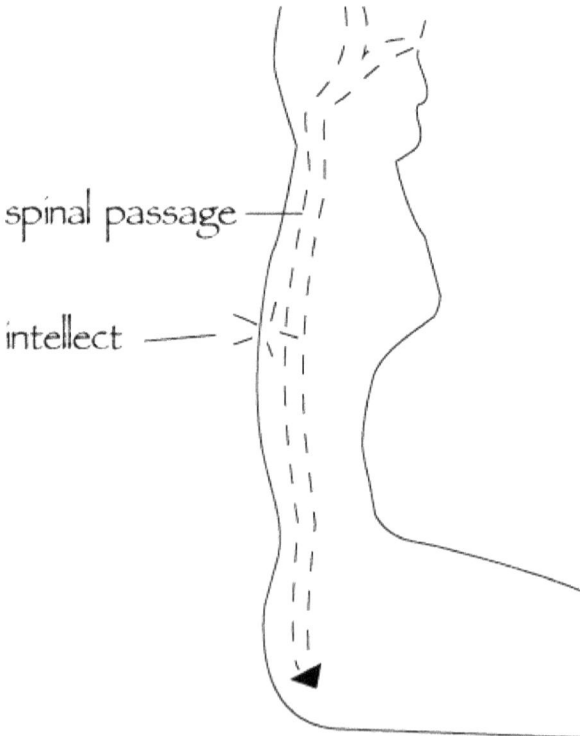

spinal passage

intellect

Babaji also said that I should find an easy passage for the intellect instead of trying a route that it is resistant to. His advice is to let it go through an easy passage, then later when its resistance to being controlled decreases, one may use to other passages.

November 14, 1999

Babaji

He said, "Yogeshwarananda, otherwise known as Vyasadeva, is your foremost guru."

Remark:

Later on that day I saw Yogeshwarananda. He said, "Here see this. Gather the light. Be patient. Sit in it. Move with it. First gather it, until it is bright. Then move a little. Then move back to its usual place. Then move a little again. Practice repeatedly."

November 15, 1999

Yogeshwarananda

He said, "Do the neck stretches. Those help to release intellect."

Remark:

This pertains to some postures where one pushes the feet over the head, as on the back. One has to be careful not to strain shoulder muscles and tendons.

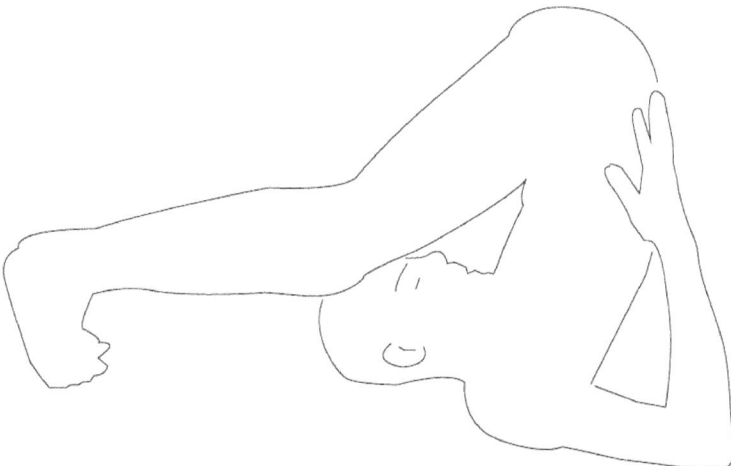

November 14, 1999

Babaji

He said, "I mastered it. So did Gorakshnath Yogiraj and other great teachers. We became perfected through hatha yoga. Draw conclusions as to why some did it and got no results. What is the reason, for the supernatural people, devas, reflecting over not having a human body."

November 15, 1999

Babaji

He said, "Gather the intellect above the neck. When it is bright enough move down and/or attempt to move down in an oval path, down the right side, up the left side continuously."

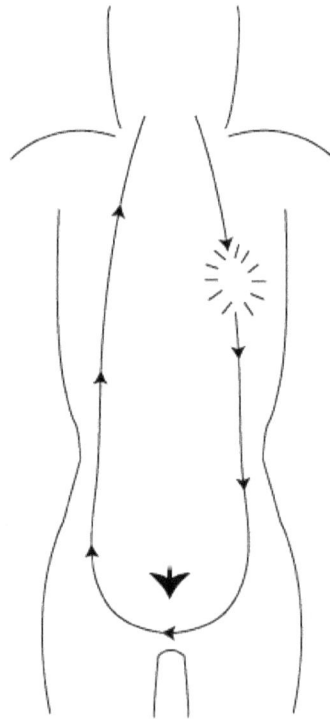

back of body

The procedure for gathering the intellect light was shown by Yogesh. That consists of causing the intellect light to stop pursuing and conceiving of outward sense objects, and to cause it to internalize on itself. By this, it glows brighter and brighter due to not dissipating its energies on excitements.

November 16, 1999

Babaji

He taught a method of seeing down into the subtle body, without going down into it, using the intellect organ to shine a light. Sometimes instead of a light, one has to see down by pranavision, which is vision through compressed subtle energy.

According to Yogesh pranavision is higher than visual vision. As I peered down, most of the energy seemed to be red but there was a multi-colored fluorescent light and a blade-like energy shaft.

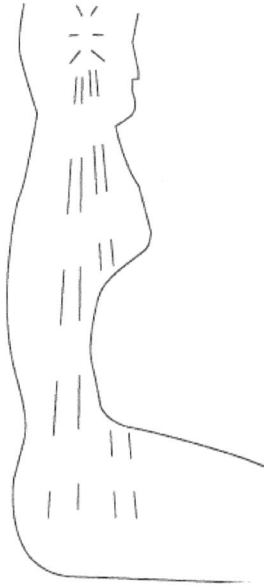

As I looked a yogi came there. I identified him as Subramania, who was the editor of the *Hinduism Today* magazine. He claimed that some years ago he had a vision of Shiva. Based on that vision, he established a pilgrimage in Hawaii. However from the description of his vision, he saw Babaji, not Shiva.

There are many persons who mistake an advanced yogin for Shiva. Sometimes, Babaji is mistaken. Sometimes Agastya is mistaken. Sometimes

Swami Rama who started the Himalaya Institute, and who left his body, is mistaken. This is because some yogis have features like Shiva. However it is not a matter of contention because the instruction of any such yogis may be the instruction of Shiva.

Once I got a sculptured form in a shop in Guyana. The form was supposed to be one of Shiva. Actually it was carved by a sculptor who thought he was producing a form of Shiva. In fact it was Babaji. In another incidence, a person procured what was supposed to be a Shiva form for me but when I communicated with the deity, I found him to be Agastya.

If one does not know Shiva personally, one may mistake a great yogin for him. That yogi may not correct the student. He may not want to damage the person's faith.

November 16, 1999

Goddess Durga

A vision of her killing Mahishasura, with other supernatural women at her side.

She said, "Give me a cube of gold daily. By the end of the day discard it as useless trash."

Remark:

This is a potent instruction. In my poverty condition, there is no way I could offer a cube of gold daily. The Goddess knows this. She either tests to see my willingness or she sets up conditions for this in another dimension where the cubes are available. With supernatural persons one may not know what is intended. Their time frame is different.

On the previous night, a picture vendor who sold pictures of supernatural persons, saw me in the astral world. He wanted me to worship Ma Durga on his behalf. I neither accepted nor rejected the request. His idea was based on my success in worshipping deities. He thought that if I worshipped on his behalf, the worship would be successful. Of course that is incorrect. He should tone his worship. My worship may serve as an impetus, an inspiration, or motivation, but it cannot be substituted for his.

Later Ma Durga told me that the cube of gold represented semen conservation in celibacy.

There are true stories of substitution of one person for another for social benefits. For instance in the Valmiki Ramayana, we hear of Rishyashringa who was substituted so that his resultant pious activity would fructify as rainfall and prosperity but such things pertain to social and not spiritual affairs. One should not confuse one for the other. In spiritual life, one has to perform the austerity and honoring of superior souls personally. One may learn from others but one is required to personally practice.

Babaji

He said, "Gather it here first. Pull till it gets brighter. When it is established, move with it to the objectives."

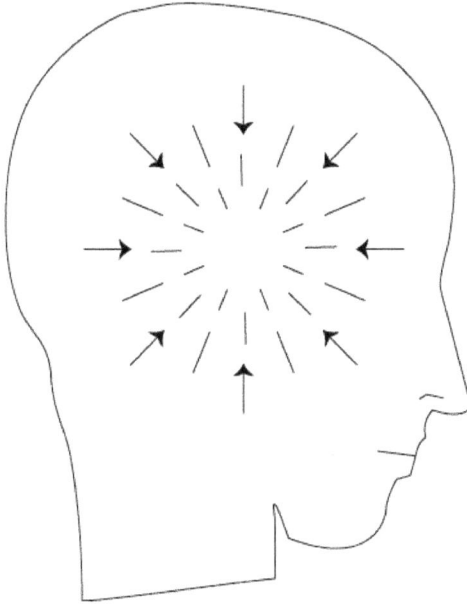

Agastya

He asked, "What is the lesson?"
I replied, "Draw in the light intensely. Redirect it daily."
He remarked, "That is good. We had no trouble mastering that in by-gone eras.

Remark:

At the time of· this communication, I practiced an intellect pull-down kriya, given by Babaji. It was a light suction, where the intellect glowed periodically.

November 19, 1999

Yogeshwarananda

I had some realizations in his association: It was that negativity toward yoga exercises, comes from good and bad non-yogic association. Such negativity should be banished each morning by doing the exercises and reaching a point where one feels that the negative energies are dissipated. During the exercises, there is a period of laziness and lack of enthusiasm. One has to work through that period, get beyond it and then begin doing the exercises in earnest. One should not stop as soon as one feels the laziness was removed but should continue further on.

There is a sense of fulfillment felt when one banishes the negative influences but that is not a completion. For completion, one has to go further to do the exercises in the positive energies which is the association of helpful yogis in the astral world.

Some of these yogins use physical bodies. Some do not. One should be sure to dissipate the lusty energy. In some sessions there may be more lust than in others. One should gage it. If there is more of that energy, one is required to do more pertinent exercises which absorb and evaporate it. After doing yoga for some years, the lusty energy may cease. Until then, one should endeavor to scatter it by doing breath-infusion.

There is also a certain curiosity interest in the intellect. That should also be satisfied. This interest has to do with transferring one's curiosity about the gross material existence into the subtle existence of one's psyche. It is important in technique yoga to transfer all interest from the gross world and from the external subtle world into the inner psyche, so that one becomes fully preoccupied with self-purity.

November 19, 1999

Babaji

He said, "I will be there for another week. During that time, be sure to attend the other teachers."

Remark:

Babaji spent a week teaching intellect glow exercises. He comes and goes as he likes. Sometimes he watches from a distance. Sometimes, I see him sitting in lotus in meditation. He is the not the kind of person who can be bothered by disciples. If he wants to instruct, he does so. When in his presence one has no desire to ask questions. One characteristic of his, is that he never demands that his disciples accept him as their only teacher.

November 19, 1999

Panchanam Bhattacharya

He is a departed yogi. He is in the lineage from Babaji through Lahiri. Such yogis become perfected, and move on from this dimension. They are hardly seen. Somehow he became aware of my efforts. He said, "Be attentive."

He wanted me to observe the relationship between the spirit's attention, the sensual energy pick-up, the intellect force and the vision orb.

The spirit's attention which is picked up or sensed by causal super-subtle energy is the most important thing that must be curbed. However that is not easy.

November 20, 1999

Babaji

He said, "It is not stable. There is instability produced by conceptions and ideas."

Remark:

This was in reference to my attempt to stabilize the intellect organ. As it is, we live in a way that denies spiritual existence. Our normal course is designed in such a way as to keep the intellect organ from being realized and seen.

November 21, 1999

Babaji

"This is the beginning of hatha yoga. This is where Arjuna was initially, before he was instructed with the Bhagavad Gita. It is strictly intellect disinterest, done by the core-self by constantly pulling back intellect's interest into itself for a constant sufficient flow."

Remark:

In the Bhagavad Gita, the curriculum for intellect yoga, the curbing of the intellect, is described in chapter two. Babaji explained the intellect as the intellect organ in the subtle form. When the intellect's interest in this world is reduced to nil and when the intellect becomes enriched in itself and becomes perceptible as a glowing light on the mystic plane, one has really completed the course of intellect yoga (buddhi yoga).

November 22, 1999

Agastya

On this day I was in the association of Agastya. He said nothing, nor did he indicate that I should do a particular practice. Thus I applied the instruction I recently received from Babaji, where he advised that I continue raja yoga as I attend to the practices given by other yogins. In meditation, I grabbed an orb, a ball of the intellect energy which had a perverse interest in my occupation. I squished it to stop the idea from expanding.

There are various ways of getting rid of thoughts which obstruct meditation. One should learn the various methods or be inspired with them. One can stop the mind from becoming a compartment for the expansion of disturbing ideas.

November 23, 1999

Shiva

He said, "Others live there too. It is no surprise if lesser ones do."

Remark:

Shiva said this after I discovered that Babaji stayed in my subtle body. Other greater personalities like Brahma, Vishnu and Shiva also stay in one of our bodies. Babaji merely by his association gives an influence which gives the benefit of progress. He helps a beginner to change the cells of the body, so that the form becomes conducive to yoga.

November 23, 1999

Babaji

He said, "Develop this again, the brow chakra stability."

Remark:

Brow chakra is the first aspect of technique yoga. Babaji always stressed that as the preliminary stage. This consists of focusing the two optic channels into one area between the eyebrows. This is the first step in trying to control the intellect organ.

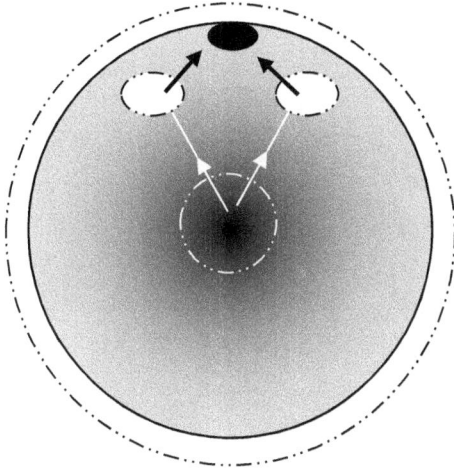

Since much energy from the intellect tracks down the two optic nerves, which leads to each of the eyes, one has to retract this energy into the intellect in order to conserve it and develop intellect stability. First however one has to focus the two-tracked optic power into one track.

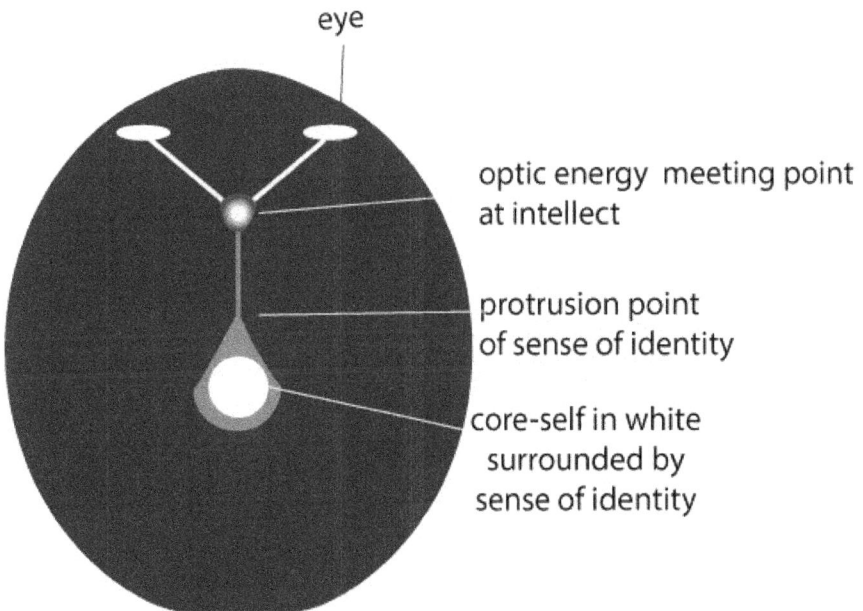

eye

optic energy meeting point at intellect

protrusion point of sense of identity

core-self in white surrounded by sense of identity

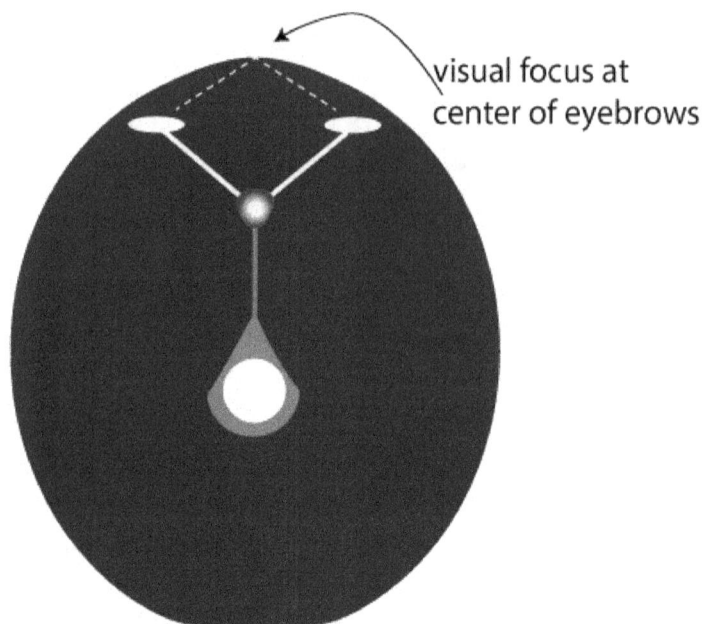

visual focus at center of eyebrows

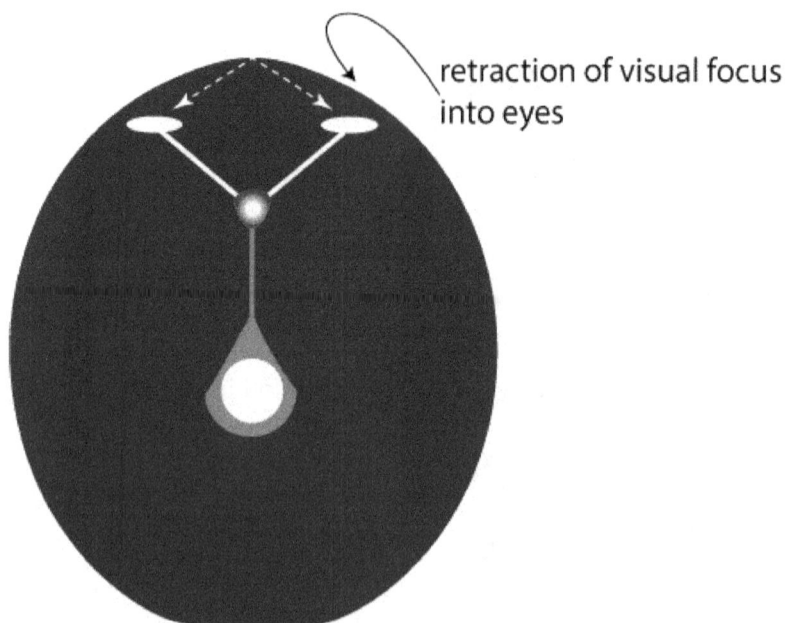

retraction of visual focus into eyes

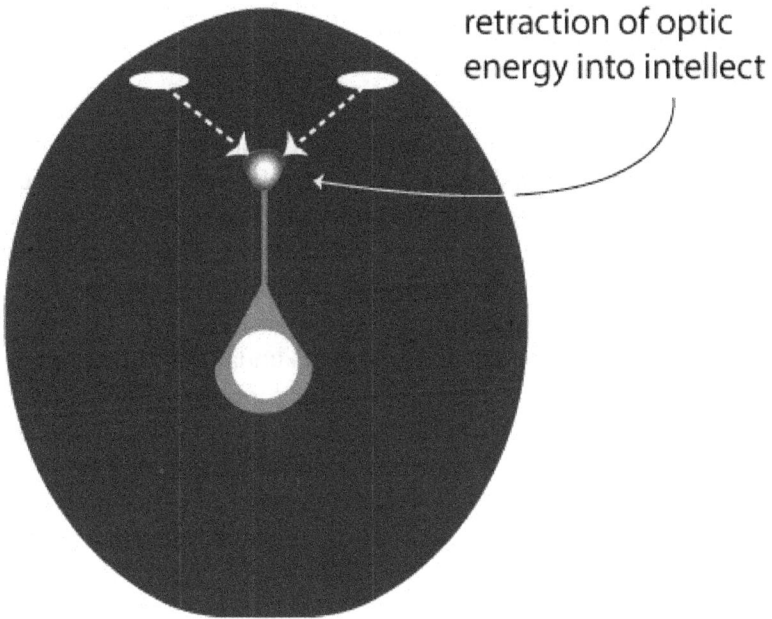

retraction of optic
energy into intellect

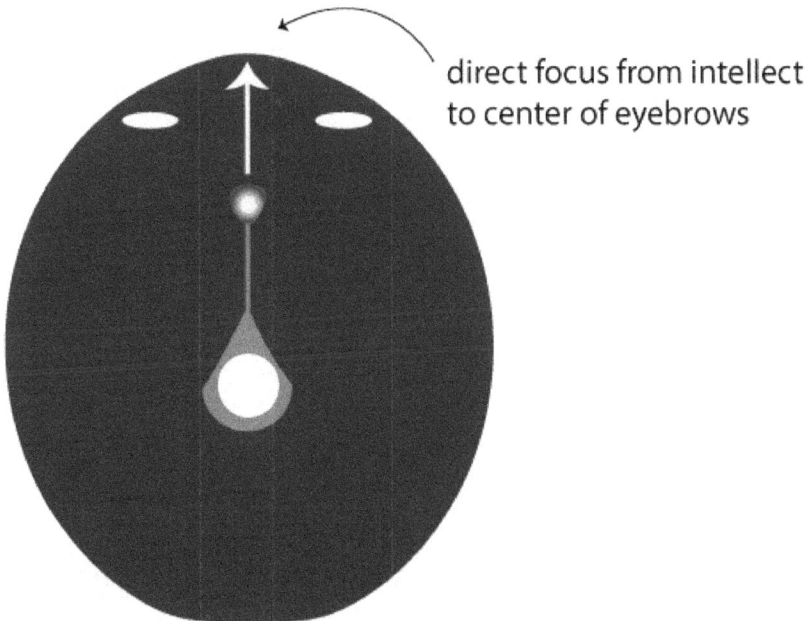

direct focus from intellect
to center of eyebrows

November 23, 1999

Babaji

He said, "Do not break the seal."

Remark:

This refers to a break in the loop of kundalini energy. Kundalini energy when experienced in normal usage is the reproductive power in the body. In simpler terms it is the lifeforce in the body, the power which runs digestion, which heals the body and which makes the body rest. That power is disrupted when energy is wasted and whenever one constructively or otherwise, express the sexual force in subtle or gross dimensions.

Generally a break in the sealed energy of kundalini is caused by ancestral pressure, brought on by the need of ancestors for physical forms. They apply a pressure from the subtle world. That force triggers sexual connections. However if one is able to develop a yoga siddha physical body, one can bypass the ancestors since one's body will be unresponsive to sexual polarity. This is made possible by advanced technique yoga, where the kundalini energy loses the sexual charge.

Here are some diagrams of the sealing and breakage of kundalini loop.

sealed   broken sealed

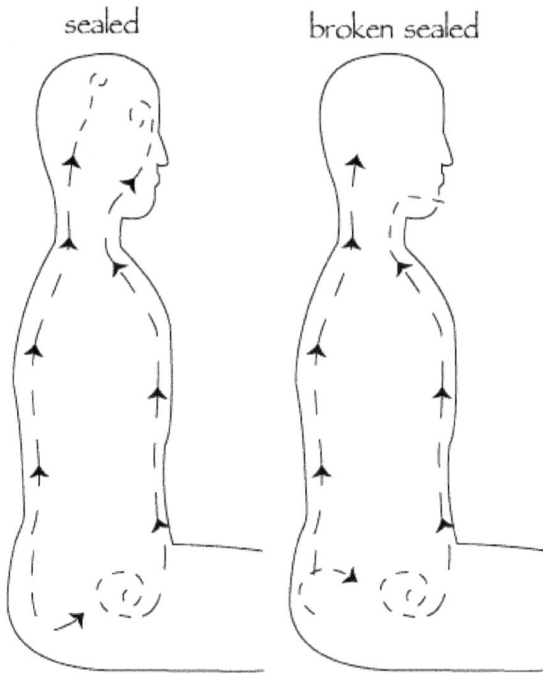

partial collapse   full collapse

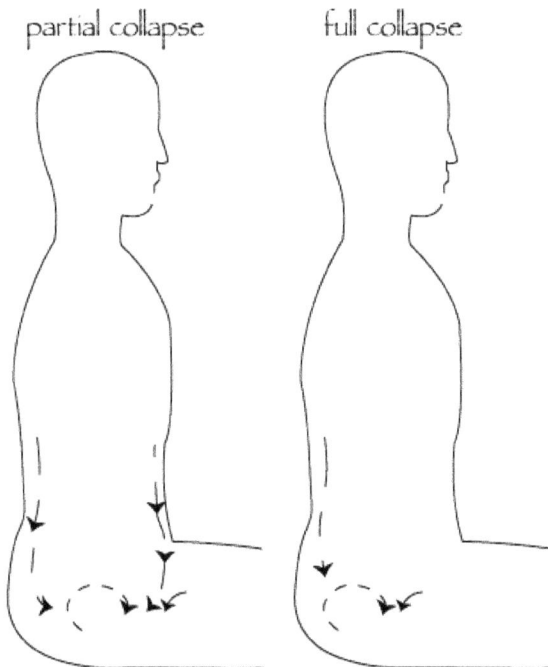

Instead of responding to ancestral pressure, a yogin who uses a yoga siddha form responds to siddha pressure, coming from mahayogins like Babaji. Everyone is under some type of pressure. Thus, the yogi escapes the ancestral force and becomes responsive to the siddha influences.

A physical yoga siddha body through an accomplishment is not a subtle achievement. It is an indication that the yogi made advancement. A full yoga siddha body is when the subtle form is free from sexual attraction. This is harder to achieve. As I explained in other books, curbing the subtle body from sexual expression is a much harder task. Merely curbing the gross body and changing its sex craving tendency is not a subtle accomplishment. It is however a source of confidence for beginners, so that they may know for sure that the attainment of a subtle yoga-siddha form is a definite possibility. Otherwise the range of yogic accomplishments, would seem to be a case of fighting a losing battle. One can win the battle. That is certain.

November 24, 1999

Balarama

He said, "That is important. Only a few can accomplish that."

Remark:

He spoke of keeping the kundalini loop closed as instructed by Babaji.

November 24, 1999

Hanuman

He said, "Use Babaji's method and see this."

He showed how to retract and subdue the small vision which is in the intellect organ.

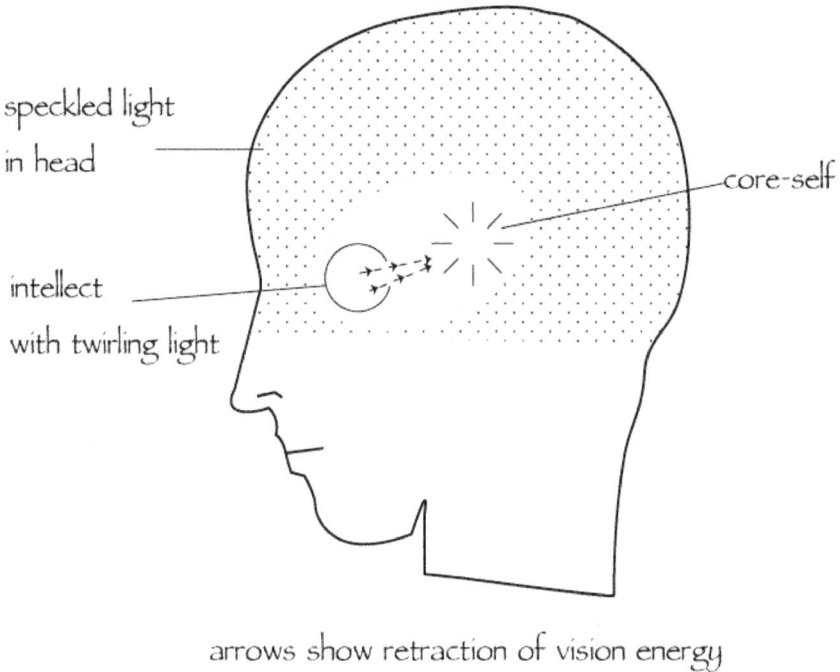

speckled light in head

intellect with twirling light

core-self

arrows show retraction of vision energy

November 24, 1999

Babaji

He said, "From within the intellect, retract that one too. That is especially incompatible with a siddha's existence."

Remark:

He spoke of the tongue orb which sometimes moves out of the intellect down into the tongue and palate. According to Yogesh this orb does not actually move out of the intellect organ but rather, it flashes a light in the tongue and palate, while remaining stationed in the intellect. He said that a similar orb appears in the tongue when activated by the continuous periodic flash. Yogesh is the master visionary of the subtle organs. He detailed these. I think that hardly a yogin is able to reach his level of clarity in the matter.

When the flashing energy is retracted from the various sense organs, one can curb those senses on the gross and subtle levels. For instance if one can control the flash of energy reaching the tongue from the intellect, then one can control diet.

November 25, 1999

Babaji

He said, "Attend to either Yogesh or Hanuman."

Remark:

This is the special feature of Babaji. He never tries to establish himself as anyone's one and only guru. He does not object to anyone taking help from others.

By his advice I consulted Yogesh, who stayed in my intellect organ. He showed where to find the taste orb and the reflection of it in the tongue and palate. I found it behind the tongue in the area of the mouth where food moves just as it is to be swallowed. It was an orb of milky light shining brightly like a bulb.

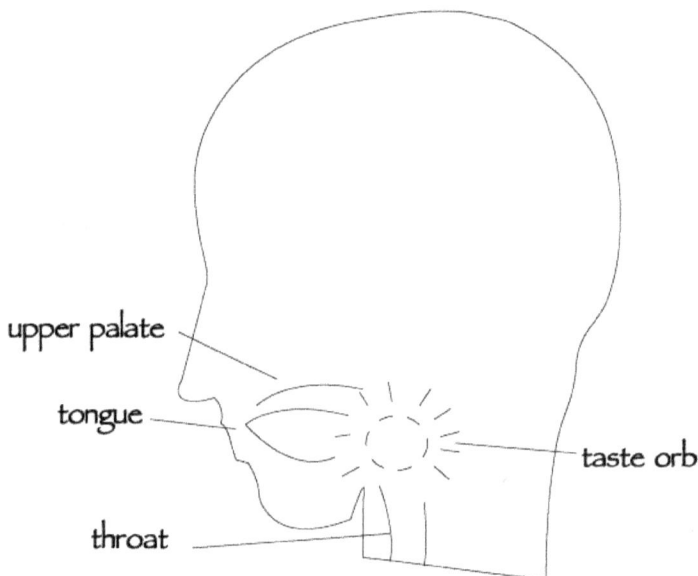

November 25, 1999

Yogeshwarananda

He showed the eye in the intellect and the taste orb which is reflected into the throat. These are lights on the subtle plane. By pranavision they appear to be multi-colored lights and moving atomic energy.

eye orb in intellect

taste orb

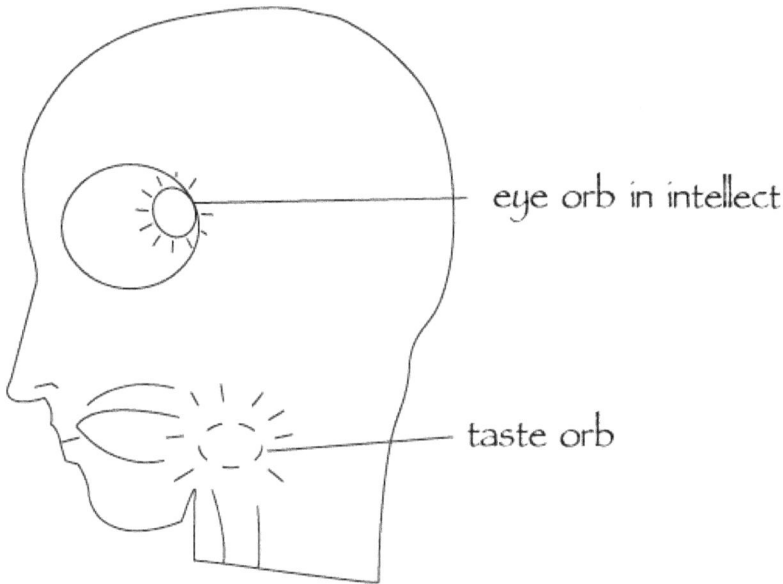

According to Yogesh, when his guru touched his head he saw the complete set of lights. That caused him to be fully absorbed. He saw all details in a matter of two days. However in my case, I saw these lights, one by one, over a period of years. Up to the date when I initially typed these remarks on March of 2001, Yogesh showed different subtle lights. In my case, it was a gradual revelation. I state this to debar persons from asking me about making them see lights. Yogesh showed these after entering my brahmrandra and penetrating into my intellect organ. Sometimes he stays there for days at a time, sometimes for minutes or seconds, and then leaves. It may be that I have some special opportunity. That is based on a yoga siddha body that I carried over in many lives. Otherwise I was not as lucky as Yogeshwarananda whose technique yoga teacher was physically available for a short time and who in that time, blessed him with complete supernatural perception.

I had used the supernatural vision before but it was involuntarily. Once I saw a four-handed Vishnu form, Padmanabha. Once I saw Gopal Krishna the transcendental cowherd boy. Both visions concerned only spiritual forms. Once I met Shiva in a supernatural forest. These occurrences were not controlled by me. They occurred by acts of providence, by those deities causing my spiritual eyesight to be activated.

No one should approach me about giving supernatural or divine sight, because if I could awarded it I would have done so already. I myself, strive for its establishment and continuity. I can tell you this however, and I state this by the blessing of Yogesh and Padmanabha Vishnu, that the supernatural and divine visions are powered by the vision of the core-self. This spirit vision if retracted from the physical pursuits, and if contained and refocused into the supernatural and spiritual worlds, would give the perception you crave. Otherwise it is not possible to see into higher dimensions. It is the same spirit vision that powers the physical sight, and the power of conception and imagination.

November 26, 1999

Ganesh

On this day, Ganesh advised that I do a technique which was shown by Yogesh. The accomplished yogin left some notations in my intellect organ. I picked up the instructions supernaturally.

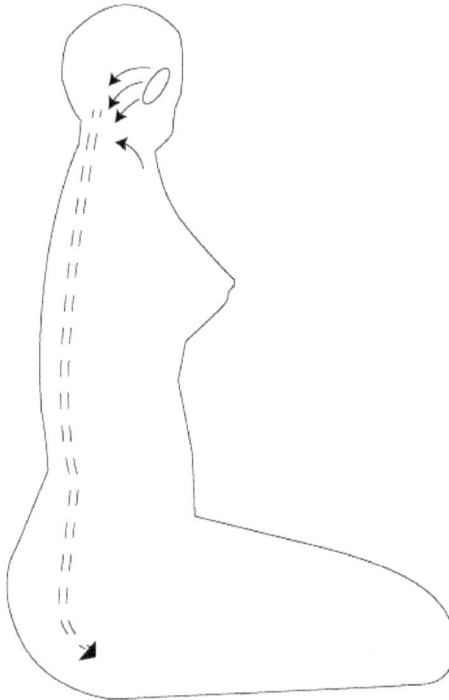

Eye orb is turned counterclockwise ¼ of a turn and then it is turned back ¼ of a turn. This is done repeatedly by will power. If it resists will power, one should observe its movement and let the will power follow its movement by keen observation. The eye orb gives of a light-effusion energy, a subtle nourishment.

November 26, 1999

Panchanam Bhattacharya

This yogi came. He showed a solar energy tube in the intellect organ. It appears that the intellect organ is multi-dimensional, such that on one level one sees certain parts and on another, one sees a different sets of operations. He showed a solar energy tube in which imagination occurs. He told me to tightly control the imagination and throat orbs.

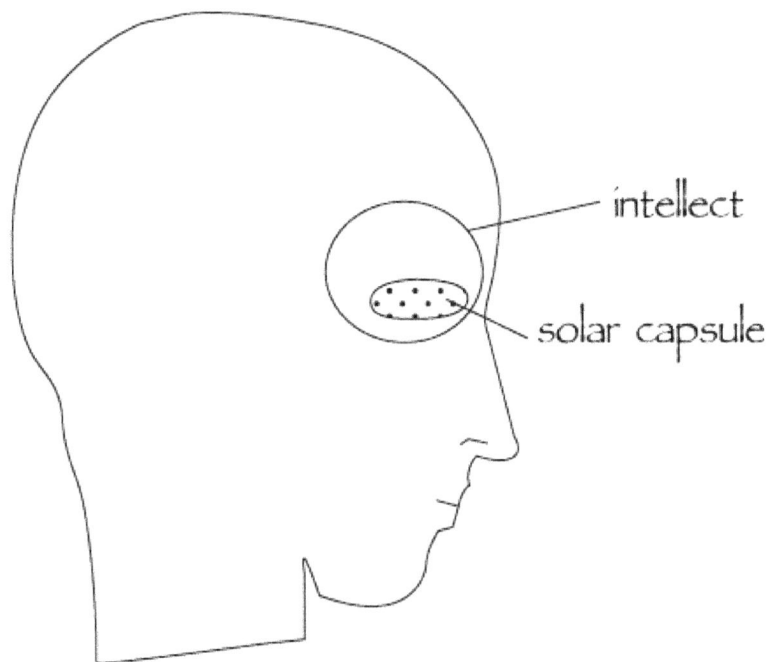
intellect

solar capsule

November 26, 1999

Babaji

This yogi came. He showed the imagination capsule orb. The same orb was shown by Panchanam Bhattacharya. This orb goes in an ecliptic orbit. It travels up and down as indicated by the dotted lines in the diagram below. When it is in the stand-by mode, not being used, the core-self is stationed in the back of it as indicated.

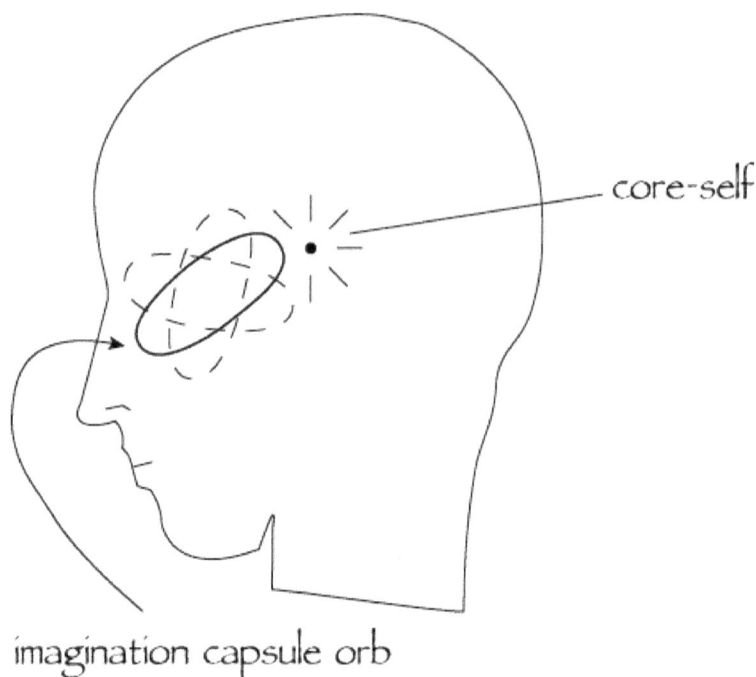

core-self

imagination capsule orb

November 26, 1999

Yogeshwarananda

He said, "Instead of imagining various things, spin the organ of fantasy. Get that under control."

Later on, I asked a question, "What is the cause of the lack of distinction of these organs."

He replied, "It is caused by too much engagement with temporary existence."

I replied to him, "That engagement is mostly non-deliberate. It occurs even when it is not desired and even when it is not deliberately activated."

He remarked, "Yes, but that does not matter. Some children whose bodies were scaled in fire, were endangered even though they did not deliberately create the blaze."

I then said, "Guruji, the imagination and other powers of the intellect take place whimsically."

After I stated this, he was silent. I did not pursue the issue further.

Babaji

He said, "That will remove the oil in the rib cage. It will remove emotions which are harbored in the subtle rib cage."

Remark:

Babaji spoke of the result of doing the bow stretch when one does it sufficiently to affect the back of the body and when one does each side separately with particular care.

Valmiki

He said, "Pull it back and up like this. Make the sensing end of it be harnessed upward."

Remark:

He spoke of the imagination orb. Persons who are bewildered as to what the imagination orb is, may find out by sitting in a dark place, remaining still as possible without disturbances. As soon as one senses that there is an image, idea or sound in the mind, one should note where it occurred, whether on the left or right side, in the front or behind, above or below the self or sense of self. Where it occurred is the location of the imagination orb. In fact the subtle mechanism which created the image or idea is that imagination orb. The trouble with this subtle organ is that it is hardly seen but its operations in the form of images, sounds and ideas is seen in the mind.

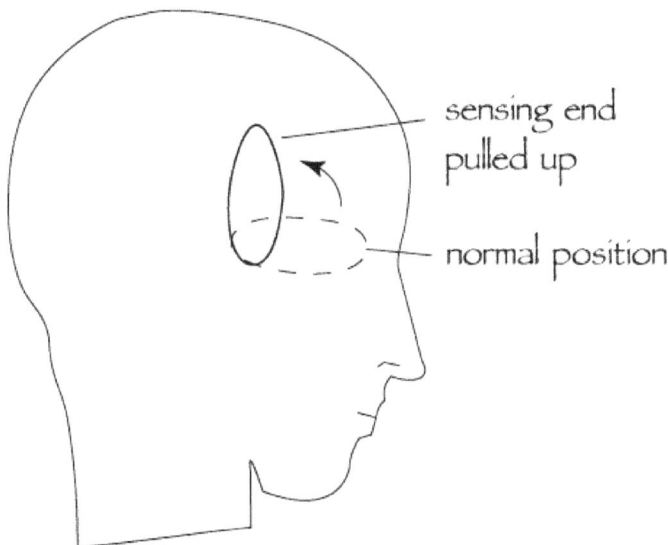

sensing end
pulled up

normal position

November 30, 1999

Brahma

He said, "Everything lean. Subtle energy clean."

Remark

This refers to the condition of the energy in the subtle body of a yogi. This is desired. It requires a tight diet so that in the lotus posture, the abdomen can be pulled up and the eye orb can be pulled into the intellect organ.

December 2, 1999

Shiva

He gave a technique which was a combination of a posture, breath-infusion and an action of pulling down the intellect organ with a spike energy.

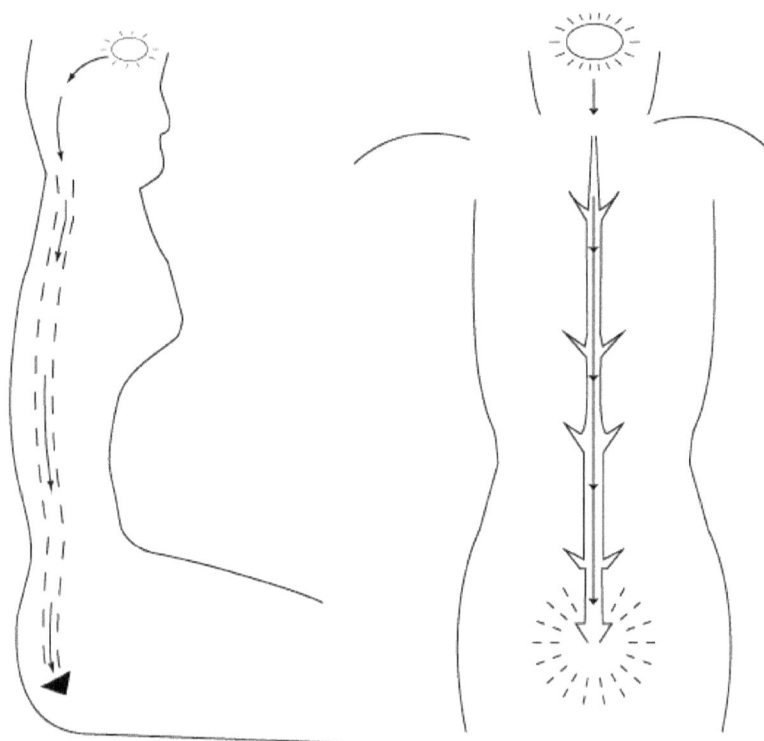

December 3, 1999

Krishna-Balarama

They asked, "What did he show?"
I explained the spike kriya, demonstrating how I was shown it.
They replied, "Do this one to eliminate the split energy."

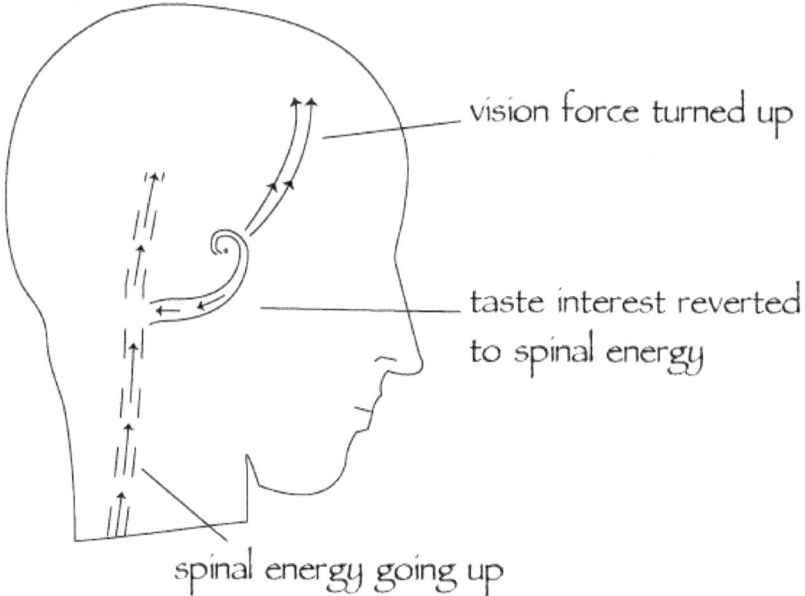

vision force turned up

taste interest reverted to spinal energy

spinal energy going up

December 5, 1999

Babaji

He explained how the subtle energy in the throat which controls eating, fears that it may be separated from the core-self. This fear causes the core to be more accommodating to over-eating. Babaji showed the fear to induce me to get rid of it, or at least not to respond to it.

December 5, 1999

Narad

I rarely hear from this mahayogin. He showed a collection of lights in the head. He showed how to stabilize them where there is light which is pursued in meditation.

Sometimes in meditation, one sees a light, which appears out of nowhere, out of the darkness within one's head. Then when one tries to focus it disappears. Narad explained that some lights act on their own to appear and would remain in view for some time, if one did not pursue them and did not try to arrest them as a focus.

December 6, 1999

Murlidhara Krishna

He said, "When will you straighten your back? Do it and more siddhas will visit you."

Remark:

This remark was given after Babaji showed some neck stretches.

Babaji

He showed a back yoke stretch, where the toes are grabbed. This causes sex energy to be released from the waist area. One should do the down-draw breath, drawing physical and subtle air through the crown of the head with the brow chakra, being pointed inward into the crown.

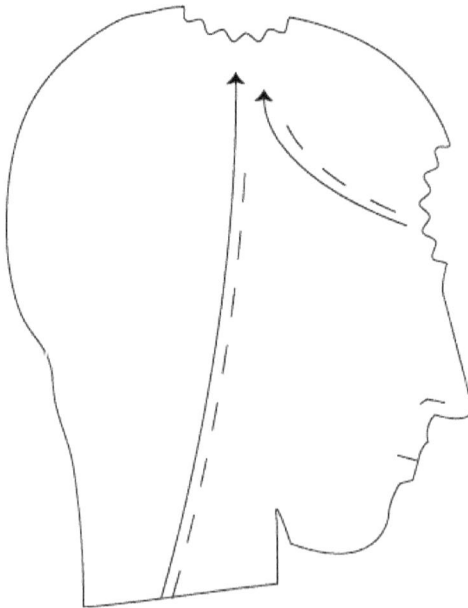

stretch

December 6, 1999

Skanda

He showed a technique for absorbing the brow chakra into the top chakra. This comes after one loses interest in the brow chakra and its benefits. The brow chakra is caused by the combined energies of the crown chakra and the kundalini force which is based at the bottom of the spinal column.

March 8, 2000

Shiva

Evacuation process

Shiva inspired realizations about the evacuation process. If one does not have prompt evacuation, and if diet is not properly regulated for facilitating yoga, the base chakra will not develop. Instead the energy at the base will remain darkish and will be sluggish. Some people use visualization. They feel that this can activate the chakras without vigorous breath-infusion and postures. Visualization works if one first purified the chakras by grosser methods like doing kundalini yoga, curbing diet, eating at the proper times, doing nauli stomach pumps and other hatha yoga exercises. One cannot influence the system merely by subtle methods like visualization of the breath going into and out of the body, or through mentally tracking the chakras up and down the spine.

In this respect the association of Shiva and of other great yogins is indispensable.

In-blast kriya.

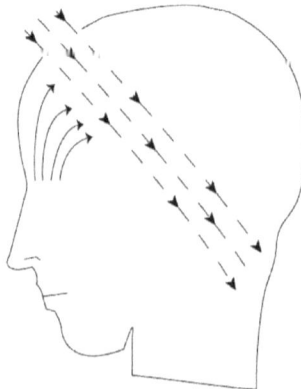

March 13, 2000

Shiva

On this day he gave a technique which is shown in the diagram below. This is done while one is in the lotus posture, keeping the spinal energies and intellect organ together by mystic contact. At the top of the forehead a space opens up from the outside. One then sees through that space. In some cases, the space is there as a space of bluish haze. Or, it may open to a clear bluish sky outside the psyche.

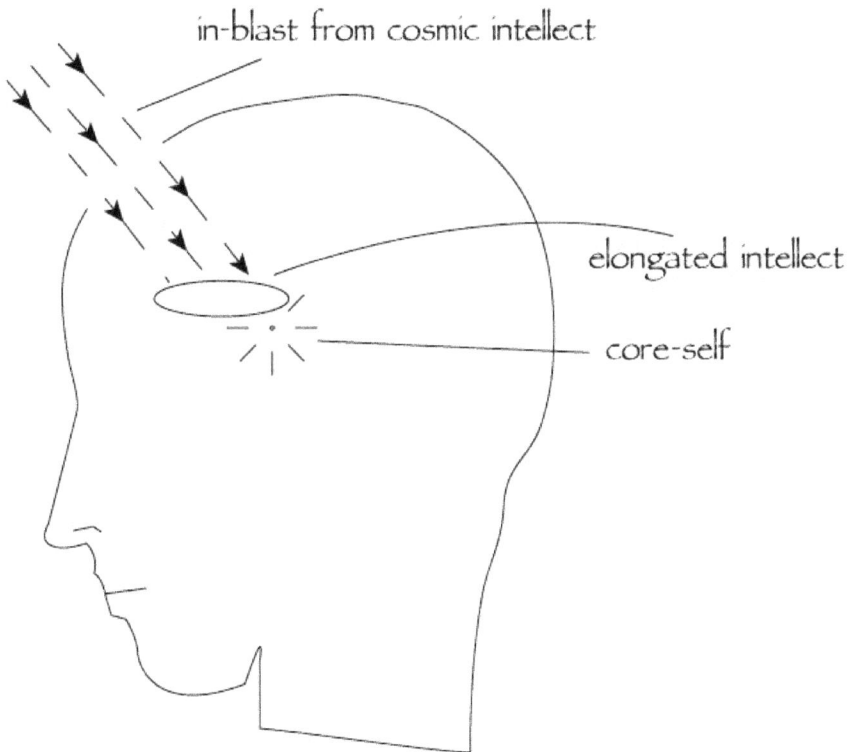

in-blast from cosmic intellect

elongated intellect

core-self

March 13, 2000

Murlidhara Krishna

He gave the same technique with a stronger blast of energy coming from the outside.

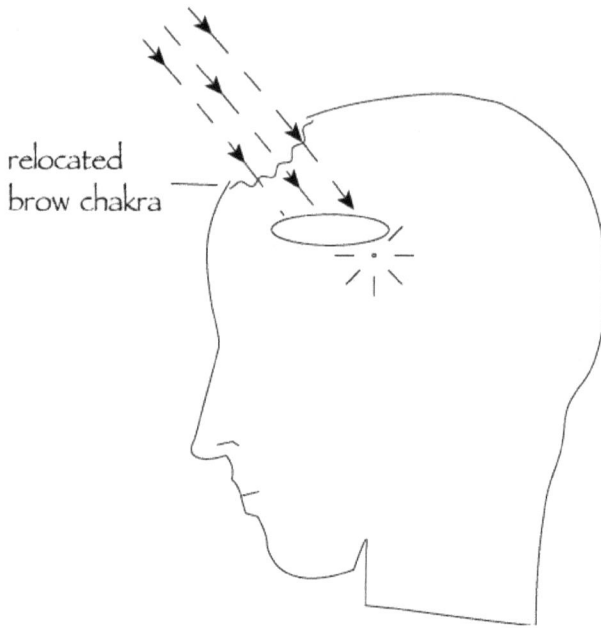

relocated
brow chakra

March 14, 2000

Shiva

He gave the same technique but with a pull-in of the chakra area.

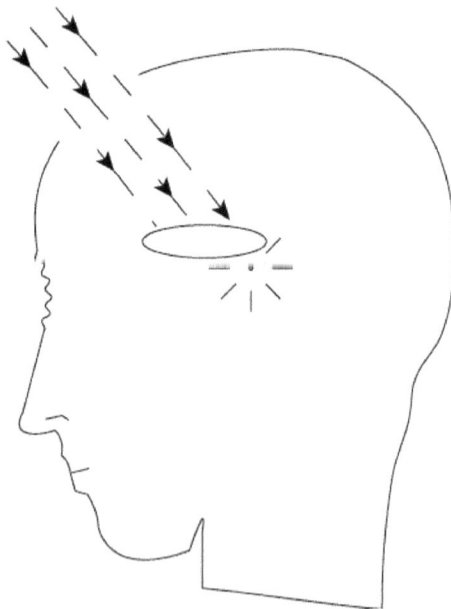

March 15, 2000

Shiva

He gave a yoni pull-up exercise. This means pulling up the female sexual opening. This is for men and women. It is done while doing breath-infusion with the eyes closed. When the body is sufficiently surcharged with physical and subtle air, one should inhale or exhale once more, and then concentrate on drawing up all sexual energies from the pubic area. One should apply the anus and stomach locks.

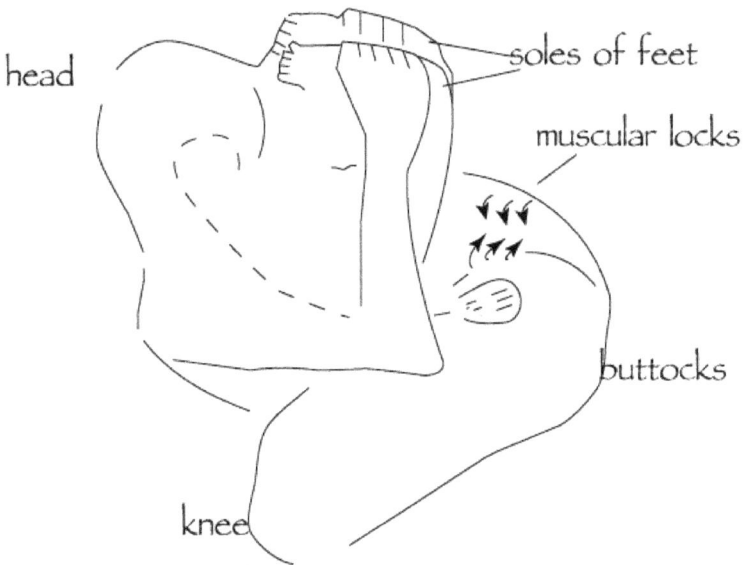

head

soles of feet

muscular locks

buttocks

knee

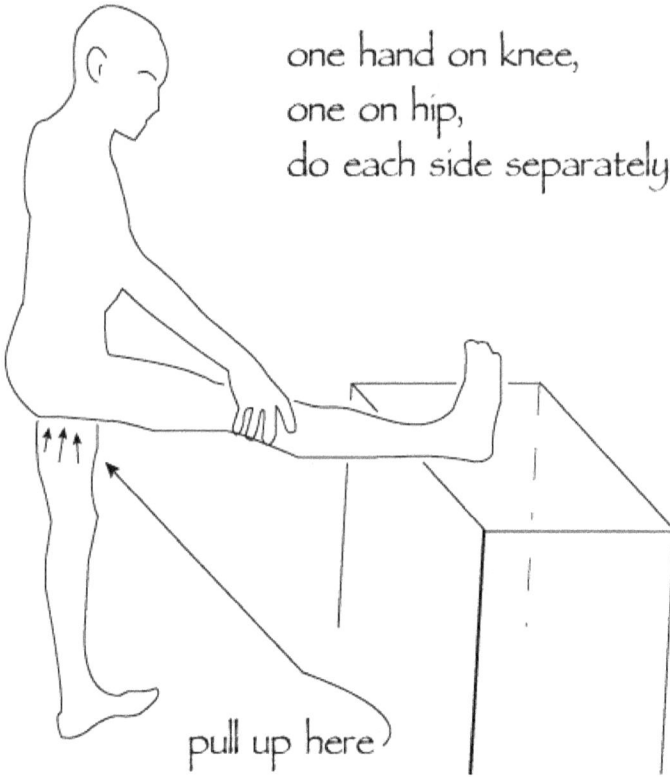

one hand on knee,
one on hip,
do each side separately

pull up here

March 15, 2000

Shiva

He gave an in-blast and brow chakra retraction procedure. This energy goes down to the base chakra. This is done after doing the morning session of breath-infusion with the body fully charged. One should, if he can, sit in lotus or easy pose. Note that the energy from the brow chakra goes to the kanda which is a small bulb in the pubic area of the subtle body.

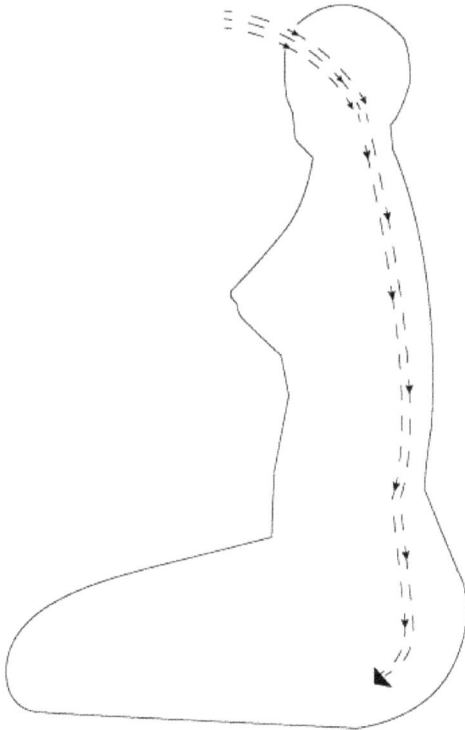

March 15, 2000

Helping the base chakra.

On this date, I made notations regarding which action helps the base chakra to become purified and to free itself from so many chores, which cause it to remain at the bottom of the body. One should do the following.

Take less food.

Do a massage of the anal muscles while taking bath.

Take more air into the body while doing breath-infusion, at least twice per day, early in the morning and in the afternoon. One may do breath-infusion after evacuation, at noon, before meals, before taking water, after rising in the morning and in the afternoon.

One should always evacuate promptly and keep track of the daily evacuations which should be regular. One should be sure that all stools are evacuated from the anal pouch.

These actions which are hygienic and physical do much to free the kundalini force, so that it can continually come up the sushumna passage in the middle of the subtle spine. In that way, kundalini energy would endeavor always for the upward ascent into the brain.

March 18, 2000

Hanuman

He said, "Be attentive to the exercises. Do not generalize. Protect your back when lifting or working. Do not be careless. Work on special areas when you do postures since each gives access to particular body parts. Do not jerk or stress the back unnecessarily."

He gave this technique.

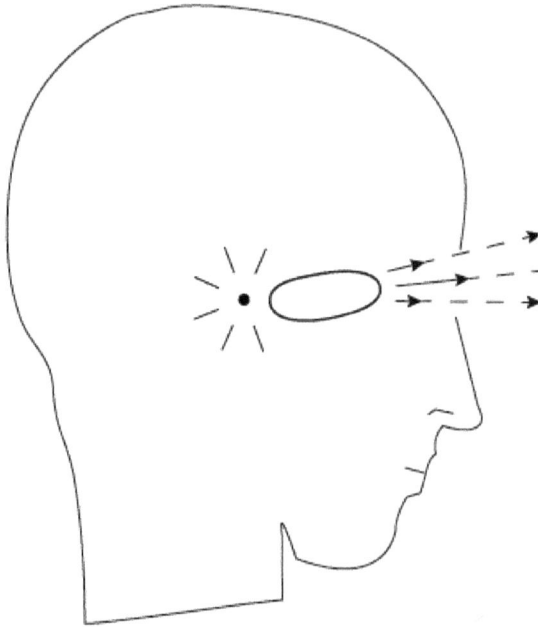

March 19, 2000

Anila deity

He said, "Needs will be fulfilled. You need not be the one to fulfill any particular need of anyone. It is best to sidestep the concerns of others. Reserve yourself for yoga. Hide yourself or they will place demands on you."

March 19, 2000

Shiva

He gave this kriya. In this one, there is no opening to the outside of the psyche.

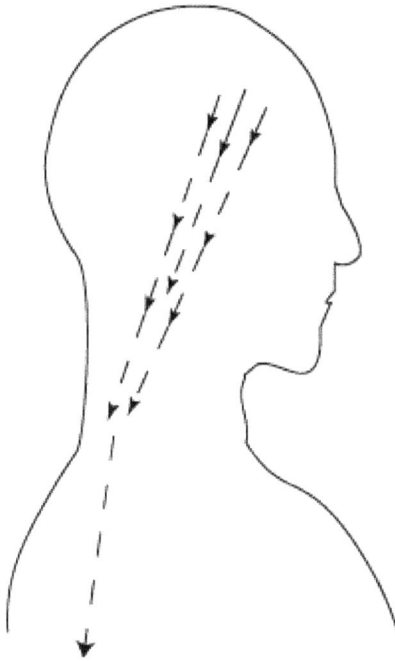

March 19, 2000

Shiva

He advised on water intake. This was for me to take water in the morning after I did exercises and meditation. This water was to remove excess chemicals from the body. This helps the kidneys to remove harmful chemicals which would harm vital organs.

I was to take water before my main meal which was at 5am in the morning. Before the meal I took half a glass of water. This water gives the body any water it needs at that time. If one does not take such water, the body will squeeze water out of the food being digested. This will make for a drier stool which will take longer to travel through the colon.

March 20, 2000

Shiva

This is a technique which uses the breath. As marked on the diagram, one pulls energy in from the top of the forehead down to the base chakra when one inhales, and pushes energy out through the brow chakra from the kanda bulb when one exhales. The points labeled are touch points which are kept track of mystically.

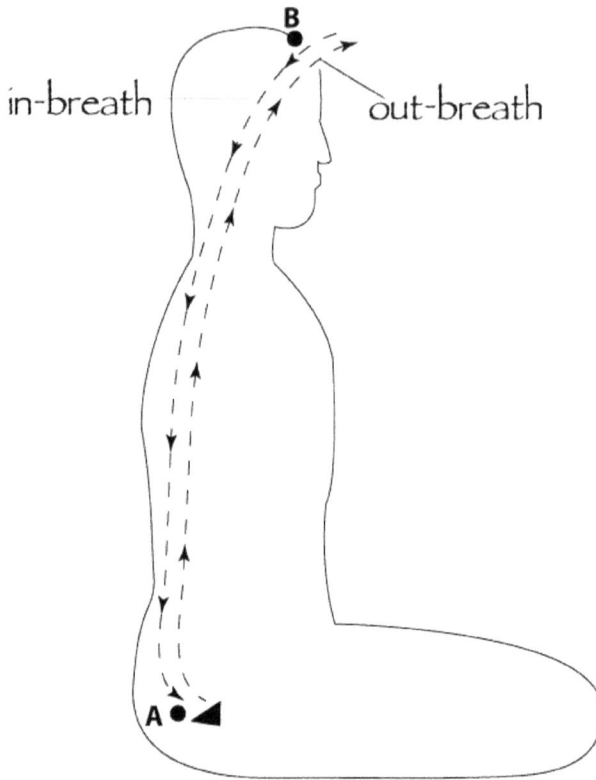

in-breath   out-breath

B

A

A and **B** are touch points

March 20, 2000

Shiva

Spinal spiral out-blast

This is done as shown in the diagram below. It is done during and after an intense session of breath-infusion.

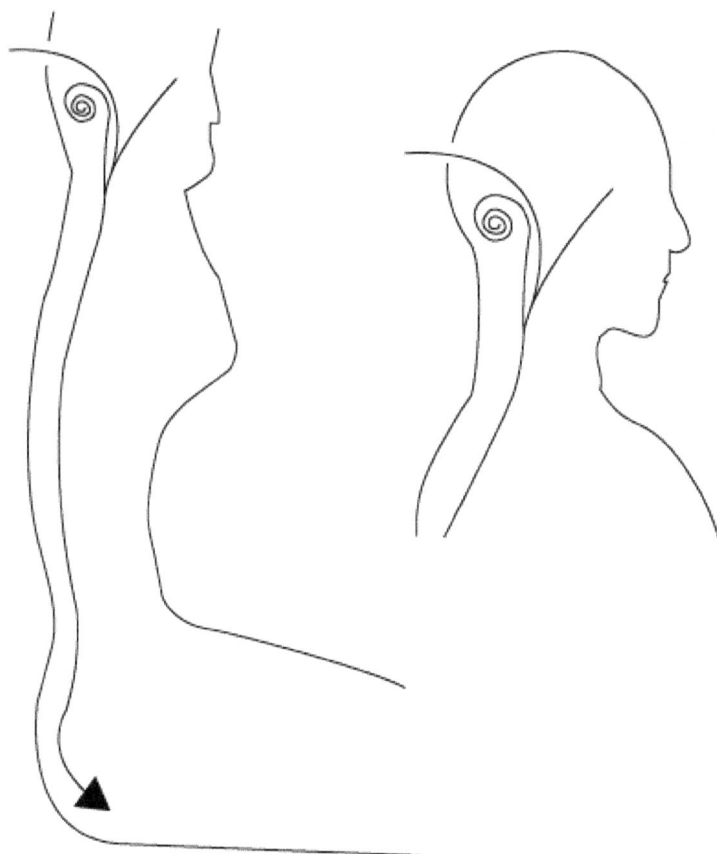

March 21, 2000

Shiva

He said, "Attentive hatha yoga practice with advanced mystic techniques, gives the mind the habit of looking within the psyche to correct faults and to observe relevant aspects of the subtle organs. Gradually the force of this practice takes hold of the mind and changes its outward-going tendency into an inward-observing one. This is the stepping stone to higher yoga.

March 23, 2000

Shiva

In-blast with inner intellect concentration

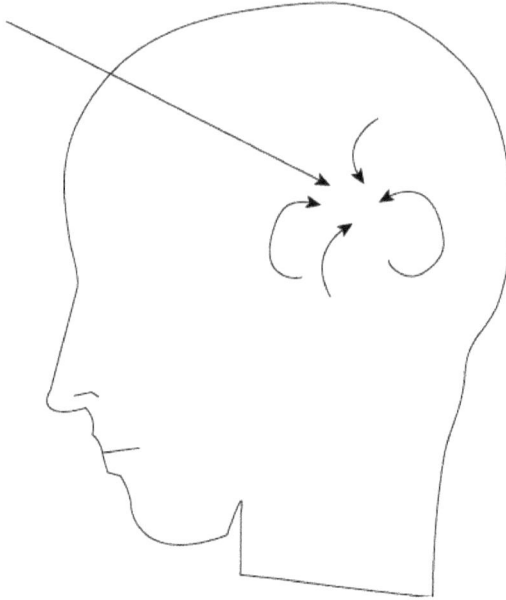

March 24, 2000

Shiva

He said, "All flirtation leads to responsibility which is sponsored by work on the basis of passion."

Remark:

This was said by Shiva when I was circumstantially forced to work with some ladies at a church. Generally, working in the material world is an impediment to yoga practice. However some work cannot be avoided. Due to flirtations with women, a male is forced to work like an animal, either physically or mentally. Mental fatigue is tagged as stress.

Flirtation, as Shiva told me, leads to responsibility at a late date. The flirtation is actually sponsored by a need for work. It is motivated and sponsored by passionate energy. Initially the work is disguised as a promise for pleasure. When the male being accepts the promise, he becomes drawn into compulsory work. This utilizes his time and pulls him into more cultural involvement through more sexual interactions and the resulting liabilities.

In my own case, for example, I can say that in this life and in many others, I worked on and on, industriously, on the basis of rebounding forces from previous flirtations. The intellect instrument in the subtle brain has a perverted sexual sense. It is continually lured into flirtations which terminate in hard mental or physical work or both.

Every flirtation, however slight, will cause a male to work hard in the future to adjust the energy to nature's satisfaction. While he does this, nature will implicate him for further employment. Thus if he is not careful, and certainly if he is not a technique yogi, he will be condemned to being a mental or physical work-horse in the material world. That is just the way it is. I know because that was my existence for some time. Every time I assume a physical body I experience this.

During the month of July of 2001, while I initially typed this remark, I began a commentary on Bhagavad Gita. That was my second commentary. That is for kriya yogins. The first commentary was to clear up the confusion regarding exactly what Krishna said in the Gita. In any case, that second commentary gave details of the secrets of how to work and end the flirtations. The Bhagavad Gita is a treatise on how to work in such a way as to terminate the work.

Everyone is being victimized in the material world, both the males and females, except that the females are set-up to set-up the males. It is all a set-up. Some people feel that the selves have no sexuality but they are wrong. Some core-selves are neuter but many are male and others are female. Various tiny seeds look alike because their natures are not activated As soon as they sprout, their sexuality or neutrality becomes manifested. It is so with the selves. Initially most of them exist in compact clusters in the spiritual sky. In that condition their potentials are not shown That is called the condition of sat or eternally existing causelessly.

If somehow or the other, the Supreme or one of His parallel divinities, take a mind to cause the expression of the individuality of a particular cluster of spirits, we see their natures expressed in certain types of worlds like this material place. Most of the worlds are supernatural.

Part 3

Shiva

He gave some inside locations for calling upon or meditating on certain divine persons and mahayogins.

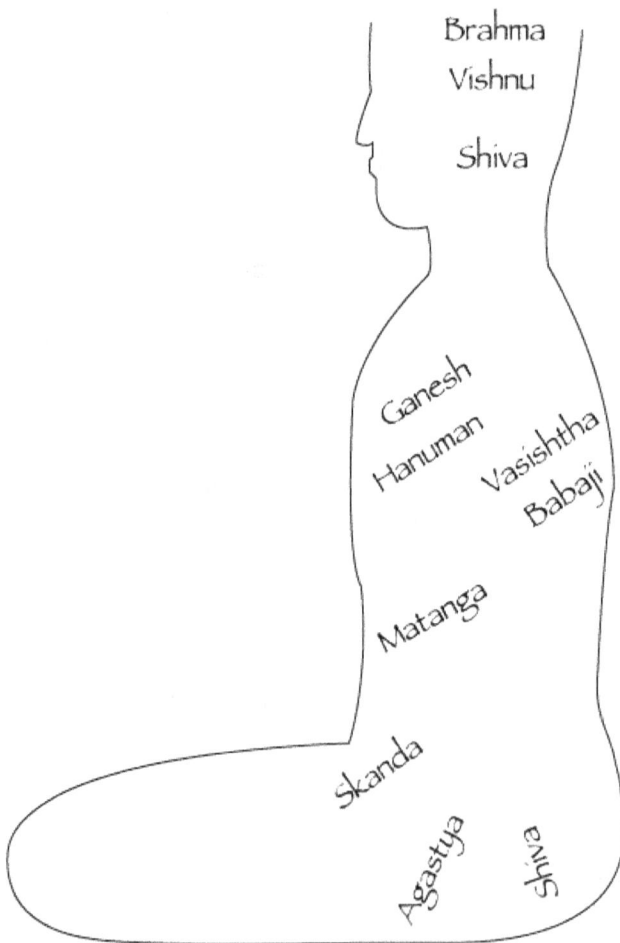

Brahma
Vishnu

Shiva

Ganesh
Hanuman

Vasishtha
Babaji

Matanga

Skanda

Agastya

Shiva

March 25, 2000

Ganesh

He said, "Sometimes you owe money. Sometimes without reason, it is taken by time. He can waste it if he desires."

Remark:

It is important to be free from non-yogic association otherwise one will be unsubmissive to providence, and will progress very slowly. Usually people feel that incidences are based only on circumstances of this life. There are a group of people who feel that things are based on the circumstance of this life and on the movement of the stars.

Besides all this, there are past lives. Those histories are the basis of the present one. That does not mean that in all cases, whatever happens to someone, is based on his or her karma or actions in the past life. There are other more pressing and urgent factors, besides a man's past actions. There are supernatural forces in the form of fate. This is pressed on him by the urgencies felt by supernatural people who could care less about what a limited spirit deserves.

In technique yoga, we want to be free from the influences of people who feel that everything is based on the present. They try to rationalize everything in the present context. They force this idea down the throat of a yogi, sometimes causing him to give up the association of Shiva.

In the case of earned income, a man is expected to spend most of the money on his family. If he has children, they take priority. Usually the mother is very protective of the children because that is the way of the nurturing energy which sponsors feminine nature. This is a very useful energy but it has no conscious idea of past lives. It has blind instinct only. Under the force of that energy, a mother expects that her husband will use every penny earned to advance family interest. However some of the earned income is due to go elsewhere because of other obligations from past lives.

On the other hand, some men waste money when they come under the influence of intoxicants or when they come under the influence of previous sexual connections. This is due to a weakness in male nature, a serious flaw in it, a persistent vice.

Over all, for most human beings, material nature was, is and will be a puzzle. They will never figure it out.

March 26, 2000

Shiva

He showed a between-thigh nadi subtle tube.

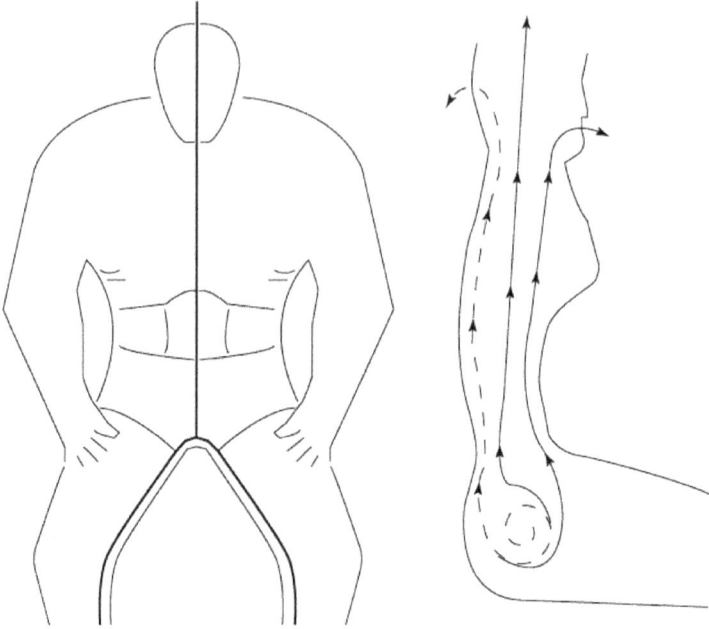

Mar 30, 2000

Shiva

He instructed me to use an abdomen-push after breath-infusion.

This is a pushing out of the abdomen while pulling up from underneath. The push is steady but done sufficiently not to strain the system. This helps to energize front kundalini. In the beginning, for at least two or three years, when one does kundalini yoga, one should concentrate on awakening back kundalini. Later on, one should work on front kundalini.

Usually for motivating back kundalini, one stops doing the rapid breathing on an inhale, and one pulls up the abdomen. In front kundalini practice, one stops on an inhale and pushes down the abdomen.

Here is a diagram of how the downward push is applied. This is also a lock, even though we generally stress that locks are upward pulls. In the advanced stages, there are locks in the form of downward pushes. This is revealed inside the body by accumulation of subtle energy and by mahayogins, who observe one's efforts and who come into one's psyche, and teach from within the subtle body.

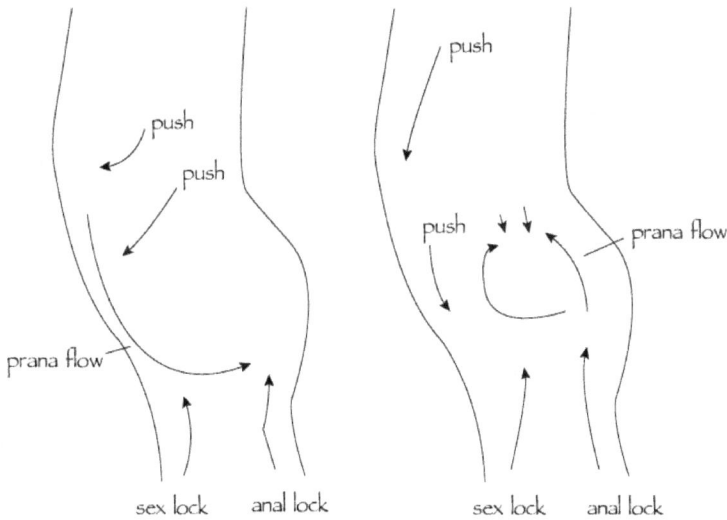

Shiva

He showed a solar plexus energy draw-out technique.

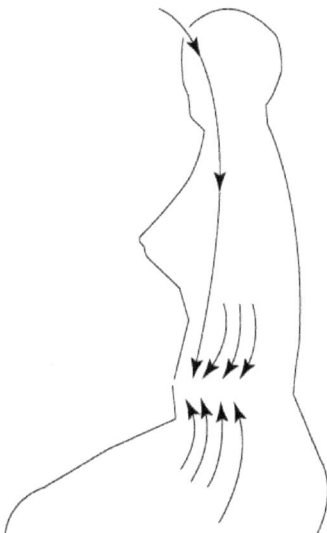
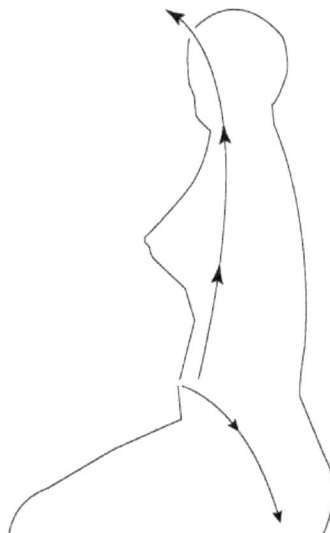

This technique for solar plexus revelation, helps one to understand what was being done when one entered the mother's womb. At that stage, more or less, one is shrunk down to being just an urge for drawing nutrients from the mother's energies. One pulls nutrients both physically and subtly. This is why one's body becomes attached to the mother's form emotionally. The attraction is physical and psychic.

After losing a body, one usually becomes a disoriented wandering ghost. One wanders about the astral places, but one does that in close association to surviving relatives and friends. It is rare also that one goes to a heavenly location. After wandering for a time, one gets worn down psychologically, because one lost every physical possession. One stays with one person whom one feels one can trust. This is usually a son, daughter, grandson or granddaughter. Sometimes one stays close to a husband or wife but usually that is not the case, because by the way of family life, a husband and wife usually have disagreements in their later years. They gradually become estranged from one another with the equivalent force which forcibly brought them together in their youthful days.

If however one stays with this wife or with the husband after death, then it is likely that if one is not careful, one will become the brother or sister of that spouse in the next birth. Usually as I said, one stays with a son or daughter or with a dear friend. Gradually by the force of time, one loses interest in regaining status and property from that previous life which one just departed. One sees that it is hopeless. One begins to feel that one will never be able to live in this physical world again. This causes anguish. From that disillusionment, one loses grasp on recent memories of the immediate past life. Then by that erasure of memory, one forgets the former body and one transforms into being an idea in the mind of the person who would become one's parent. From that position in a tiny idea body, one becomes a sexually-charged emotion. From that one gets very near to the sexual apparatus of that would-be parent.

By getting near the sexual apparatus, one becomes a sexual urge in the person's form. Then one enters into the testes of the male person who may give one a birth opportunity.

When at last, one's energies get the chance to be squirted out into a womb in a sexual intercourse either through a willing or unwilling sexual contact, one assumes a small form as a sperm, and hustles up the birth canal and is instinctively and emotionally drawn to the uterus. At that place, one becomes attached both physically and emotionally.

Being greedy for material life, because of the anguish of having lost a body, one draws nutrients from the mother physical and subtle forms. From that one forms into an embryo.

April 2, 2000

Shiva

He said, "For the purpose intended take help when you get it. Cooperate with the charged subtle energy. Move faster."

Remark:

Sometimes a yogi, and at other times, a supernatural authority like Shiva, will gave help on a particular day in relation to certain subtle passages that may open in the subtle body. Sometimes, one has a vision of something on a subtle or super-subtle plane. One should flow with the instruction, inspiration or revelation, temporarily leaving aside regular practice.

In technique yoga, there are set procedures which are followed on a daily basis. From time to time, a technique yogin gets an instruction to change his method. This can be based on advancement to a higher level or digression to a lower one. Besides this, there are changes made on a daily basis by the practice itself. For instance, while doing morning breath-infusion one may be inspired to focus on a certain part of the subtle body. This may only be for one morning or for two, three or four mornings. Then one may switch to another procedure.

One should temporarily gave up a set procedure, if the charged subtle energy bore new passages in the subtle body on a particular morning or if one has a certain vision or sees or hears a certain great yogi or supernatural being. One should follow the lead of a new inspiration. After it was productive, one may return to regular practice, or even adopt a new process.

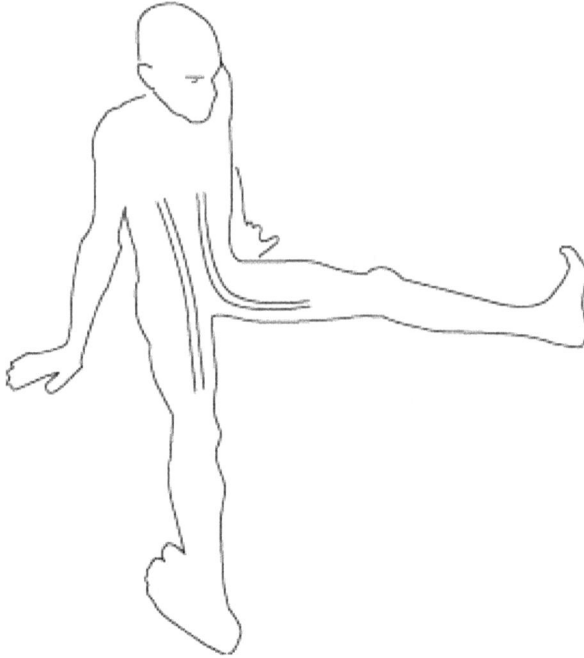

April 2, 2000

On this day I had an inspiration about a subtle charge which opened and revealed a passage that runs down the middle of the sexual area, and then up to the heart area. This was discovered while doing breath-infusion.

April 4, 2000

Shiva

He said, "If there is less pollution, there will be less kundalini sensation and less gap between normal consciousness and raised kundalini consciousness. Less food causes less impurities and less lust, causing more fresh subtle energy to flow. It produces less craving for sensations.

On this day I did this posture and realized these subtle tubes.

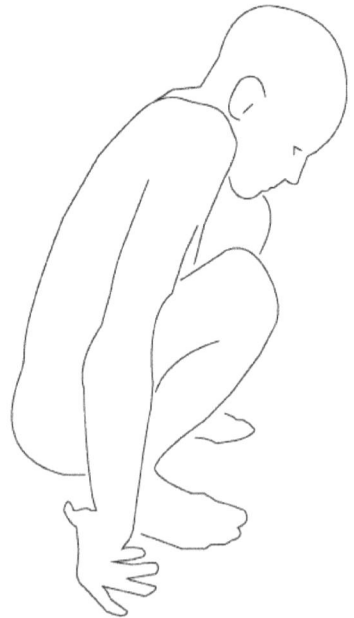

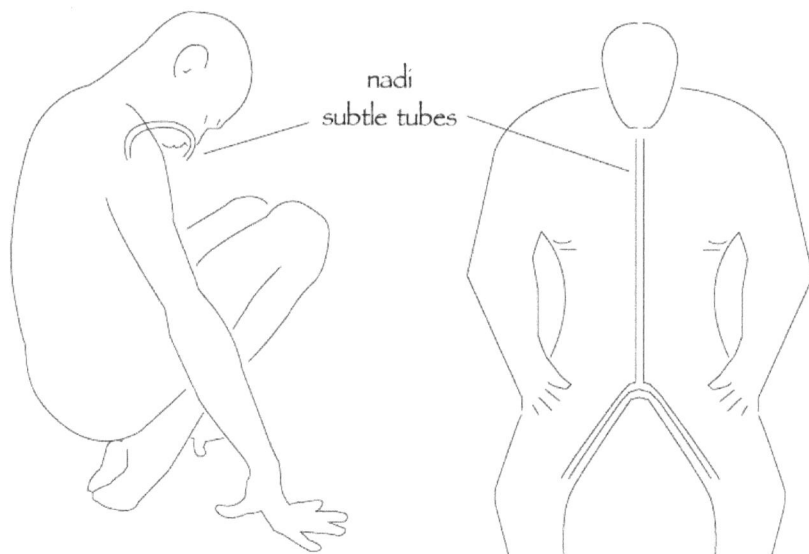

nadi
subtle tubes

Remark:

Yogesh explained that the kundalini force is based on the flaring up of the bhasvara fire. This is the same energy which stimulates the navel chakra and which causes digestion. It is subtle but it has a gross counterpart. It is fed by food nutrients, oxygen (prana) and carbon dioxide (apana). Yogesh explained that at a certain stage the bhasvara fire is eliminated.

People are fascinated with kundalini chakra but it is not such a big issue in the advanced stages. It is however, very important in the beginning, when one should arouse it daily and clear the subtle nadi passages with its fiery force. Unless kundalini is aroused daily, one will never purify the subtle body sufficiently. Subsequently, one will remain on the lower stages. When I advise that someone practice daily, I usually get a weak statement for compliance or a blank look. If one does not practice daily, he or she will not cause kundalini to remain in the brain.

April 5, 2000

Shiva

He said, "Do down-draw or breath-infusion to the lower abdomen. Do the lip-lock, by stiffening and puckering the top lip slightly. Draw under and stiffen the bottom lip. Push the abdomen out after rapid breathing ceases."

Remark:

This is an example of getting an instruction while doing exercises. When one is so inspired, one hears a voice, usually in the head or chest area. It is a subjective voice. However, by following the instruction, one gets results. In this way one increases confidence in clairaudience.

Mentioned above by Shiva was the lip-lock. This lock is usually not mentioned in hatha yoga books. There are many bodily locks which are not mentioned. Books give an outline, an overview. For more particulars one should practice. As one practices one is shown the way, either by a yogi who uses a physical body or one who uses an astral one only.

Sometimes, one gets help from yogis who passed beyond the need even for subtle forms. One receives such instructions from the causal plane.

April 6, 2000

Shiva

He said, "It is best to bow by doing a difficult procedure."

Remark:

This was a comment for a change of method by substituting the practice of a difficult technique for bowing down. Stated differently, I was to do a difficult technique instead of bowing down before the picture of Shiva. The same energy used for bowing would be used to complete a difficult mystic action.

On this morning, he gave a three-point concentration which involved being aware of the kundalini chakra, the kanda bulb and the ahankara sense of initiative.

April 7, 2000

Shiva

He said, "After intense breath-infusion study the distribution of the air absorbed."

Remark:

This is the study of rechak or the arrest of breathing after an intense session of breath infusion which ends with an exhale. Immediately after a session, one may cease breathing for some time without strain. One can trace the movement of subtle energy as it courses throughout the subtle body, travelling through subtle tubes.

If the subtle body is not fully surcharged with fresh subtle air, one will find that the mind will still impulsively create ideas. Those are memories coupled with incoming thoughts.

Sometimes, the mind gets caught in the flow of pranic energy and attains a trance stillness or special movement. Sometimes the kundalini energy moves up as a tingling sensation or as a streak of light. Sometimes it moves up the front middle or back of the body. Sometimes it moves to the right or left side. Sometimes it flashes brilliantly and illuminates various areas of the psyche.

April 9, 2000

Shiva

He said, "Take the intellect to the charged subtle energy. Bring them together. They should work cooperatively. The intellect should be close by when the subtle feelings act during sleep."

Remark:

This is an instruction to get the two powers to work for spiritual advancement. Usually these powers work at odds. Or they work closely for the purpose of procuring sense enjoyments which are costly. For instance, in sexual intercourse, they work closely. The intellect schemes to achieve sexual contact. It joins with sexual feelings as they both explode in a burst of light during flashes of sexual pleasure. However the core-self has to get these two functions under control and cause them to work for emancipation.

April 9, 2000

Babaji

He said, "As a yogi, be sensitive to the subtle energy in food. Good results cannot come from polluted energy. The vegetables should be fresh. Stale, yellow or old vegetables should not be used."

Remark:

This was an instruction in food selection. Babaji began living in my body during the year of 1998. From then on, he closely checked the food preparations. If a certain vegetable was yellowed, he instructed that it be discarded.

April 9, 2000

Shiva

He said, "Learn more and more of the subtle, subtler and subtlest sensations. Addiction to the gross excitements discourages and eliminates subtle perception. Study the absorption of the breath. Notice its movements here and there."

April 10, 2000

Shiva

He showed how strenuous labor causes much subtle energy to be exhausted out of the subtle body. Then extra rest is required. In meditation after strenuous labor, one sees that polluted subtle energy and used protein was vacated from certain parts of the body and psyche, as if they were eliminated from certain storage places in the physical and subtle forms. One also sees the gross and subtle cells packing new energy in the blank spaces.

Hatha yoga causes old energy to be moved out of storage places while new energy is packed in by doing breath-infusion. The solar plexus is the chief place for taking complaints from the various cells about energy losses and for giving new-energy which will be stored in blank areas.

People who do neither hard work nor hatha yoga, have much old energy stored like old things long forgotten in a dark out-of-the-way closet. This old energy influences them to avoid strenuous work or yoga practice. If they are asked to work, they become reluctant and assume a sour non-cooperative attitude.

April 11, 2000

Shiva

He showed how sugar creates greed and ruins yoga. When one eats sugar, or sweetened foods, the appetite increases artificially. One then eats more than necessary. That ruins the practice. A little sugar in some part of a balanced meal is alright.

April 11, 2000

Shiva

Right-eye vision overflow.

Under Shiva's influence, I experienced a right subtle eye vision overflow, such that the visual energy flowed in all directions and perceived all directions simultaneously.

That is a natural capacity of the subtle body. Since the psychological energy is focused on the physical side, one loses subtle perception. Some take narcotic or psychedelic drugs to experience the subtle body but such action causes a backlash in terms of causing the subtle body to become even more unavailable. It is best to practice yoga if one wants to be conscious of the subtle form.

April 12, 2000

Shiva

He said, "The postures should be specific. Stretch carefully while paying strict attention to the particular parts being exercised. Do not generalize. Each of the asanas stretch particular areas."

He gave a technique. A white-bluish light, which is the compressed shrunk intellect organ, moves into the heart chakra and causal cove area.

April 13, 2000

Shiva

He showed how to move the intellect organ into the throat. Once it enters there, it may become elongated like a capsule or like a slim rectangular body. It is then completely out of the head.

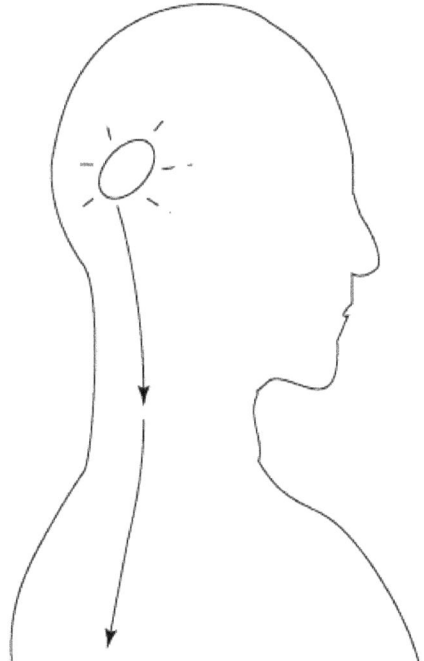

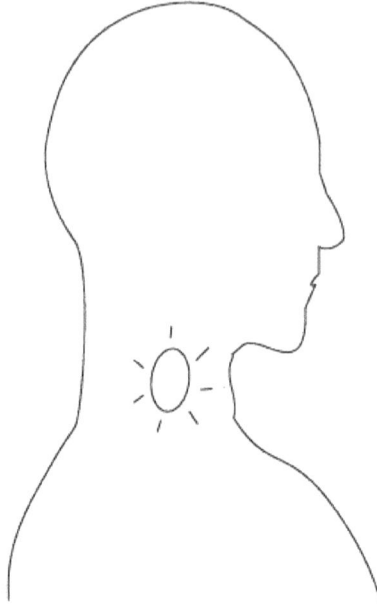

Some realizations in association with Shiva

Celibacy is important for stability of mind. Otherwise by being involved with sexual intercourse, the mind gets excited and exhausted alternately. In addition, females have the menstrual cycle, which is a monthly event. This affects males indirectly. One should be distant from the fluctuations or endure an unsteady mind. Without equilibrium, on cannot meditate effectively.

Another aspect is diet control. The cells of the body are involved in acquiring nutrition. This is why we see that even though a person may dislike obesity, the body may still have excessive fat. The cells may have desires to be filled with food nutrients. One has to get free from food cravings. One should do whatever is necessary to achieve that.

April 15, 2000

Shiva

He instructed that I see Agastya, who gave a death-withdrawal mystic action. This technique is used at the time of death of the body. It is written that Krishna and Balarama used yoga when leaving their specially-designed material forms. Unless one is prepared beforehand, he cannot leave the body in the ideal way. Many persons who follow various religions hope that circumstances will be in their interest at the time of death. The idea is go to God's paradise hereafter.

A definite procedure is to reach that special place while one has the gross body, and to practice getting there repeatedly before the body dies. This is not easy. There are many pressing demands which disrupt the effort and forestall the development. However, a yogi should endeavor no matter what. We can learn from those who are preoccupied making money. These people instruct by their example of how to always keep the objective in mind.

Day or night, in light or darkness, they plan to make more and more money. I had the opportunity to be near wealth-seekers. It is wonderful how they think of money concerns no matter what. Even sexual indulgence, a habit that disrupts many yogis, is not as important to those who constantly acquire money.

Agastya schooled me about the necessity for the breaking off of the sex down-link, the pulling up of the emotional feelings and the kundalini. He said that unless these are done there is no question of applying the death withdrawal technique.

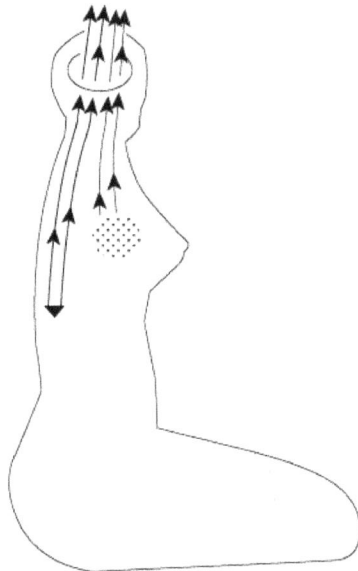

I include diagrams of the required mystic actions. In any case, the sex down-link must be broken. One must pull up the kundalini chakra and the emotional feelings that keep falling out of the causal body into the subtle form from the bottom of the causal cove.

old technique   pull-up technique

A man can say what he likes and believe in any God that suits his fancy. He can have any of those assured spiritual masters who promise salvation, but if he has not accomplish this before death, he will not go to a spiritual paradise hereafter.

April 16, 2000

Agastya

He introduced me to a great yogin from the South India. This powerful yogi was known as Thirumullar. He discovered psychic actions which could reform wayward human bodies. He showed the vrikrodhara technique which cause the removal of abdomen-genital, anal-buttocks negative energy. He showed how some yogis eliminate their astral genitals and are no longer attracted to astral sexual intercourse.

Thirumullar showed the hanging light in the lower chest. He instructed that I do breath-infusion in the lotus posture and bow down to Lotus Devi in special postures. This goddess is known as Sarasvati Ma.

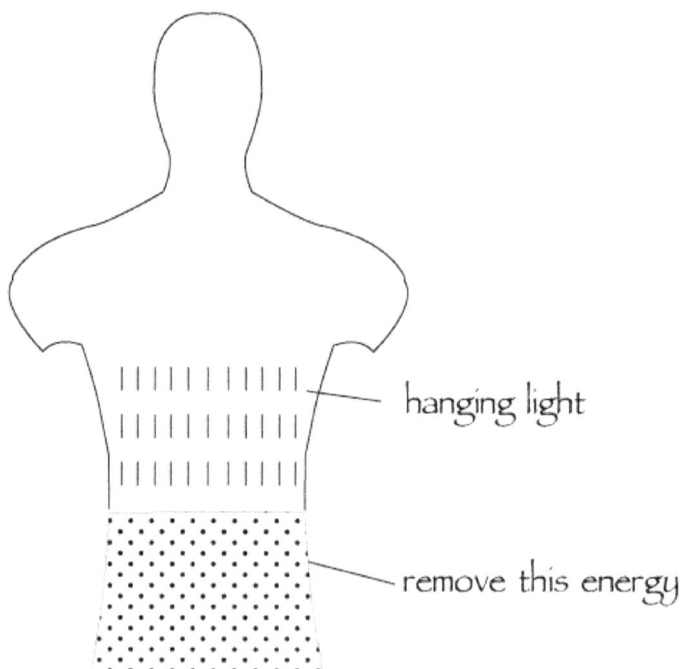

Thirumullar showed how to lean forward in lotus with the elbows out at angles, while putting the palm on the soles of the feet and doing intensive breath infusion to get the physical and subtle air down in the body using it to lift hormones that were stored in the lower torso. He showed various twists in lotus posture which cause release of hormones in the lower back, and stirs polluted subtle energy and upsets the thighs ability to store sexual fluids. The thighs support sexual impulse and frustrate celibate efforts. Special exercises keep the thighs from fulfilling their mission which is to keep the yogi involved in sexual intercourse on one level or another.

Agastya made a remark, telling me that since the Upanishadic period, those who went south developed stronger and more vulgar digestive process, which these psychic actions eliminate. He said that Thirumullar was the first to perfect these psychic actions to that degree.

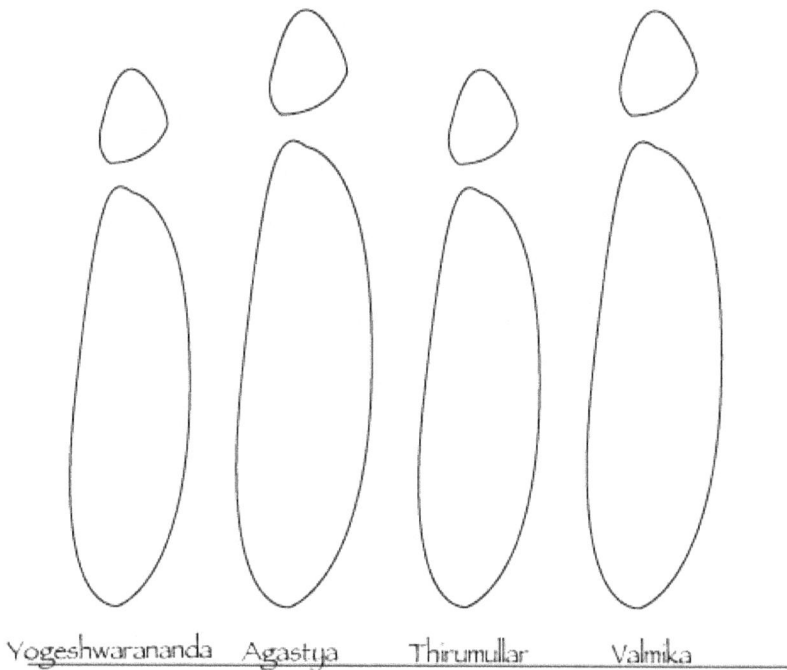

Yogeshwarananda   Agastya   Thirumullar   Valmika

South

Thirumullar sits to the left of Agastya. One other aspect is this: In technique yoga, we are not addicted to or proud of a sampradaya, institution or lineage. We do not have a siddhanta, dogma or theology to defend and protect. We have practice. The practice changes from time to time. We are not fanatical about a guru. We are honest about the desire for progression. Technique gurus are not possessive of students. The student is free to go to another teacher for special assistance or even to try methods which may prove to be useless.

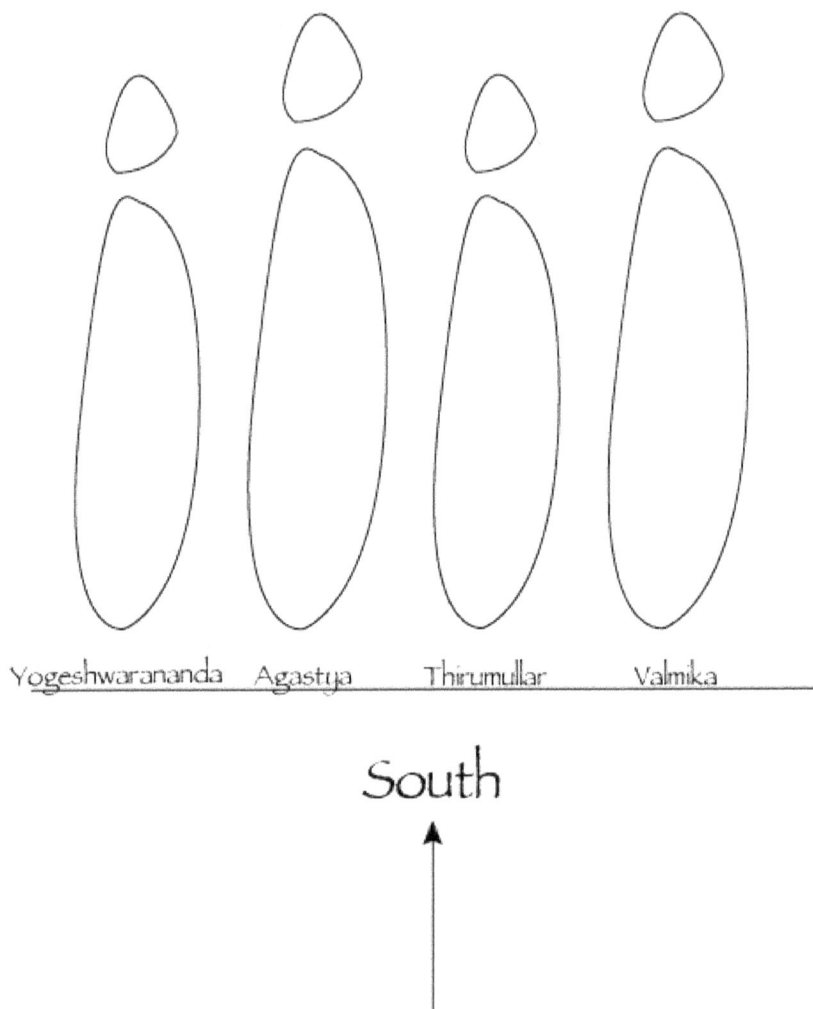

Yogeshwarananda   Agastya   Thirumullar   Valmika

South

April 16, 2000

Shiva

He said, "Get in the habit of taking baggage at each step. At the time of death, you will be compelled to carry everything which was not incinerated by yoga techniques."

Remark:

This pertains to the subtle aspects of the psyche. Those are the only things which go with a person at the time of death when the gross body must remain on this side of existence. A man may not want to carry his sad nature or depressive energy but he will have to if these were not eliminated by psychological techniques.

In yoga practice one may work with the kundalini force or with the charged subtle energy in some part of the psyche or with the intellect organ, but at the time of death, one has to manage these aspects either in an efficient or inefficient way. Shiva advised that I manage them now.

April 16, 2000

Thirumullar

He said, "This is kundalini pulling itself up, relocating above the brow chakra, above the digestive mechanism, changing its anchor point."

Remark:

After much practice in kundalini yoga, one reaches a stage where the kundalini chakra gets up and leaves its anchor point at the base of the spine. This comes after honest practice at diet and sex energy control.

Thirumullar showed the pulling force in my body. It was slightly above the navel chakra.

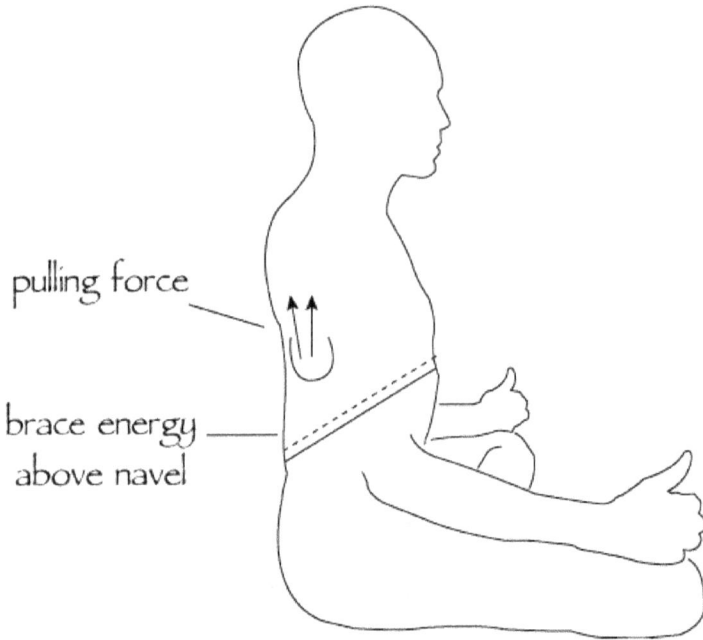

pulling force

brace energy
above navel

April 17, 2000

Thirumullar

He gave a neck holding-point for kundalini chakra. From that place one moves it to the bindu point in the lower back of the subtle brain.

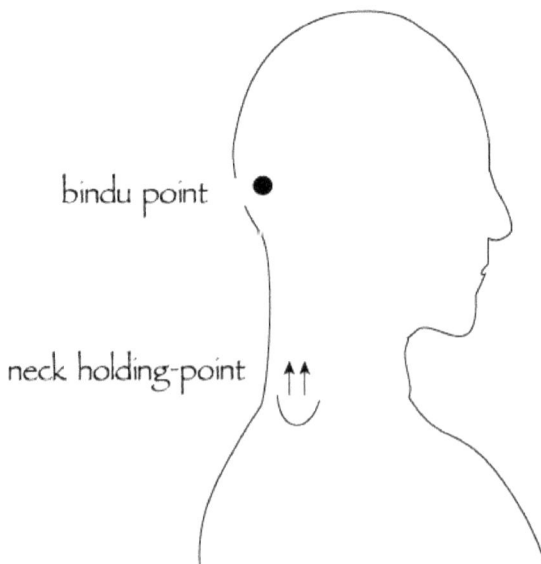

bindu point

neck holding-point

Shiva said that I should remember the whole psyche. He remarked, "Stop taking a part of it. Passengers must carry their belongings. No porters are there to assist aspiring yogis."

Thirumullar explained sugar addiction. He said that sugar ruins sense control.

April 14, 2000

Thirumullar

He said, "The lower attention should be on clear pranavision and not on heightened sensation."

Remark:

The attentive energy of the self is split into parts. It is not one whole energy except when one enters a transcendence zone or heightened states of concentration. The lower part of it, usually craves heightened sensations. In the material body, these culminate in sexual pleasure. This tendency of that lower attention has to be changed so that it becomes addicted to pranavision. Pranasight comes from the steady practice of kundalini yoga and from technique practice which causes one to peer down into the lower trunk, seeing through the subtle energy molecules. Each of those tiny molecules is surcharged as a miniature super-tiny eyeball.

Thirumullar made these remarks, "Once the three lower functions are cleansed and then burnt off, there will be a blank feeling especially in relation to food. Do not give in to it. Do not try to fill the blankness. Get used to it as a normal condition. For instance, when it is put to the ear an empty narrow-mouth bottle has a sound. If however, the bottle is filled with a liquid, the reverberation disappears.

"Do not fill the emptiness when you become aware of it, otherwise you will develop the habit of irregular eating. Accept the emptiness as a desirable feature."

April 19, 2000

Shiva

He said, "Fire up this tube between the orbs."

Remark:

That was to be done while doing intense breath-infusion and focusing the charged subtle energy in the areas shown in the diagram.

Thirumullar directed a lotus over-stretch. This is done while the body is seated in lotus posture with the hands on the knees and the elbows pointed outwards. One stretches to one side then to the other. This is done after surcharging the subtle body with breath energy.

Yogesh taught intellect yoga, the disciplines through which one gets mastery of the intellect organ in the subtle head. I was to protect the intellect from sunlight and artificial light during meditations, protect it from exhaustion by carefully regulating my interaction with the material world, by not thinking impulsively, by refraining the intellect from thought detection. This would increase the accuracy of the intellect's perceptions, give it stability in meditations and cause it to ignore temptations.

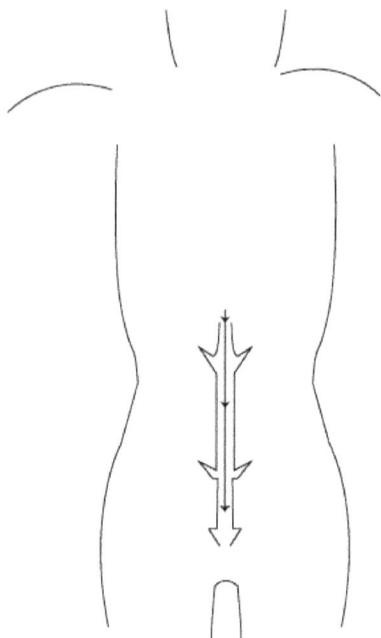

April 19, 2000

Shiva

He said, "Make yoga time. Place the mind in the body to continue today's practice."

Remark:

I got a technique from Thirumullar. This was a meditation in the lower back of the body. Shiva reminded me to practice this during the day, even while driving a vehicle. Those technique yogis who have jobs, should try their upmost to practice in any spare time, and at any time when their jobs do not require much concentration. Whatever little practice a yogi does, accumulates.

Thirumullar gave a meditation for focus in the lower back.

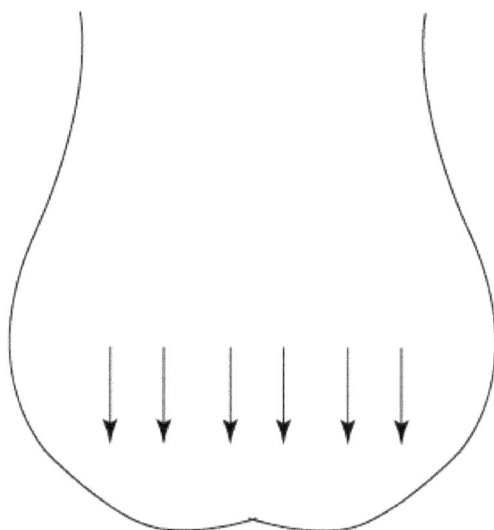

April 20, 2000

Shiva / Thirumullar

Under their conjoint guidance, I realized that if one is successful at diet restraint and proper breath exercises which cleans the trunk of the body, the subtle energy at the lower part of the body, takes on the same quality as the energy in the brain. By this, the consciousness becomes more purified due to clarity in the subtle form.

April 21, 2000

Skanda

He said, "Here is a blessing for higher yoga above the stomach."

Remark:

While saying this, he put his foot on my head. By his grace I got a new base above the stomach area. This is due to success with celibacy yoga and with navel-region clean-out. Kundalini yoga is meant to activate and ignite the base chakra. This concerns cleaning the anal region. Celibacy yoga concerns clearing the pubic section and thighs. That releases and purifies the second chakra. After that one should do navel psychic actions to clean the digestive system. Once this is done, the kundalini energy may relocate above the navel.

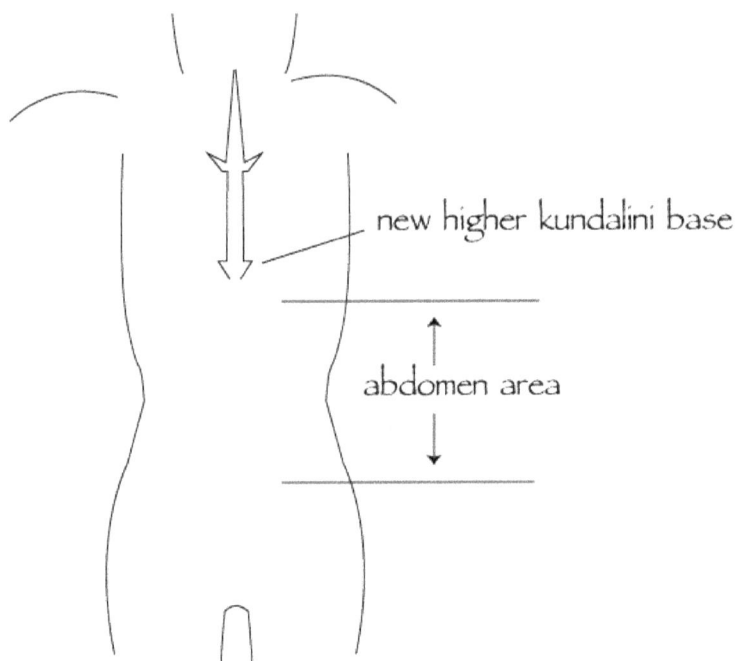

new higher kundalini base

abdomen area

April 21, 2000

Shiva

On this day, he confirmed the blessings of Skanda. He said. "The reduction in meals causes the relocation of kundalini above the navel. Once the lifeforce gets in the habit of moving upwards, it will gradually ascend. With sufficient practice, after a time, it will remain stationed in the brain.

"This is not based on desire but on practice. It is not a visualization. It comes on by proper hatha yoga postures and pranayama breath-infusion which purifies the subtle form. When the resistances and impurities are removed, kundalini has no reason to remain in the lower trunk of the body.

April 22, 2000

Shiva.

He said, "The cleanest subtle energy becomes manifested by the removal of front and back kundalini. It is not based on a mindal attitude alone. He gave this technique.

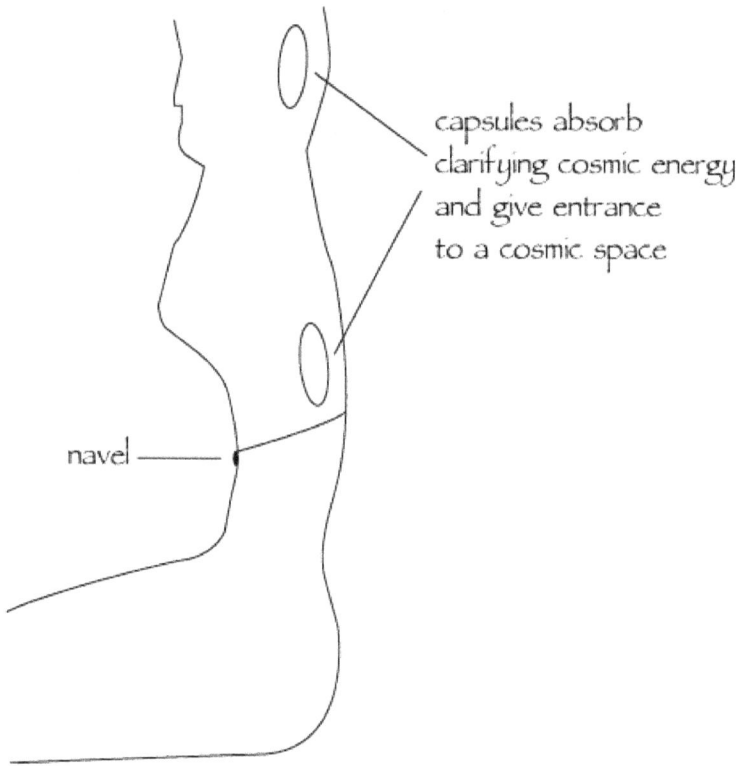

capsules absorb
clarifying cosmic energy
and give entrance
to a cosmic space

navel

Front and back kundalini are eliminated by steady yoga practice, mostly by a steady breath-infusion or by other effective pranayama, like alternate breathing with retention before switching to the alternate side. However, one must do asana postures along with the breath infusion. Once the purity is attained, the kundalini and the sexual hormonal energy, do not linger in the lower trunk. This is a physical, psychic and mystic process which depends on physical actions in postures and breath-infusion. Since the subtle body is intermeshed in the physical and is affected with it, these physical actions are psychic.

April 22, 2000

On this day by the influence of Shiva, I began to consider that along with postures and breath-infusion, one must be sincere in the practice. One must take due care and become proficient, otherwise one will get only partial results. One must respect the practices, doing them attentively.

April 24, 2000

Shiva / Thirumullar

Under their influence, I got a technique which had a bottom-abdomen light. This technique is manifested after one achieves the purity through which the kundalini chakra moves up to the navel permanently.

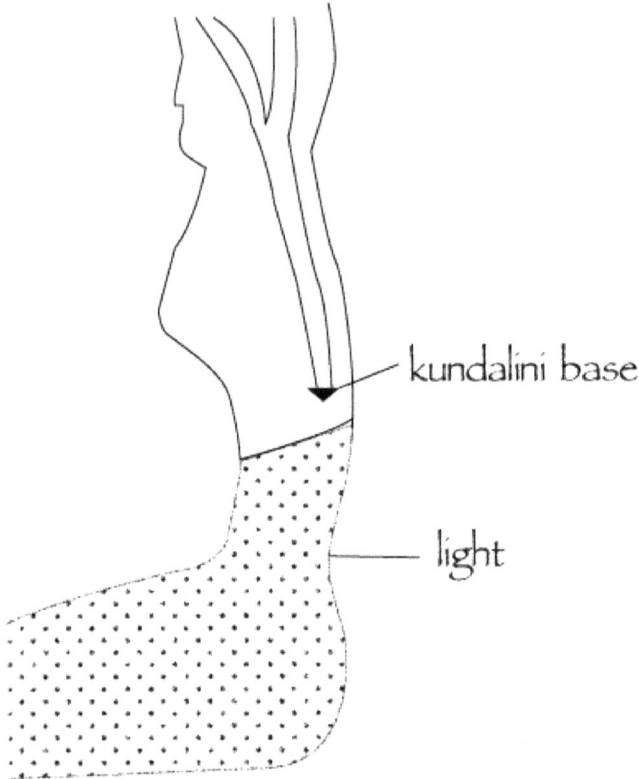

kundalini base

light

April·24, 2000

Shiva

He instructed that with breath-infusion, I should move the kanda up to the higher abdomen area. The sexual organ would remain in its usual location with its capacity for begetting physically but the subtle sexual mechanism would be changed.

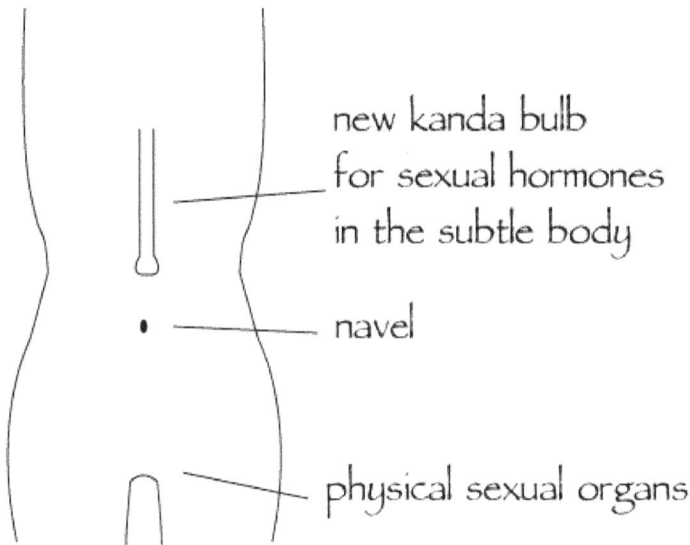

new kanda bulb
for sexual hormones
in the subtle body

navel

physical sexual organs

April 26, 2000

Shiva

He gave a short-kundalini pull-up kriya. This is a preliminary procedure for eliminating kundalini. Initially, when I typed this remark on August 1, 2001, I noticed that Yogesh got rid of his kundalini completely. In that way, he has nothing to do with creature survival on any level. It is a wonderful achievement. Right now, he seems to exist as just an idea on the causal plane. At least that is how an embodied being would regard him.

Once a person is used to gross life, he feels that someone who does not have it, does not exist, or he fantasizes about the glorious existence of those beyond gross perception. The truth is that unless we become retrained to defocus from the physical and the lower subtle levels, we cannot perceive anything beyond that, and as such, anything in the higher dimensions would appear void.

Shiva gave a technique for a short kundalini pull-up with intellect and sense-of-identity retraction. This is a pratyahar sensual restraint that takes one to the causal plane.

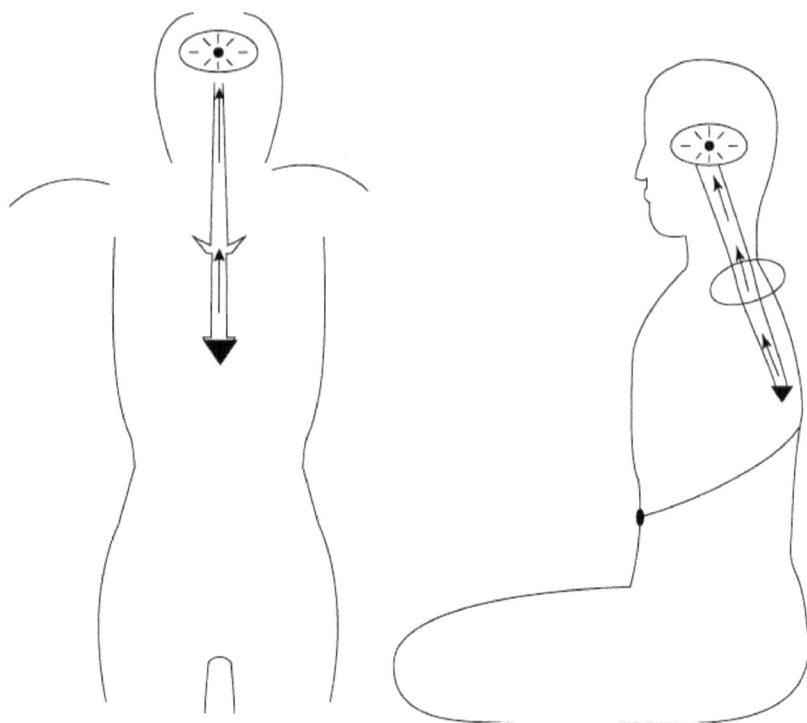

April 25, 2000

Shiva

He gave a technique for pulling up energy in the legs. One makes the effort to relocate the base chakra moving it higher and higher in the body. One must also retract other lower energies which are subsidiary to the base.

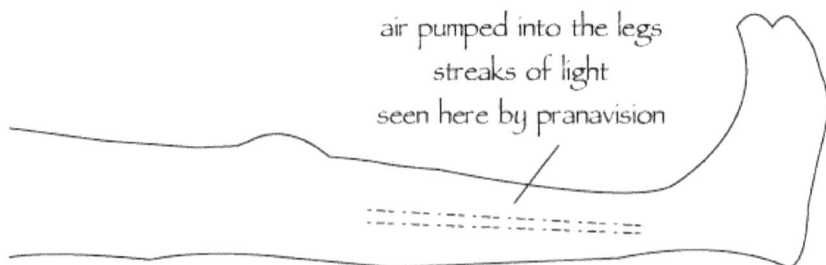

air pumped into the legs
streaks of light
seen here by pranavision

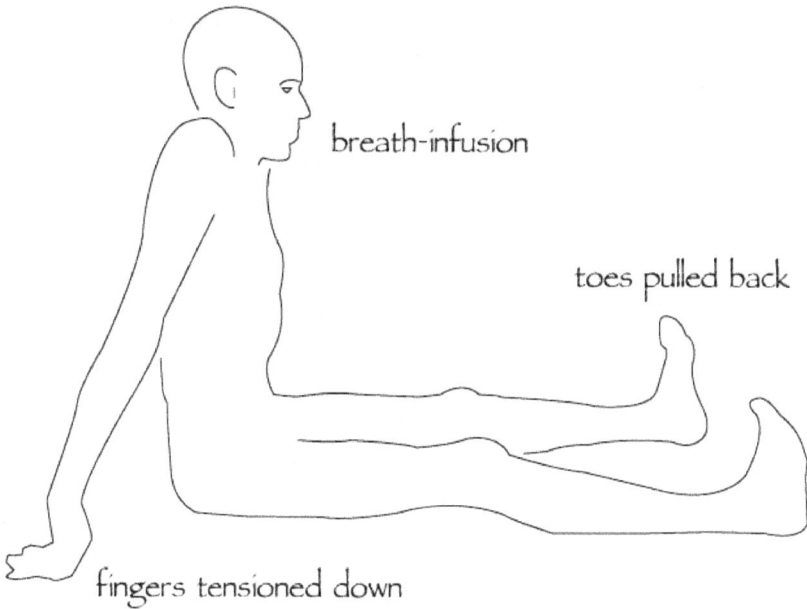

breath-infusion

toes pulled back

fingers tensioned down

April 26, 2000

Shiva

He said, "Write this down."

Yama moral restraints and niyama encouraged activities represent social life in the material world, but in the higher practice, it is the social activity between the core-self and the subtle organs like the intellect, which is regulated.

The asana postures represent kundalini being anchored at the base chakra. Pranayama breath-infusion represents kundalini relocated to the chest area.

April 26, 2000

Shiva

He said, "Mystic actions, not imagination."

Remark:

At this time I lifted kundalini out of the base chakra by diet improvement and by more breath intake. Initially one does this by pushing polluted energy out of the body. This occurs by surcharging the subtle body with fresh subtle air. The fresh subtle air develops an electric charge and drives the pollutants out. In the more advanced stages one uses diet restraint. This also means eating only a certain amount at a certain time of the day.

When kundalini is pushed out by the subtle surcharged force, the kundalini returns to the base chakra as soon as that pushing force subsides. Practically speaking, for a beginner it means that it will return as soon as he ceases the rapid breathing exercises. This may be compared to a snake in a hole. If somehow or the other, one can harass a snake in its hole, the creature will leave the residence but it will return as soon as one stops the inconvenience. But if somehow, one can remove the hole, the creature even if it returns will not stay there. Similarly, if one pushes kundalini up by using rapid breathing surcharges of air, kundalini will leave now and again but it will return.

When however, one curbs diet and permanently surcharges the psyche with fresh prana, the kundalini will no longer return to the base.

As I indicated elsewhere, the first thing to do for diet reform is to stop eating late in the afternoon or at night. Of course one must use a vegetarian, fruitarian, dairy products diet. Late eating obstructs yoga. Gradually one should stop it altogether. One should train the body to take a full meal early in the morning.

Kundalini chakra is addicted to sexual expression. One has to fight that tendency until it is curbed or is forgotten by the psyche. Sexual intercourse is hardly necessary unless one is duty-bound to generate infant bodies. Otherwise it is quite unnecessary, but somehow it has a way of asserting itself. One must work to become celibate by doing the appropriate disciplines.

May 1, 2000

Surya

He said, "Dump him but do not let him know. He is categorically unfit to advance. If he ever calls, I will alert you. You can beam down, so that he keeps thinking that you are similar to him."

Remark:

This was some information from the sun-god Surya. It was about a man who wanted me to associate with him. This person felt that he and I were on par. Actually, he is not on par but it is not in my interest to clarify this. Sometimes for some reason or the other, a person gets this feeling that he is on par. Of course it is not important for me to know this. But if the person becomes a nuisance, a deva, a supernatural person may intervene, telling me what to do in relation to that person.

Each of the atmas or core-selves is in a particular category. If one mistakes himself for a higher personality, one will make mistakes. Some persons who think that I am on par, may cheat themselves because they do not take my association in the proper way. Instead of approaching submissively and getting help to advance, they engage either in rivalry or familiarity. They remain on a lower stage.

Because I came to this low point of existence, many other male beings and even some females like to pitch themselves to me, to show that they are on par. That is alright but it will not help them to become elevated. In all seriousness what is valuable about me is the practice. That is it. I myself am not important. It is the practice that will cause elevation.

May 2, 2000

Shiva

He said, "Read about Takshaka in the Mahabharata."

Remark:

This is in relation to my association with those who feel that they are on par. By that feeling they cannot be assisted effectively because they position themselves in a way, whereby they cannot be taught the practices. It is not that I am superior, because after all, we find that if a man is superior in one area, he is inferior in another. For instance, if a man compares himself to an insect, there are many obvious areas of superiority but the insect has advantages too, like its ability to fly and it capacity for rapid crawling movements. It may even crawl up a vertical wall, something that is impossible for a human being, no matter how great he may be.

But besides all this, there is spirituality. Each of the atmas or core-selves is of a certain category. One has to know the category of self and not walk on the toes of superiors.

The worse people are those who took a spiritual master and then got from him, the feeling that he is the greatest and that subsequently they are also the greatest for having a connection with him. These people can hardly be assisted unless their false pride is broken.

In the story of Takshaka, King Parikshit committed a crime in insultingly honoring a yogi by putting a dead snake on his neck. It was an insult in the disguise of honor. Later, Parikshit who was himself a devotee in good standing, was cursed by the yogi's son, but without the yogi's approval.

At first when the King became aware of the curse, he took a repentant attitude. Then he felt it was okay to be cursed like that. The curse was fatal, demanding that a magical snake creature, named Takshaka, bite the king fatally. After some time, the King thought it over. He decided that it was his duty to try to prevent Takshaka from killing his body. Everything was to happen in a certain time frame, hence some counselors told the king that if he could avert Takshaka at a certain time, the snake could do nothing after that danger period passed.

However Takshaka was no ordinary creature. He was determined to kill the king's body, somehow or the other. He was empowered with a valid grievance towards the royal family. Takshaka, felt compelled to fulfill his mission of ruining the dynasty. There was no better way to achieve this, than to kill Parikshit's body.

As Takshaka journeyed to Parikshit's hideout, he met a brahmin medicine-man named Kashyapa. In a discussion, Kashyapa revealed to Takshaka, that the poison was curable. Kashyapa said that he had the antidote to it.

It was demonstrated to the snake man, that the antidote would revive the king. At that point, Takshaka, that very intelligent snake-person, made a proposition to pay Kashyapa. Explaining to the medicine-man that no one does anything without getting something in return, Takshaka proposed to pay Kashyapa not to apply the medical services which could revive the king. Agreeing to that, Kashyapa was paid. Takshaka then went in disguise as a fruit worm and killed the body of the king.

May 2, 2000

Thirumullar

He gave a stub-kundalini kriya.

This is experience after an intense session of breath-infusion, after one assumed lotus posture and allow the subtle body to recline while on the back while the gross one remains in lotus posture. One sees with pranavision perceiving the lights which pass through the astral air cells of the lungs. In this practice, if all passionate energy is not removed from the psyche, the intellect will keep running back to configure thoughts. Here is a diagram.

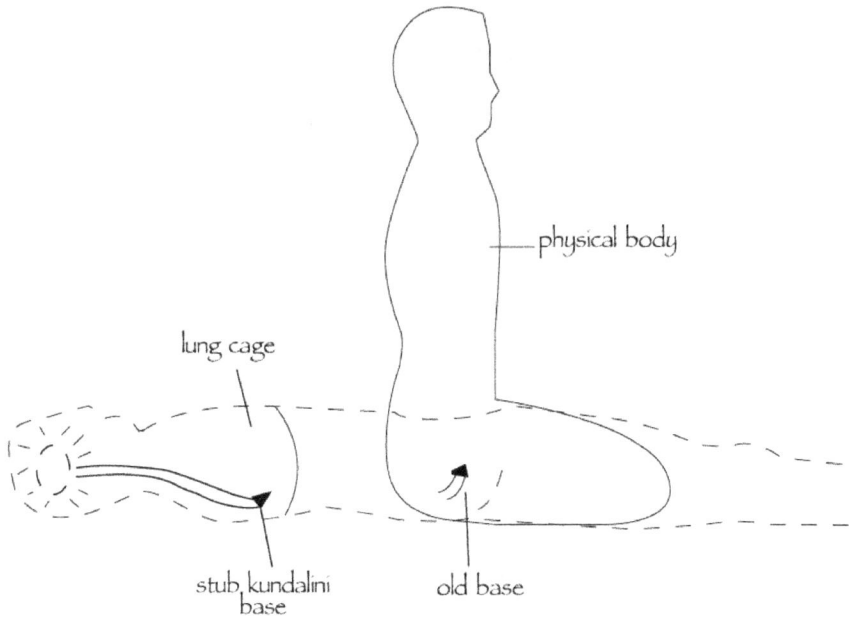

physical body

lung cage

stub, kundalini
base

old base

May 3, 2000

Babaji

He showed a stub bliss energy concentration process. This is called naala-chitta. This is found at the throat as in the diagram below. If the mind drifts off while seeing this or while trying to perceive this, one should make the mind say the vibration of it mentally.

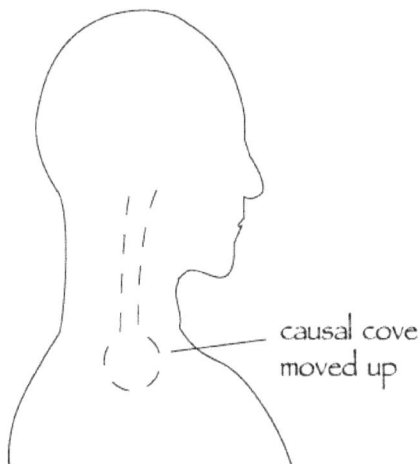

causal cove
moved up

Part 4

May 4, 2000

Shiva / Thirumullar

They gave a technique for stub-kundalini. This is done with the subtle hand only. The physical hand remains on the thigh while the physical body is in lotus posture. One holds the stub-kundalini with the subtle hand.

physical body

arms on thighs

subtle body
right hand clutching
stub kundalini

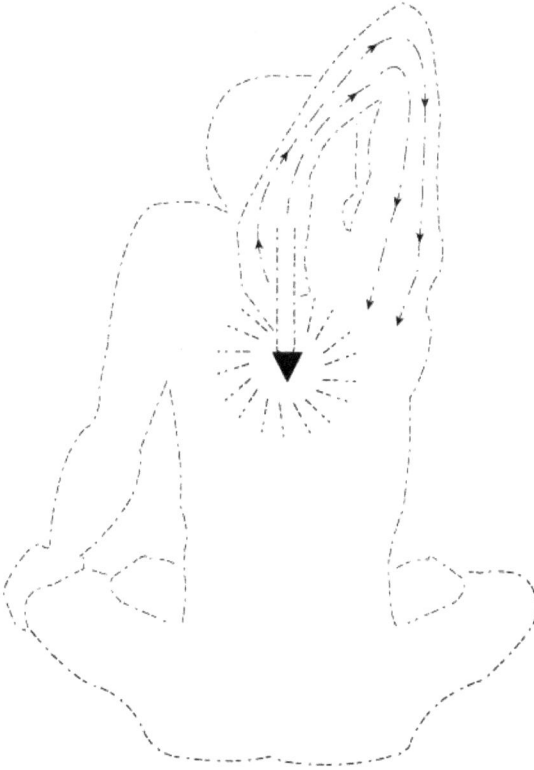

May 5, 2000

Shiva/ Thirumullar

Shiva said that because of its concentration of power, the stub-kundalini is more able to immobilize the intellect. After doing an intense session of breath-infusion, one does this in lotus or easy pose. Please note that stub-kundalini is the kundalini energy drawn up or moved upwards and concentrated in focus upwards.

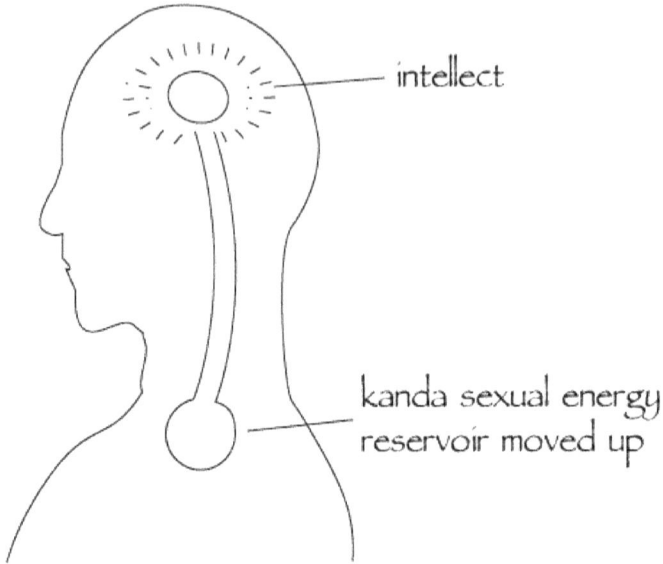

intellect

kanda sexual energy
reservoir moved up

May 5, 2000

Shiva

He said, "Remember the location mantra. Put all spare focus mildly on the stub-kundalini. Use the subtle hand to grab it."

Remark:

This was an instruction to keep doing the morning kriya, during the day. A yogi who must engage in cultural activity or in making a livelihood, should during the day keep in touch with the technique used in early morning meditation. If there is an extra focusing power, it should be applied to the practice, otherwise it will naturally seek out destructive sense objects, which deter yoga success.

May 6, 2000

Shiva

An experience of the bliss sheath (ananda kosha)

Remark:

This bliss sheath is a subtle form in which one experiences a cool type of happiness, without a pressure for enjoying it. It is not an imposing type of happiness nor one that brings on cravings. One experiences this while in the subtle body grabbing the long-stalk kundalini. It has a blue-white transparent color of light energy.

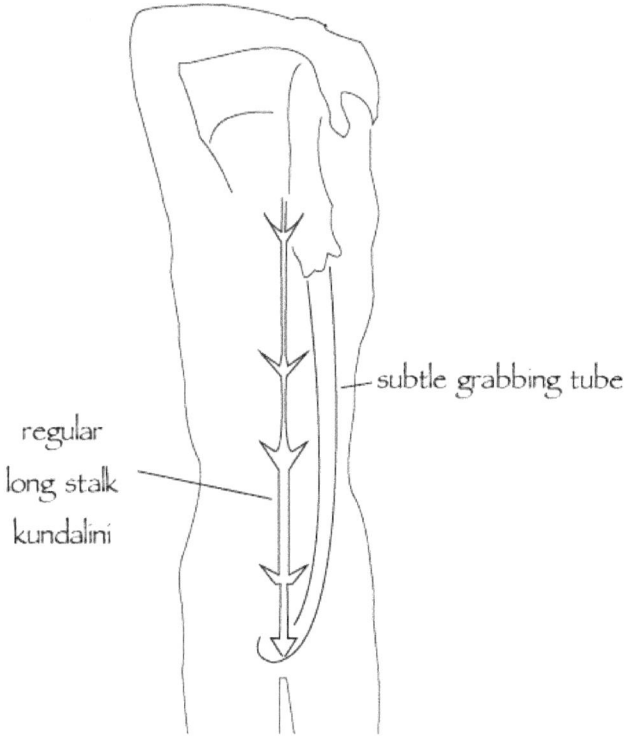

regular
long stalk
kundalini

subtle grabbing tube

May 9, 2000

Shiva

He gave a triangle pose for removing drowsiness and yawning. This is done with breath-infusion, while the person practices celibacy yoga. It does not work if there is no celibacy yoga. There are two poses in which to do this.

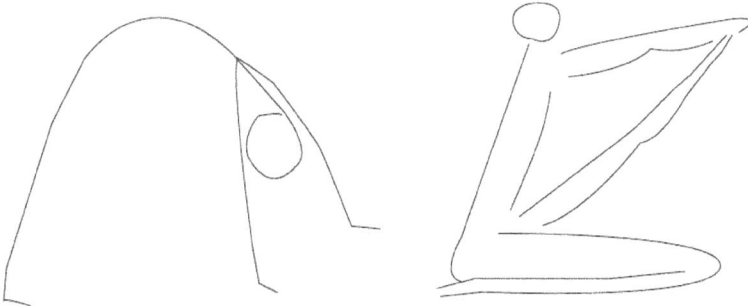

May 9, 2000

Shiva

A sex-energy movement technique

This is a bow stretch pose in which breath-infusion is done. The bow stretch is used in advanced celibacy to release hormones which builds up in the chest area. There are variations of the bow stretch. These promote celibacy.

This one moves the sex energy out of the lower groin and the under-abdomen into the chest area, from where it is moved by other more difficult bow stretches.

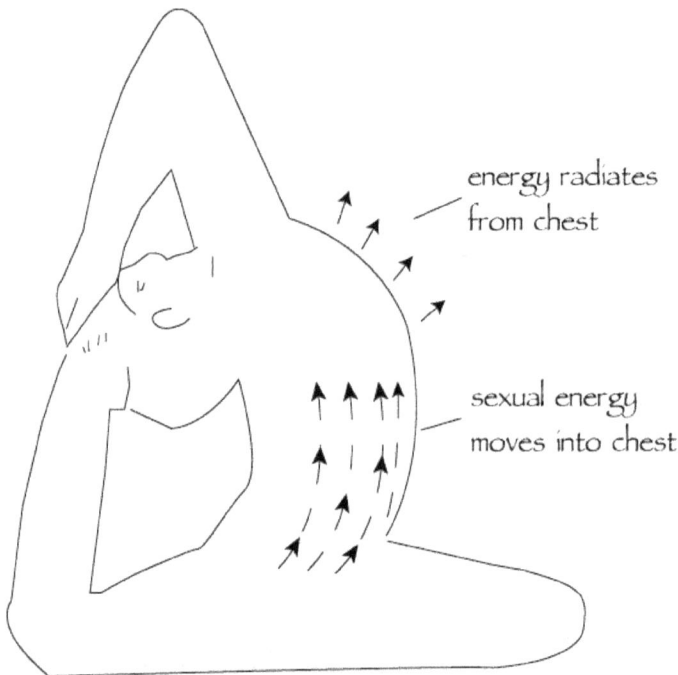

energy radiates from chest

sexual energy moves into chest

Shiva

Stub-kundalini

This is an even shorter stub-kundalini. By doing these exercises, one eliminates the kundalini energy. With kundalini one is forced to perform cultural activities in karma yoga as described in the Bhagavad Gita. If the kundalini is eliminated, one can move on from karma yoga into jnana yoga which is devoid of mundane cultural acts. Karma yoga, by the Gita, means to be involved in cultural acts without having to perpetuate the involvements.

In jnana yoga, there are no such entanglements. One's practice is then rapidly consolidated leading to advancement in the seventh and eight stages of yoga. That is dhyana momentary spontaneous focus and transcendence zone prolonged spontaneous focus.

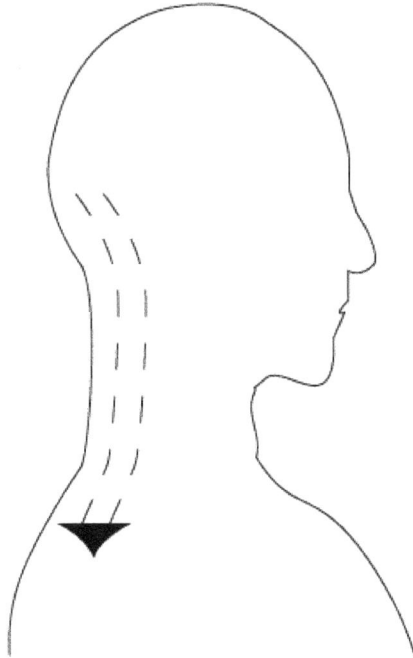

May 10, 2000

Shiva / Thirumullar

Lung chakra

By their influence, I saw the lung chakra and the nadi that leads down to the lung. This is seen in the subtle body. One sees either two small chakras or one large one, depending on if the energy is separated or united in the lungs. These have bluish spikes with little red and white dots.

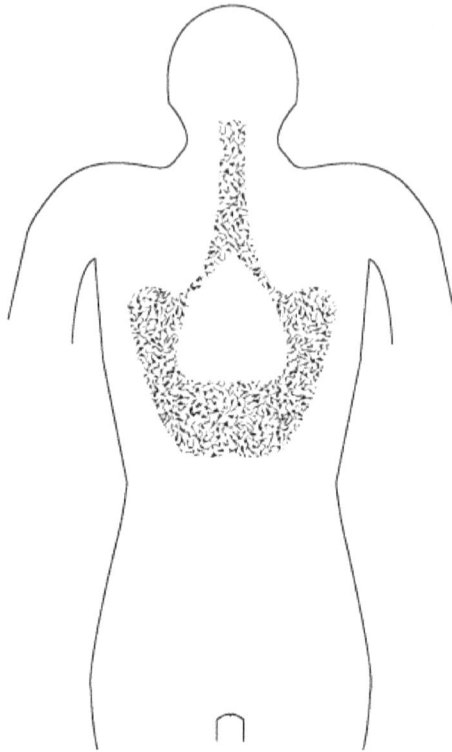

May 10, 2000

Shiva

By His influence I realized that if one looks down into the body while doing postures and sees the pains caused by the stretches, in time one will see inside the subtle body by pranavision and by psychic vision from the intellect. This leads to transcendence zone prolonged spontaneous focus and to position focus. Position focus is when a person can use a position as a point of focus just as he may use a sound for focus.

This is different to having to vibrate a sound with vocal words. In this case, a sound is heard inside or outside the psyche. The sound must come from the subtle world. One focuses on the sound. In that case one does not create physical speech. The energy one would use for creating a sound can be invested in hearing the naturally-created or naturally-occurring sound. One also does this with a position or location, as the place of focus. Postures aids one in concentration. It aids one in getting the mind and intellect out of the habit of peering outside into the physical and lower subtle environments for excitements.

May 10, 2000

Shiva

He instructed that I hold lower kundalini with the left hand, and use right hand for holding stub kundalini. One may do this one at a time or simultaneously. This refers to the subtle hands only.

May 11, 2000

Shiva

He said, "A faster-moving higher grade of subtle energy gives objectivity to the intellect which gives it separation power. Thus one gets the ability to curb the intellect and to wean it from the lower pursuits."

May 11, 2000

On this day I experienced a bright swirling light at the bottom of the lung area. In this case, the two lung cages appear as one container. It was a very bright light.

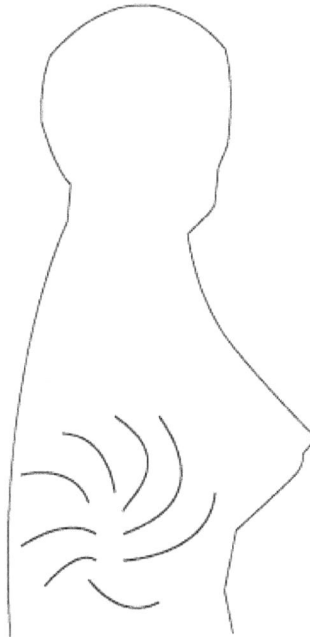

May 12, .2000

Shiva

He asked about the lung chakra.

He said, "Why is it not given importance?"

I replied, "This is because the ascetic may not have the proper focus. They follow incorrect diagrams. They may eat too much. They may be sexually-distracted. They may be attached to sensations and excitements. There are many ascetics and associates of ascetics who have favorite excitements, which they cannot give up and which they justify and sanction as religious principles or as sanctified activities."

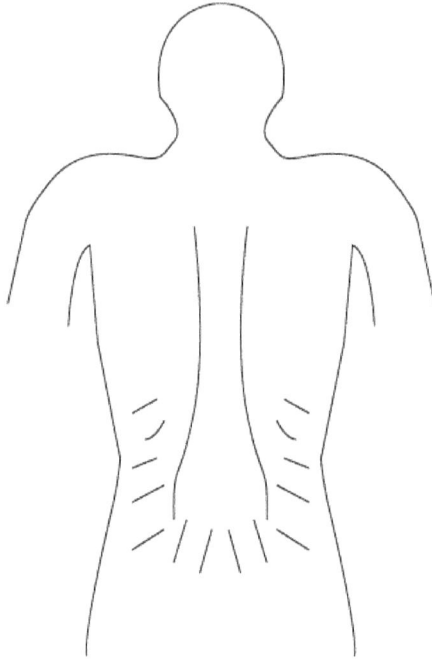

May 12, 2000

Shiva

He stated, "Running around the block and other artificial means of exercise like jogging and using exercise machines is not the same as working like a slave. Slave labor is better because it dissolves used subtle energy which is lodged in the subtle body. Much physical endeavor uses up excess food protein. Those who sit have sit-and-think jobs. They cannot have clear nadis unless they eat very little."

May 15, 2000

Shiva

He said, "That area may be cleansed. Try to do this posture with ashwini mudra."

Remark:

This concerned cleaning the base chakra. If this one is ignored the yogi cannot be successful. Kundalini chakra is usually housed at the base chakra. Thus if the housing is dirty and if the light there is of a dark hue, the kundalini will be sluggish.

There are patron deities of each of the chakras. As one advances, one sees them from time to time. The ancient yogis left diagrams showing these deities and giving their respective names. The chakras also respond to certain vibrated sounds, as mentioned by ancient yogins. As far as the deities are concerned, sometimes one deity leaves and another takes his or her place. Sometimes, one sees two authorities. They use miniature subtle forms.

While I did these purificatory techniques for the base chakra, I saw a pair of deities, a male and female. They said to me, "By your practice, there is light here now."

While doing the posture below, one should do ashwini mudra, pushing out and pulling in the anus area. This should be done slowly and carefully without straining any part of the excretion apparatus.

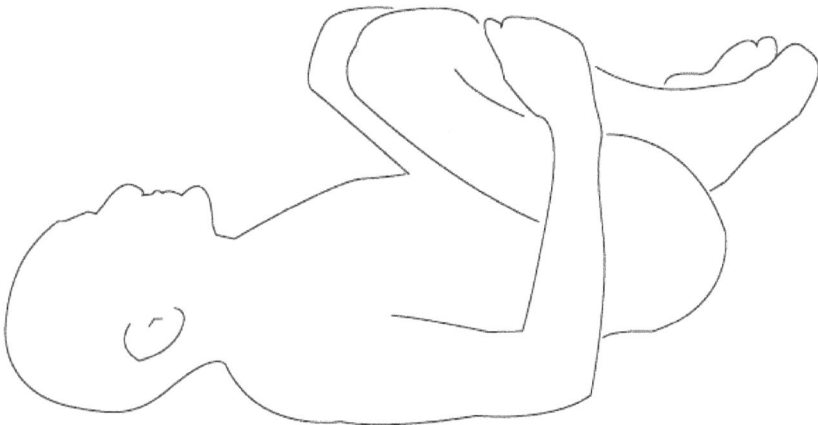

do ashwini mudra / anus lock

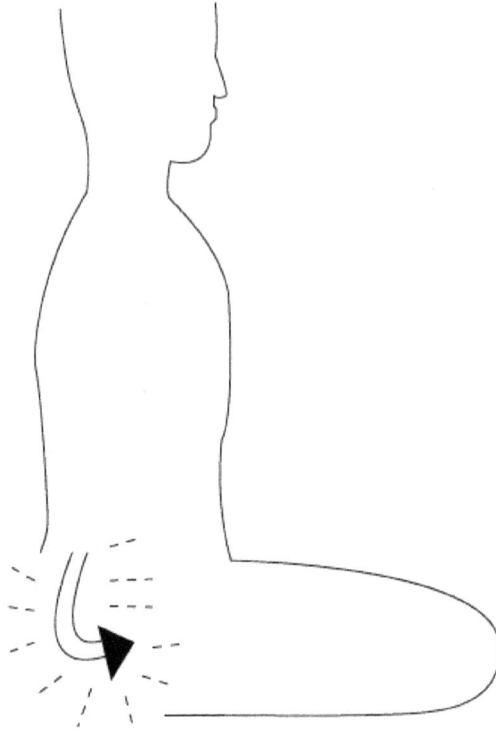

May 17, 2000

Shiva

He said, "Write about releasing the lifeforce from the excretion chores which are excessive. When that area is dark due to lingering or excessive stools, more elevated deities avoid the area. Explain the relationship to celibacy."

Remark:

The lifeforce has to be relieved from excessive digestion, excretion and sexual stimulation. If however one eats too much, he will in turn excrete too much. That will cause the lifeforce to linger in the lower area. This in turn causes an increased sexual indulgence.

There are many people who have no sexual indulgence but who are not celibate either. This is because even though they maintain morality externally, they are not sexually resistant on the emotional and psychological planes. They show a moral face physically, while on the subtle level they are sexually-indulgent.

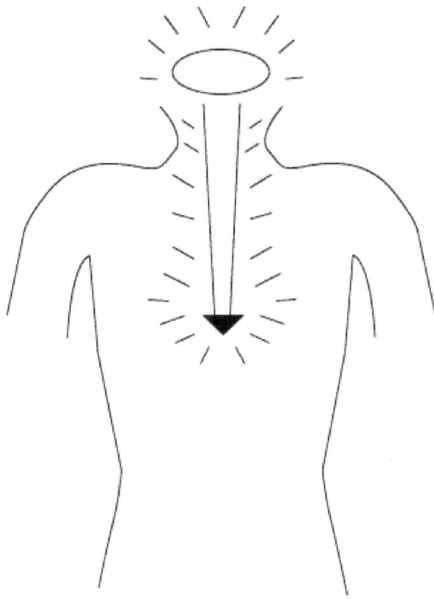

May 18, 2000

Shiva

By following his instruction, I developed a crystal clear light in the base chakra. This was due to having stools moved out of the body early in the morning. This occurs by eating the main meal once a day in the morning, and by doing postures and breath-infusion.

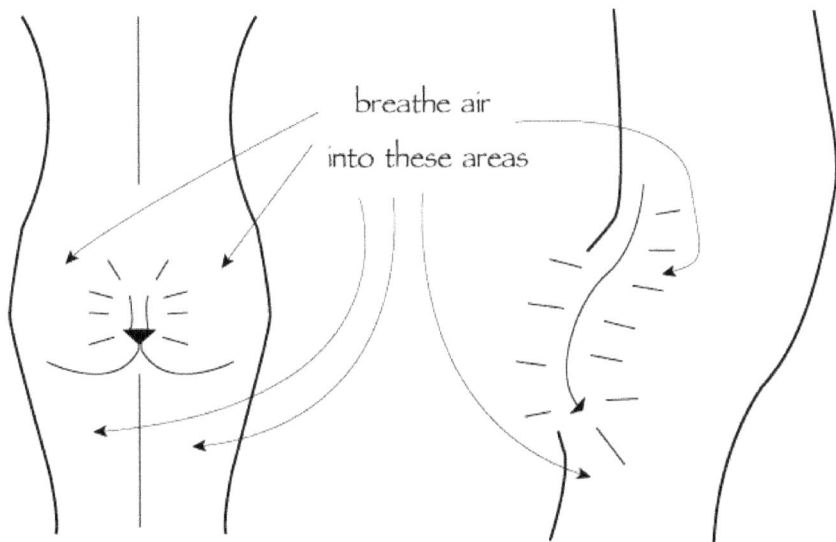

breathe air into these areas

Shiva

He said, "See this light at muladhar chakra."

Remark:

This was a success for me due to consistent practice with early evacuation, one meal per day, doing intense breath-infusion with postures and muscular locks.

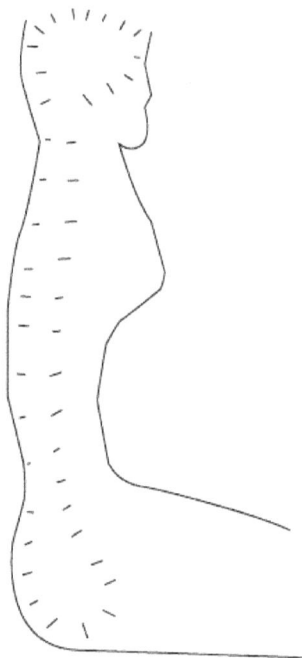

May 20, 2000

Shiva

He said, "If there are stools, the muladhar cannot be penetrated or cleansed."

Remark:

Vishnudevananda who assisted me in asana postures, once explained that it was necessary for a yogi to have only one meal per day and to evacuate as early as possible. He said that in the very advanced practice, the stools of the previous day are excreted before eating that one meal per day.

Shiva / Babaji

Under their influence, I realized that subtle energy seeks out the same, while mere sensation seeks out sensation. Surcharged subtle energy is different to mere sensations. One has to train the psyche, so that the surcharged subtle energy will pursue inner sensations. This is done by doing yoga stretches with breath-infusion and causing the attention to be focused inside the psyche.

May 24, 2000

Shiva

He gave a throat check-point cross-chakra.

Remark:

This check point occurs where the taste and food absorption subtle energies meet.

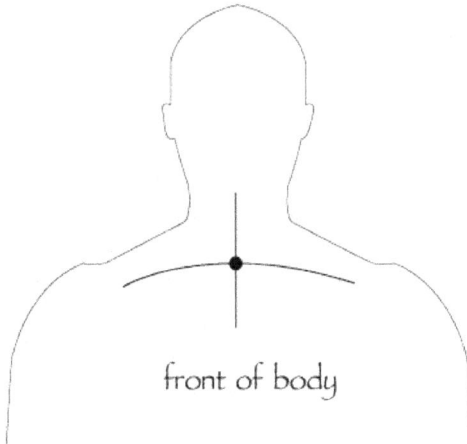

front of body

May 25, 2000

Shiva

He instructed, "Take this down. Bring this up with it. Hold it down. Let it give brightness to the kanda kundalini to float it up."

Remark:

Kanda kundalini is a rare kundalini energy, not usually mentioned in yoga books. First there is spinal kundalini which operates through the spinal sushumna passage. This is the most known kundalini. There is frontal kundalini, which comes up the front of the subtle body.

When this frontal kundalini is activated regularly one gains control of diet. Those who specialize in back kundalini may not have the diet under control. If a person gets front kundalini activated, one can know for certain that his diet is being brought under control.

Apart from the back and front systems, there are two side kundalinis. Then there is kanda kundalini which originates in the sexual energy reservoir in the subtle form.

Shiva instructed that I take the intellect organ down into the kundalini energy at the kanda bulb. This makes the energy of the bulb become lighter. It moves up as willed by the yogi. Otherwise the energy there is like a viscous liquid, like honey.

May 26, 2000

Yogeshwarananda

He said, "The back straightens as soon as the root chakra is cleansed and the liquid area is constrained."

Remark:

The back of the yogi straightens even more as soon as his base chakra is cleansed and as soon as his sex area is properly constrained by the celibate actions. Yogesh regards the sex area as the liquid producing area. Mystically one sees subtle liquid in that region.

The straightening of the back refers mostly to the spine of the subtle form. The gross body may not show an increased straightening since that body may be old and infirm for a particular yogi, but the subtle body may keep adjusting even in the case of a yogi who uses an aged physical form.

May 26, 2000

Shiva

He brought to my attention that family affairs keep a yogi from flourishing since concentration energies naturally go to family concerns which in turn discourages yoga focus.

Shiva showed how the abdomen of a yogi pulls up once he expels stools early and eats a main meal only once per day.

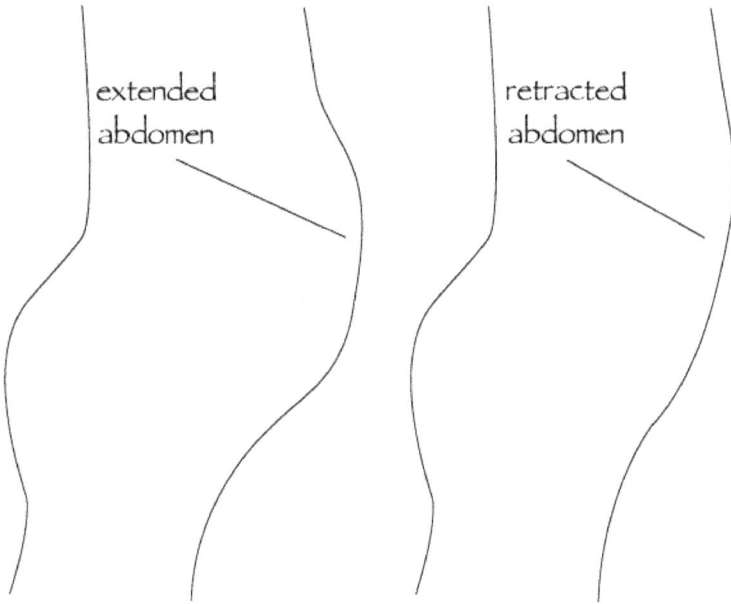

extended
abdomen

retracted
abdomen

May 26, 2000

Shiva

He showed that the removal of stools is essential to the brightening of
the light at the base chakra.

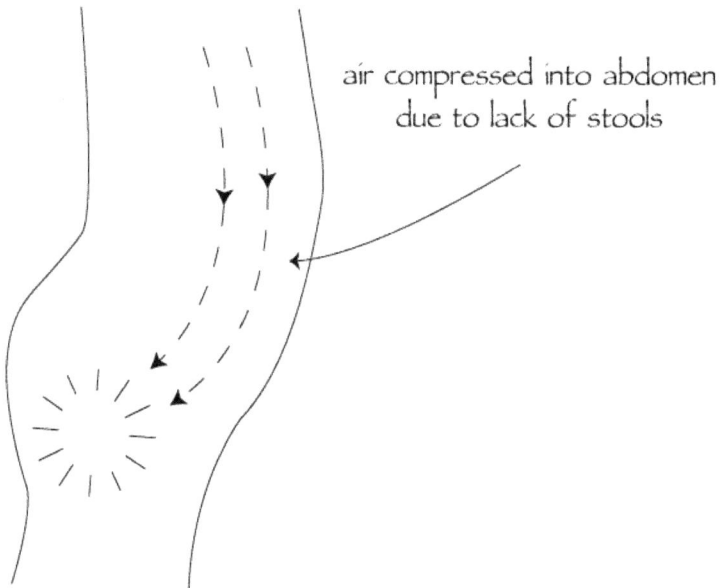

air compressed into abdomen
due to lack of stools

May 30, 2000

Shiva

He showed that the stool deity wants to stay in the body but he must leave the area if there is no stool. When there is no waste, the chamber where he stays becomes blank. Then another more elevated deity, a miniature supernatural person, comes there. They do not stay there together. A yogi should encourage the blank-chamber stool-deity to come by keeping the body as cleared of stools as possible, by diet control, proper posture and breath-infusion.

In the Valmiki *Ramayana*, there is a story that relates to this. That is the tale of Tatika, a witch who was the embodiment of nutritional greed. Her body was killed by Rama as advised by Yogi Vishvamitra. Because she was a woman, Rama was disinclined to killing her body. Vishvamitra encouraged Rama to kill it without hesitation. This was due to her criminal activities which were promoted by greed. In other words, this story can be applied to technique yoga practice, in the sense that we have to kill off the Tatika witch and the greed habit which we have for over-eating and taking in more protein than necessary. Tatika was big, fat and stout, a giant of a woman. She is represented by excessive nutrition.

It is said that later a similar person took birth as Putana and tried to feed her breast milk to Krishna. Putana smeared a poison on her breast. Subsequently because of that motive. Krishna killed her body, by extracting its life air. Here again, we may apply this in our technique practice by realizing that if we maintain nutritional greed, we will be killed because a poison will be smeared in such a way as to deter spiritual progress.

Krishna liked milk. He took much from the gopi cowherd ladies. When he dealt with Putana, he focused on her lifeforce and not on her milk. The application is that we should focus on improving the condition of the life force. To do this, we should be detached from nutrition. So long as the yogi ardently seeks out nutrition, he cannot gain control.

May 31, 2000

Shiva

He showed the photo development room of the mento-emotional energy. This is the place where impressions and mental imprints are converted into pictures, which are viewed in the intellect organ and which motivate a person in cultural activities.

Some desires come from past lives, some from the present, and some come from future times which we have not experienced. By supernatural power, some persons can project into our consciousness desires from the future which they may force any of us to live out a desire which really applies to our future, and which we cannot properly integrate now. This is why our present civilization develops so many gadgets which are futuristic. We are being compelled to do this by others who are in the future time spaces but who have the supernatural power to force us to manifest their ideas.

Some other desires come from others who are in our time space but who have the supernatural power to force us to fulfill their desires.

Some other desires come from others who are in our time space but who by their proximity cause us to work for fulfillments. These desires usually exist in miniature coded forms until they are brought to various photo rooms either in the intellect organ, the conscious or subconscious mind spaces. Once they get into the photo development rooms, a human being is all but forced to enact them. In technique yoga, as explained by Patanjali in the *Yoga Sutras*, we try to eliminate these imprints. If they are not curbed, one cannot attain higher yoga.

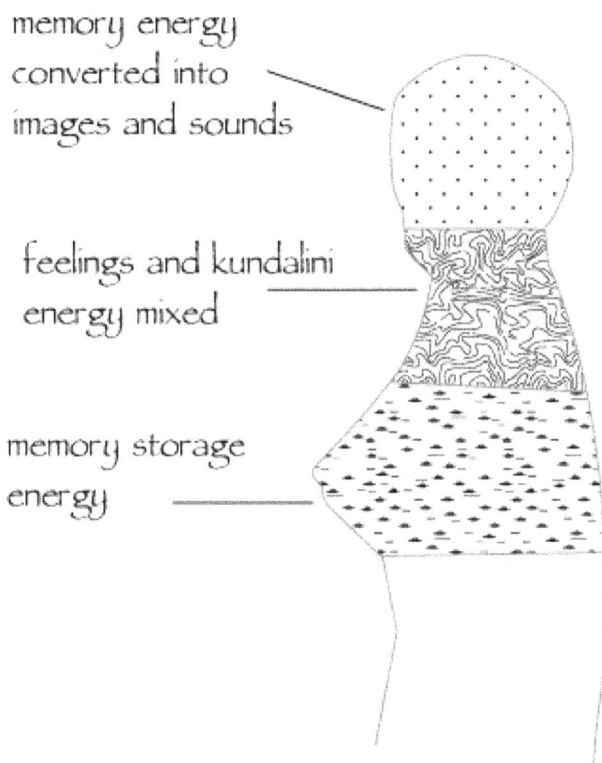

memory energy
converted into
images and sounds

feelings and kundalini
energy mixed

memory storage
energy

June 1, 2000

Shiva

He said, "A cleansed lower chakra produces clarity to this point. This cleansing frees one from petty desires which would require the lower pollutions from manifesting. Controlled eating and prompt evacuation are essential."

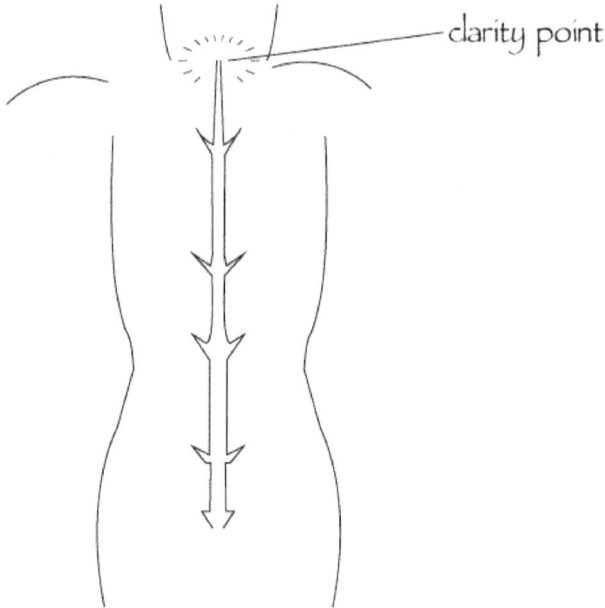
clarity point

June 3, 2000

Shiva

He instructed, "Replace all bowing down with a firmer yoga practice."

Remark:

This was a stipulation of Shiva for me to increase yoga practice by not prioritizing external formalities of worship. At one stage, one gets hung up on such routine actions of worship and honor. One feels that by doing these, one will make advancement. One makes a certain amount of progress by the external worship, but one must go for more serious yoga practice and adhere more closely to the instructions for purification of the psyche.

On this day after careful observation, I realized that sugary drinks, foods and fruits, causes one to get a quick boost of energy and then it tires the material body and fatigues the subtle form. A yogi should stay as far away from sugar as he can.

Air passage to base front loop

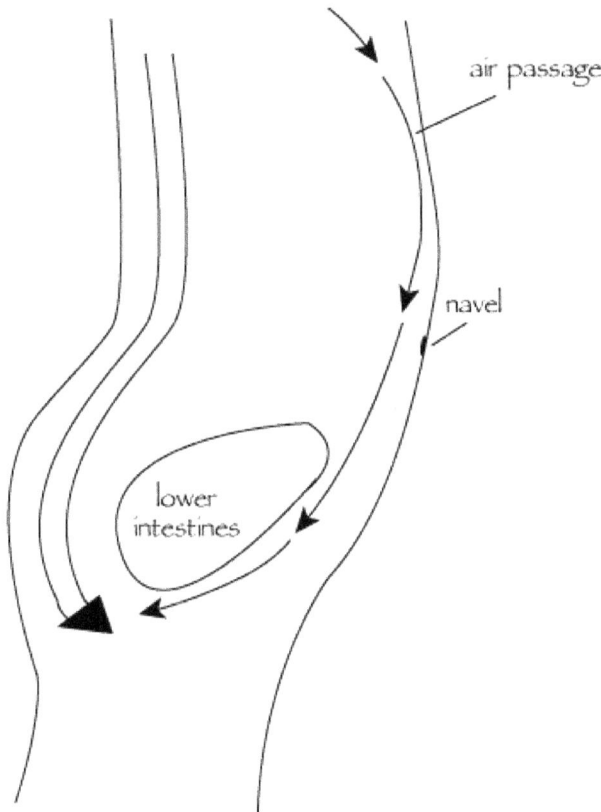

air passage

navel

lower intestines

That was from Shiva.

It concerns pushing down fresh breath energy through the front loop of kundalini energy. This may be used when stools are still in the body, but when they are not in the anal pouch and cannot be evacuated as yet. While one does rapid breathing or even alternate breathing, one may do this in order to get the infused breath energy to the base chakra.

If one's sexual energy was not held in reserve and was absorbed by breath-infusion for some time, the energy will pass through the pubic area without being absorbed, otherwise the sexual area will absorb most of the energy and only a little of it will reach the base chakra.

There is a base deity, a supernatural person in a miniature body, who resides at the base, when there are no stools in the intestines. If there are stools that person will not manifest there. The stools cause a psychic darkness. This person may be seen mystically. Or one may see him by subtle energy vision.

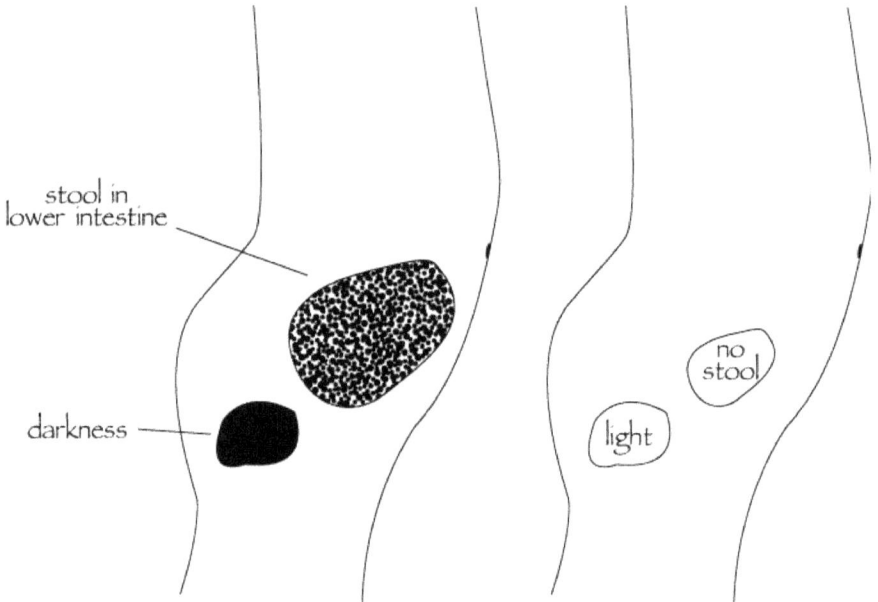

stool in lower intestine

darkness

light

no stool

June 3, 2000

Observation

While doing postures and breath-infusion, one should pay attention within the psyche to see changes which are made when the energy moves. The yogi has to make observations of his nature so that he can take steps for self-reform.

I noticed that the swallowing mechanism is related to the lower intestinal movements. Sometimes after one eats, one is able to evacuate because the swallowing mechanism which operates during eating, causes a trigger in the lower intestines to move stools into the anal pouch.

In hatha yoga, there are neck, throat ad swallowing exercises which are done. These cause a more regulated evacuation because swallowing is connected to stool movement.

June 5, 2000

Shiva

Zones of light

These were seen during exercises. A dark area where stools accumulated was also seen.

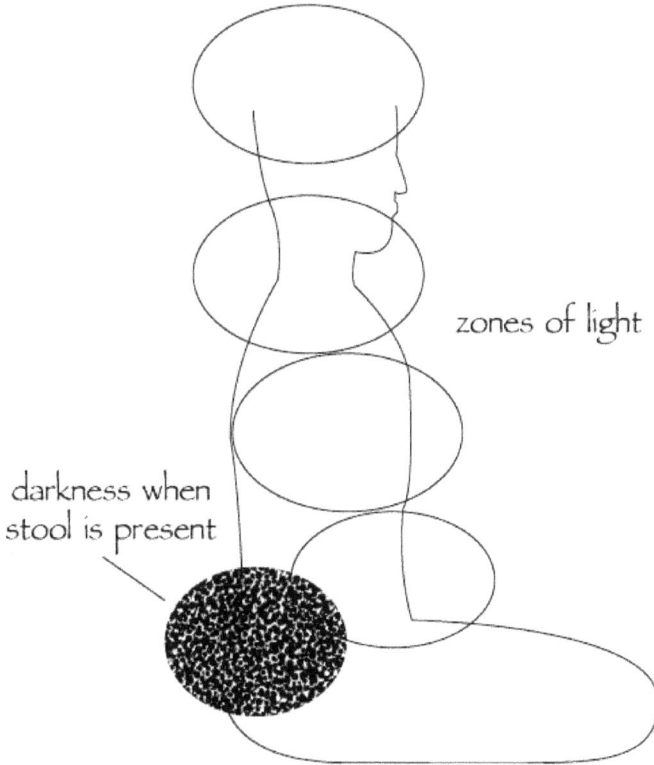

zones of light

darkness when
stool is present

June 5, 2000

Shiva

He gave some assistance with a pratyahar sense withdrawal technique. This was for stopping the intellect organ from its reactive functions. Unless this organ is made to cease such thinking, it cannot function as an internal light.

There is a privacy in thinking and in day-dreaming. One may enjoy this hidden viewing in the mind. In technique yoga, one realizes that this is a waste of valuable energy which could otherwise be used for converting the intellect organ into an internal light for seeing the sky of consciousness.

June 5, 2000

Yogeshwarananda

He questioned, "How is it possible that I touch you and you see light?"

I replied, "It is due to yoga austerities and by your interest which reinforces my aspirations."

He then said, "You may touch others in turn too but it will have no effect if they do not qualify."

Remark:

This hinges on following the austerities and abiding by the rules for practice. At this phase, a rule was that I should not use my psychological energy to respond to argumentative thoughts which come from persons who are not yogis. Some persons become annoyed because I show no interest in their affairs, or because I do not want to be dragged into discussions over this or that, or settle problems and disagreements. However I should complete the yoga practice by sticking to the rules given by great yogins. One cannot advance in yoga if one remains involved.

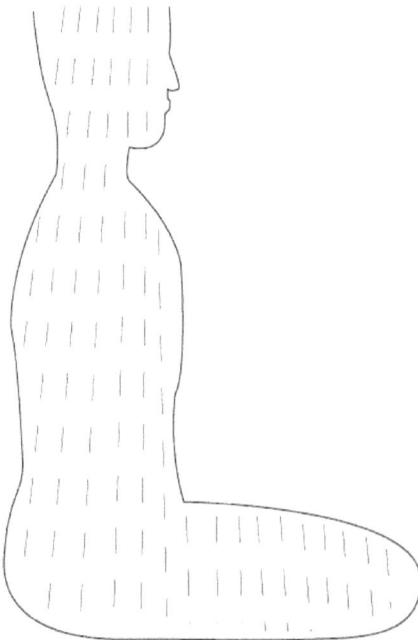

June 6, 2000

Yogeshwarananda

He showed a light which was confined within the subtle body and which did not shine outside of it. This is a light which helps one in pratyahar sense withdrawal. When one sees or senses this light, he gets an assistance that calms him down and makes him become resistant to the need for external sense contact.

June 7, 2000

Yogeshwarananda

He caused me to observe that the brahmrandra light shun down. The energy from it, soothes the organs of the subtle body. This energy descends in waves, one after the other, passing through the subtle body and then disappearing.

June 10, 2000

Yogeshwarananda

He said, "Stay under the shelter of the brahmrandra. I reside here. Contact with me is easy here."

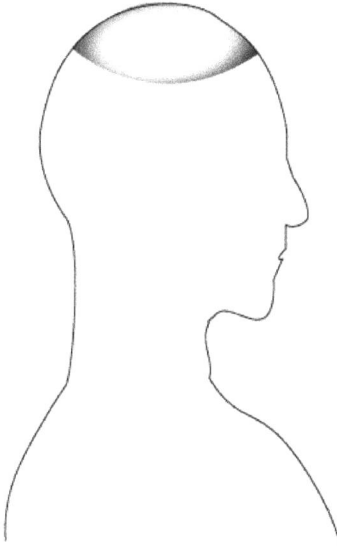

June 9, 2000

Yogeshwarananda

He said, "From up here we have no need for that."

Remark:

Yogesh looked down from the brahmrandra as I was about to take a meal. He showed some needle-like energy tracks in the throat. He indicated that until these were removed, I cannot stay in the brahmrandra area.

June 10, 2000

Yogeshwarananda

He advised, "Do not prevent the progression but do not add to it either. Whatever time allows you to do will be cumulative. The removal of karmic fixes will help indirectly to get the passion deity (Rajguna Devata) off your back. This happens mostly due to a willingness to pay. Of course he will stooge you but that cannot occur if you are vigilant and keep in touch with great yogins."

Remark:

This was advice about getting away from the field of insightful cultural activities (karma yoga), a field which only permits one to do the advanced austerities in spare time. When one is restricted by cultural obligations, one makes little progress. One keeps on in the cultural field without any relief from the material world. Such a yogi is, in a sense, condemned to be absorbed in social, cultural and political activities, with yoga as a side feature.

The karmic fixes or circumstances for palatable and unpalatable involvements, are set on by the Universal Form of Krishna. One cannot safely avoid social duties without getting Krishna's permission. But still such situations have a danger.

The yogi is victimized not by the Universal Form but by passion deity (Rajaguna), a supernatural personality, who works in conjunction with the stupor deity (Tamaguna). These two entities being powerful organizers on the social plane, would like that such a yogi remain on hand to work like a draught animal in the material world, carrying one responsibility after another in the quest of family, country, religion or whatever.

While writing notes for this journal in the year of 2002, I completed a Bhagavad Gita commentary for kriya yogins. Much of this is explained in that book. I reached the stage of getting a waiver from the Supreme Being, from Krishna. I will not be in a position to be victimized by the Rajaguna person. By the mercy of Shiva, I threw the tridents in the corner. I will no longer be poked by their three sharp points.

The key feature is to stay in close touch with the great yogins. If one cannot do so, one is doomed to be victimized by the passion and stupor deities (Rajaguna / Tamaguna). One will be stooged by them. Their agents are present here and there as anyone who is not a liberated soul.

June 12, 2000

Yogeshwarananda

He showed the front brahmrandra orbs.

Remark:

These are mostly in the forehead. They come into concentration when one tries to focus on anything or if they are attracted to objects spontaneously.

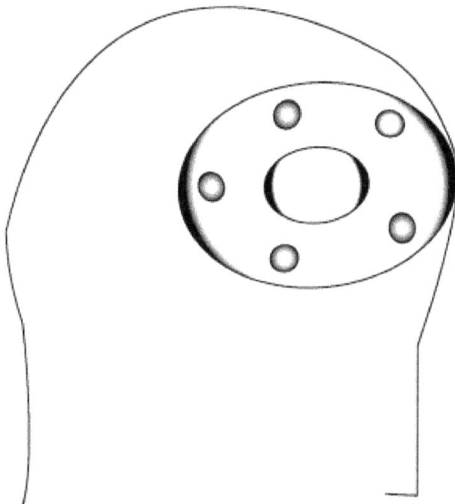

intellect with

five sensing orbs

June 12, 2000

Yogeshwarananda

He said, "They can be differentiated. See this. Check how they move and focus. Practice internal transcendental focus."

Remark:

This was an instruction force to see the sense orbs which are in the forehead. Yogesh was in a miniature subtle body, showing them in the top of my head.

June 14, 2000

Shiva

He showed the round kundalini, which is experienced when one does breath-infusion and postures and has stools which are not evacuated.

Sometimes stools do not go down into the anal pouch. In that case, if one does exercises, the energy may go around the body in a different way.

Prompt stool evacuation is important. To achieve this one has to do various types of stomach pumps. One must also pump sufficient air into the lungs so that the system becomes more energetic.

Yogeshwarananda

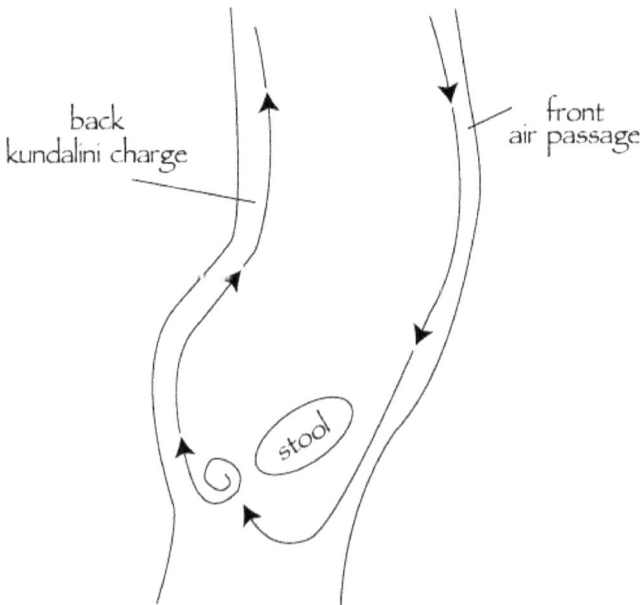

back
kundalini charge

front
air passage

stool

He said, "Try to stabilize it. Conserve it. Stop its interaction with thoughts. Train it to seek the inside only."

Remark:

This applies to the intellect system of orbs. It is part of the internal transcendence focus.

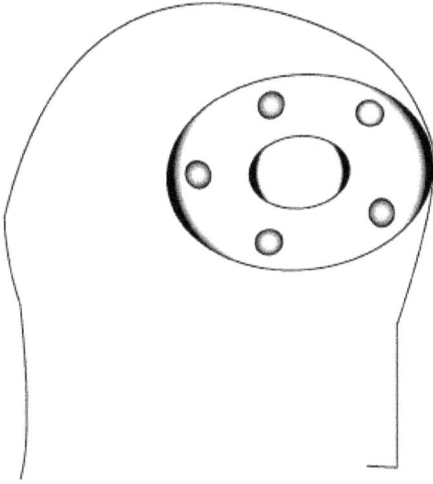

intellect with
five sensing orbs

June 15, 2000

Yogeshwarananda

He showed a stabilizing concentration which was done under the umbrella-like head orb.

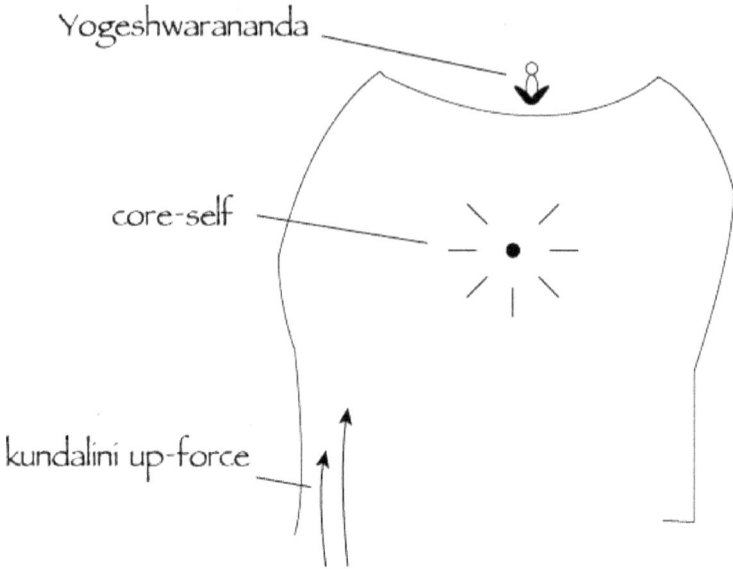

Yogeshwarananda

core-self

kundalini up-force

June 17, 2000

Agastya / Yogeshwarananda / Shiva

Under their combined influence, I experienced a particular nadi subtle tube. This tube in the nose was opened with sun-charged fire energy which was infused by rapid breathing. The body was in lotus posture with elbows out.

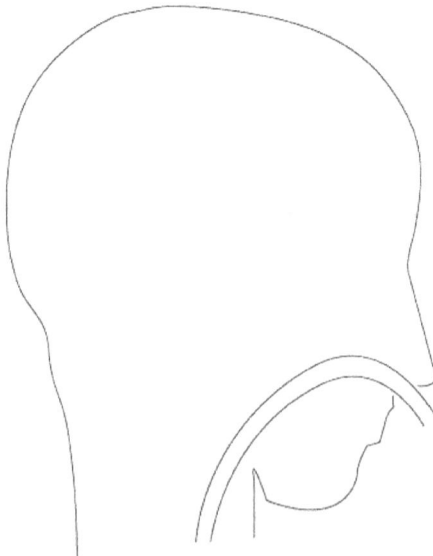

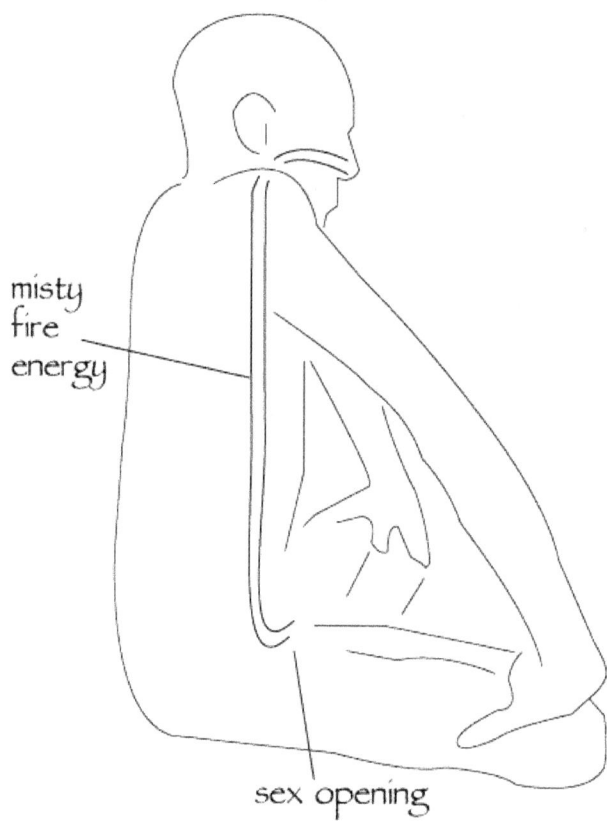

misty
fire
energy

sex opening

Part 5

Agastya

He showed a posture which is done with the subtle body. While doing this one stands on the knees of the physical body with the hands supporting the back as shown. One then stretches the astral form backwards. These exercises are particularly for the subtle form. These prepare a yogi to continue yoga in the astral world after the death of his physical system. If one is unable to develop that practice one will take another gross body, to complete the austerities. In taking that body, one may become preoccupied with social life and so waste another birth. It is important to get the subtle body in the habit of doing the exercises directly, so that its tendency to rely on doing it through the gross form is removed.

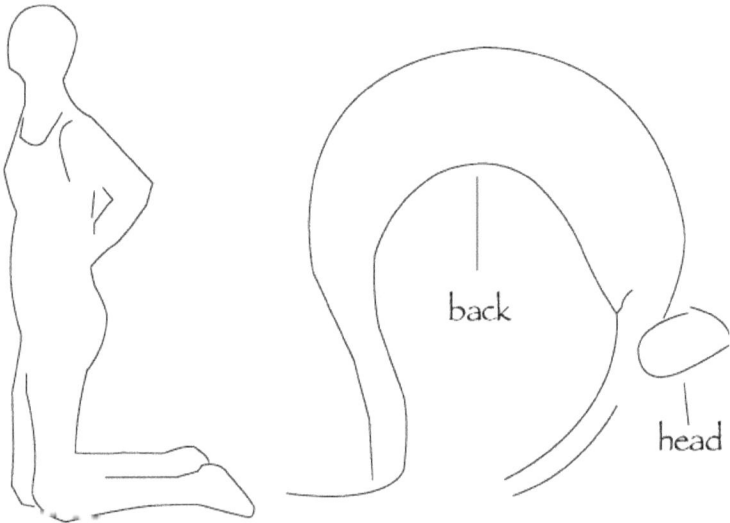

June 18, 2000

Yogeshwarananda

He instructed, "Begin the transcendence sessions."

Remark:

On this date Yogesh ordered that I begin sitting for long periods at least twice per day for the purpose of getting my psyche in the mood for transcendence. At first I used to sit like this for five or ten minutes. Then gradually I increased to twenty minutes, and then to half-hour or longer. I will increase this over a time to three or four hours.

To facilitate the transcendence meditation, an isolated rural environment is required. One should sit long enough to cause the disturbing sensuality to calm down, so that one can transfer the attention elsewhere to the sky of consciousness. Usually people sit for a time for meditation but as they do this, the disturbing sensuality keeps on with its movements of thoughts, picturizations and symbols. This does not stop unless one gets a higher subtle energy into the mind. That is done by breath-infusion and by an efficient set of poses in hatha yoga. One must also master celibacy yoga. One must be sincere in the effort to get away from the harassing sense objects. When all this is achieved one may transit to transcendental levels during meditation.

Even though in the developed countries many people claim to meditate, they are not doing so. People feel that relief from stress and ease of the mind by listening to mood-altering music, is meditation. That is incorrect.

To understand meditation one has to study Patanjali's *Yoga Sutras*. For yoga success one needs isolation. The idea that one can meditate in a modern city amidst the hustle and bustle, is not Patanjali's. A particular lifestyle in a particular simple environment brings on meditation. Trying to meditate amidst modern living is a praiseworthy effort but it is not the same achievement which the isolated ancient ascetics demonstrated.

June 19, 2000

Yogeshwarananda

He showed the operation of sense focus in slow motion. This focus must be seen in slow motion in order to understand how the psyche focuses through the intellect organ. Sometimes, the senses activate other parts of the psyche directly, without being checked by the core-self or even by the analyzing intellect.

In the feminine psyche, this happens regularly. This is why males and females have difficulty understanding each other. It is because their psyches work in slightly different ways. In males, the senses are usually checked by the analytical part of the intellect. In females, the senses bypass that analysis and directly motivate the psyche.

June 19, 2000

Yogeshwarananda

He said, "Transcendental absorption is important. It is the only position from which you can transfer the objectivity felt on the physical plane. Here now, see how the subtle energies respond without permission, independently."

Remark:

He showed a fantasy movie in a theatre in the astral world. Some children viewed the film in which the characters were projected among the viewing children. This causes the children to exhibit high emotions. I observed that my feelings were responding with excitements too. The point is that the feelings have to be shielded from exposure to sensual involvements. Due to their nature, they cannot help but respond even to illusions. Thus the yogi has to go into isolation.

This was seen at the third eye, the brow chakra, at the command of Yogesh.

June 20, 2000

Yogeshwarananda

He taught that each physical nerve has a subtle counterpart. By being attentive to the physical nerves during postures, the mind learns how to track the subtle ones. This is the advantage gained by being attentive to asana postures. Even though it is physical exercise, it causes the mind to develop subtle perception.

June 21, 2000

Yogeshwarananda

He showed a tratak technique. In this one, the eyelids are closed but the eyes remain open behind them, in such a way, that the energy which surges down the optic nerves, pours out of the subtle eye sockets. If one does this after doing an energetic session of breath-infusion, one may feel a white light coming up from the bottom and the same type of energy coming from the top at a slant as shown in the diagram. One should try to eat less and less food as one increases the pranayama practice. One should decrease the interest in social complications, so that one would have cleaner emotional energy in the psyche. Too much excitement ruins yoga.

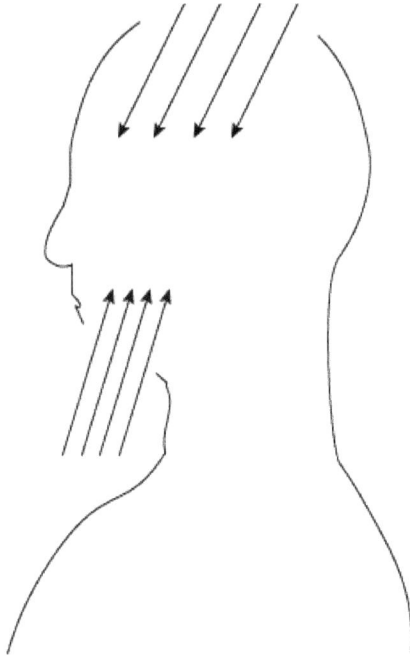

June 2, 2000

Yogeshwarananda

He explained that water, as compared to milk or any other fluid, used during the day, blocks some passages for a short period. Other liquids, depending on their protein content blocks for a longer period.

Remark:

The effects of foods must be carefully studied by a yogi. For success, he should do whatever is necessary to make advancement. One should work with the self to understand the psyche and judge responses to various foods. One should regulate diet to facilitate practice. The hard and fast rule is advancement. Do whatever causes that.

On this day, Yogesh counseled me to funnel my psychological power in the brahmrandra area of the subtle body. I was to study top vision and see how it may be tracked into the brahmrandra area. He suggested trying a head stand posture to orient the mind to the top-of-the-head nerves.

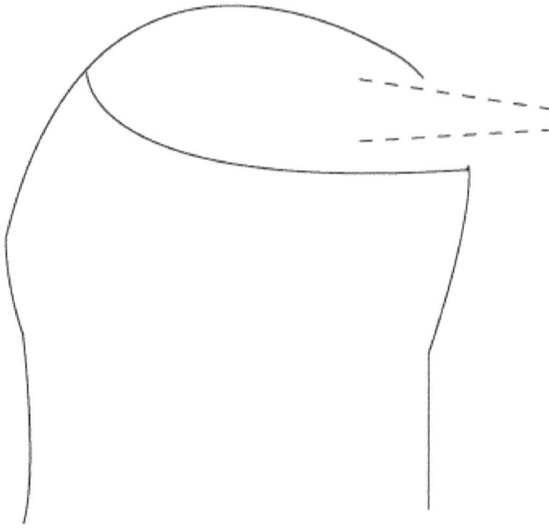

June 23, 2000

Yogeshwarananda

He gave a preparatory meditation for development of the brahmrandra. If this is done consistently, then eventually subtle energy will shoot up to the brahmrandra. One will develop the bubble body in which brahmrandra is the only opening.

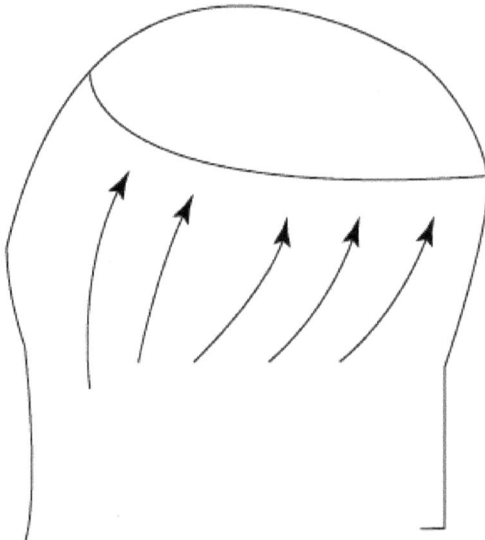

Remark:

It should be noted that some readers may develop a desire for visitation by Yogesh. I cannot promise that he will visit anyone. I know this much. He retreats more and more into the causal plane. In the years of 1998, 1999 and 2000, I used to see him much but in the year of 2002, I hardly saw him because he retreated. Many great yogis vanish from this existence and cannot be contacted from this level. However their information which was recorded by me or by anyone else, has potency.

June 26, 2000

Yogeshwarananda

He advised that I develop this meditation further. In the diagram below, the number of orbs are not accurate. At the time of this vision I could not accurately count them. I did not have the required clarity.

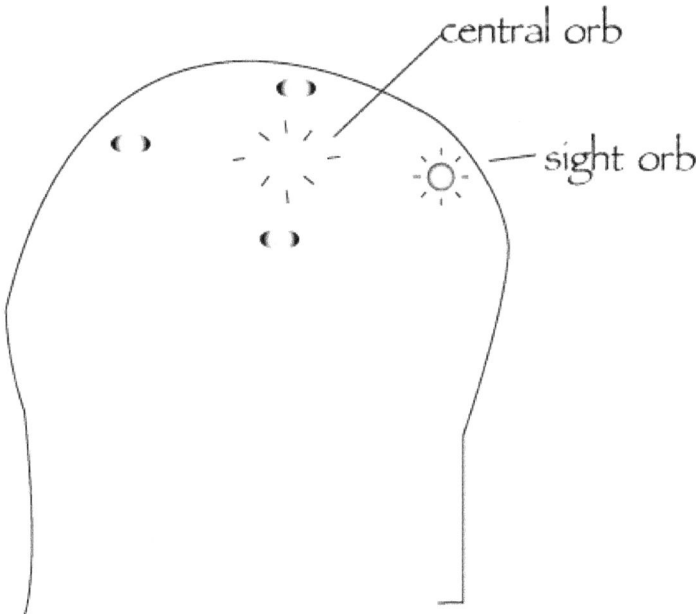

June 27, 2000

He said: "Gather it here. Collect it here."

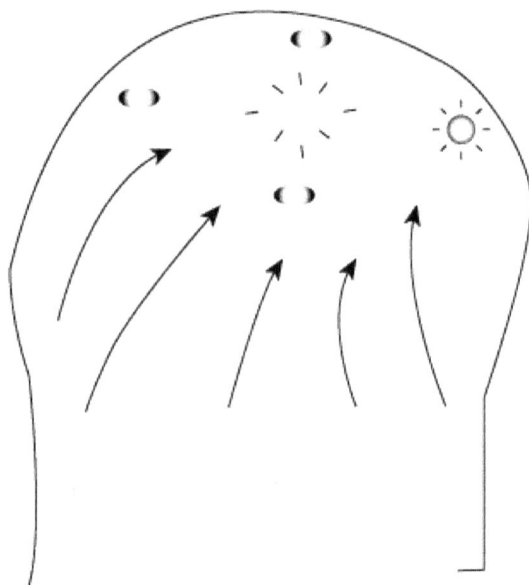

Remark:

At the time of these instructions, I did not realize that later kundalini chakra would be eliminated. There would be instead a blueish bubble-form. This form is sometimes called a higher pranamaya kosha (sensitive energy body). Siddha Nityananda introduced me to that form sometime in the year 2002. However it was these exercises that caused me develop it. Brahmrandra must be developed by these practices.

June 28, 2000

Yogesh checked my practice on this day. At the time, I lost track of the brahmrandra, due to preoccupation with thoughts. I was in a lower orb where the thoughts come from bad association. This bad association is from yogically-disinclined persons and even from religious associates, from anyone who is not serious about yoga. It is a struggle when you have to associate with such people. They cause the advancement to be retarded.

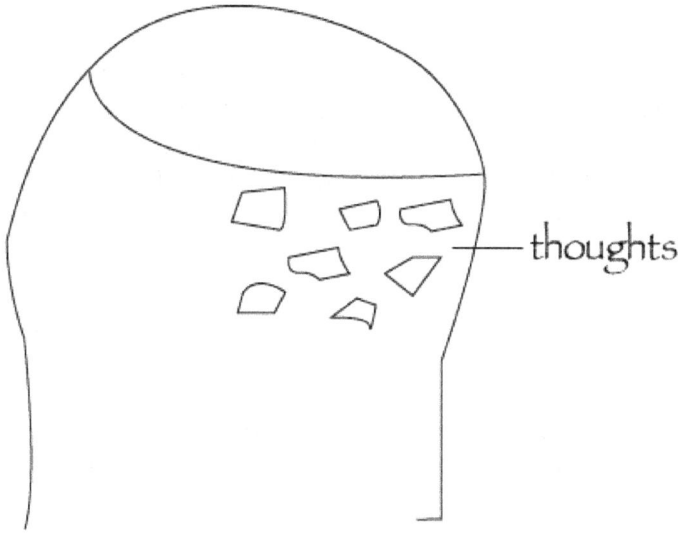

thoughts

July 7, 2000

Yogeshwarananda

On this date, I was in Guyana. I noticed that my progress was slowed considerably. This was due to have to associate with so many people who do no yoga. These include religious folk.

I did however advance in thought reception and control. I attained a distance-detachment from incoming thoughts. By that, arriving thoughts which were traveling fast, seem to be slow. I viewed from a safe distance. They landed in the mind and fizzed out.

Yogesh was present at a considerable distance from me because my brahmrandra was not as activated because of negative association. As soon as I resume the practice, I will be in close contact again.

July 11, 2000

Yogeshwarananda

He sent this message, "Death of sensual energy withdrawal is the same as energy attraction. That has to be eliminated, otherwise brahmrandra cannot be developed. Essentially those attractive energies form into sensual forms of the opposite sex, for the purpose of progeny generation on the ground level."

Remark:

Sensual energy withdrawal is dead, or sensual energy withdrawal practice ends, when one takes in too much association from persons who are not introverted. These could be religious people. Once the introspection comes to a standstill, one is thrown back to the social plane. Ultimately that leads to its highlight which is sexual indulgence. From that comes Shiva's trident, which pokes one with responsibility. Responsibility causes the end of yoga practice, because one becomes preoccupied with social duties. More or less, that is the sum and substance of this life. This is pravritti marga or the acceleration of cultural activities in order to make facility for ancestors to get infant forms.

For a serious yogi, it is a matter of saying, "To hell with Shiva's trident. To hell with Krishna's karma yoga plan in the Bhagavad Gita."

Essentially these two aspects are identical. However this does not mean that a yogi should disrespect either Shiva or Krishna. O no! We have to understand that the trident pokes us because of where we are positioned. The karma yoga becomes mandatory because of how we are situated in the creation. Thus a yogi gets smart. He takes to technique yoga to purify the psyche of the need to be involved.

July 19, 20000

Yogeshwarananda

He said, "Then this was open all around. Then gradually after some eons, it closed in the back, here. Then on this side, there was an opening here. At first it was all-seeing. Then the vision narrowed. Then the small slot closed. These opened in turn. Now you should reverse the procedure. Free yourself from the closure."

Remark:

This is a description of the evolution of physical vision, coming from the first vision which developed in the subtle body, long ago. This is a purely mystic activity. Yogesh went back in time. He went into the causal zone and returned to describe it.

In the procedure, he recommend that I was to close the external vision, the energy which courses down the optic nerves of the physical body. After doing this, I was to open the slot vision in the brow chakra. Then after some practice, I was to open the spherical vision. Look at this diagram.

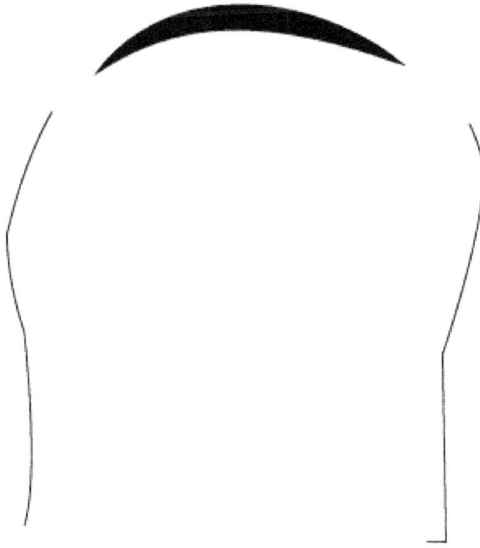

July 25, 2000

Yogeshwarananda

He instructed that I turn subtle energy in a circular direction as shown in these diagrams. These practices cause subtle energy to be more submissive to one's desire, otherwise one remains as a slave to it.

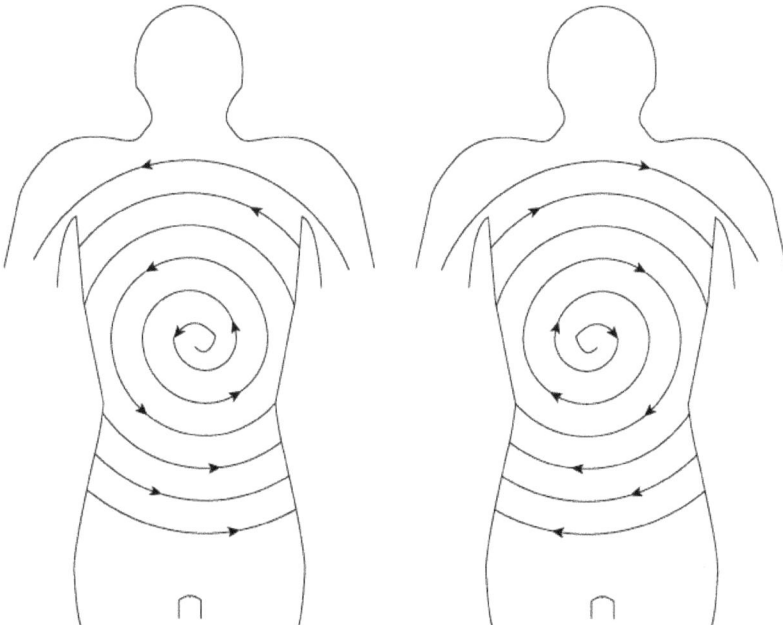

July 26, 2000

Shiva

He said, "Decide and practice. The decisions must be followed by practice."

Remark:

For success in yoga, one should practice with the help of advanced yogis. This gives a maintenance power, otherwise one will begin in a huff and puff and then stop practicing altogether.

It is not a good thing to give instructions to those whose life style will not permit the time nor energy required for practice. If one gives such persons advice, one will lose the required enthusiasm.

July 27, 2000

Yogeshwarananda

He gave a technique to practice after doing an intense session of breath-infusion, followed by down-draw breaths.

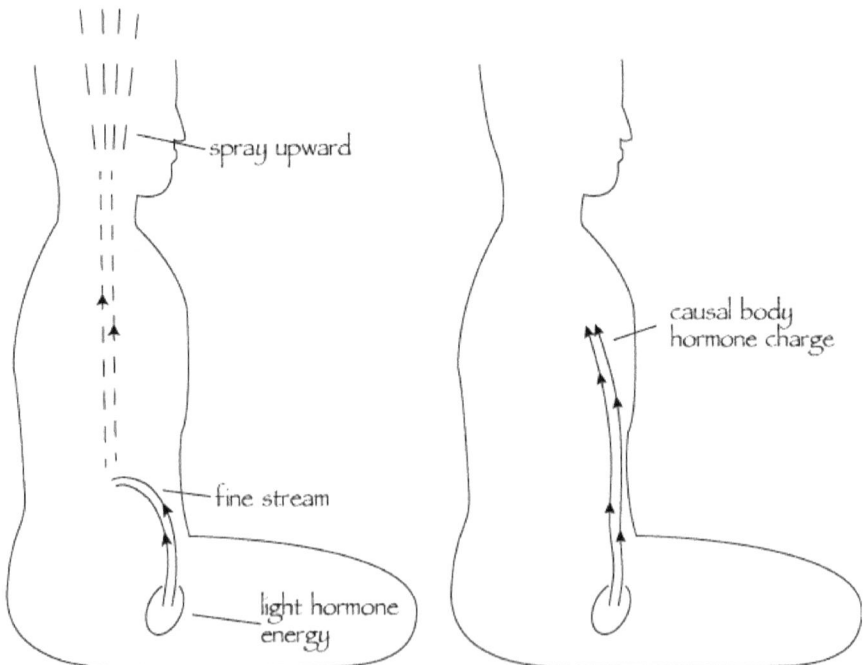

July 27, 2000

Lahiri Mahasaya

He came to check my practice. He gave some self-criticism energy and showed some orbs. Regarding the self-critical energy, one must get this from an advanced yogin. It so happens that one does not develop the self-critical energy on one's own.

double touch-points

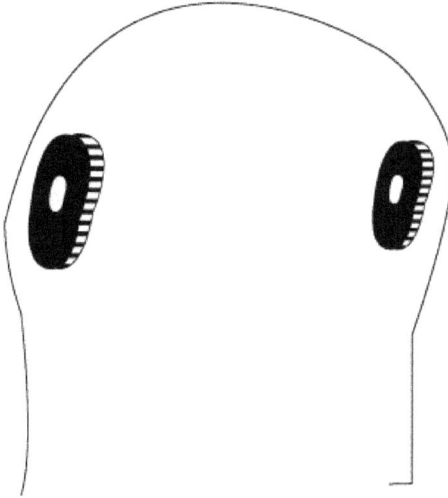

July 28, 2000

Yogeshwarananda

He gave a certain kriya. The energy movements are shown in this diagram.

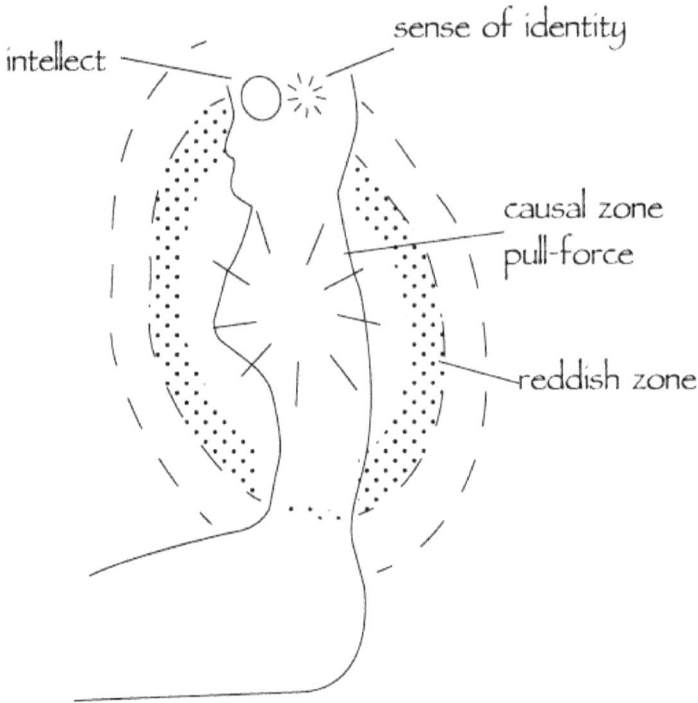

intellect

sense of identity

causal zone

pull-force

reddish zone

July 30, 2000

Yogeshwarananda

He said, "Talk to the mind. Once it is separated and you see its sensitive intelligence, always appeal to it, while engaging the lifeforce in the required habits."

Remark:

At the date for notations about this remark on April 2, 2002, I forgot that Yogesh said this. However he must have told me this because I followed this advice for some time prior. This is good advice to be applied after one passed into the 6th stage of yoga, that of dharana concentration, deliberate linkage of the attention to higher concentration forces. Until such time, this cannot be effective, since one cannot separate the core-self from the other components in the mind.

The mind, though depicted as an inert object, is highly sensitive and intelligent. In the advanced stages one may appeal to it for cooperation. One may influence it to strive for spiritual success. Ramakrishna, a tantric yogin of repute, used to talk to his mind. Sometimes he would say, "O mind, why do you want tobacco? Do you not know that it is ruinous?"

Like that he was rated as a crazed man by persons who did not understand advanced practice.

Sometimes secretly I talk to my mind saying, "You are a bad mind which ruins yoga. You have no interest in advancement. What friend are you?"

In that way I would appeal to my mind, while intimidating it. Somehow the mind would respond by trying to help with practice, and by curtailing undesirable tendencies.

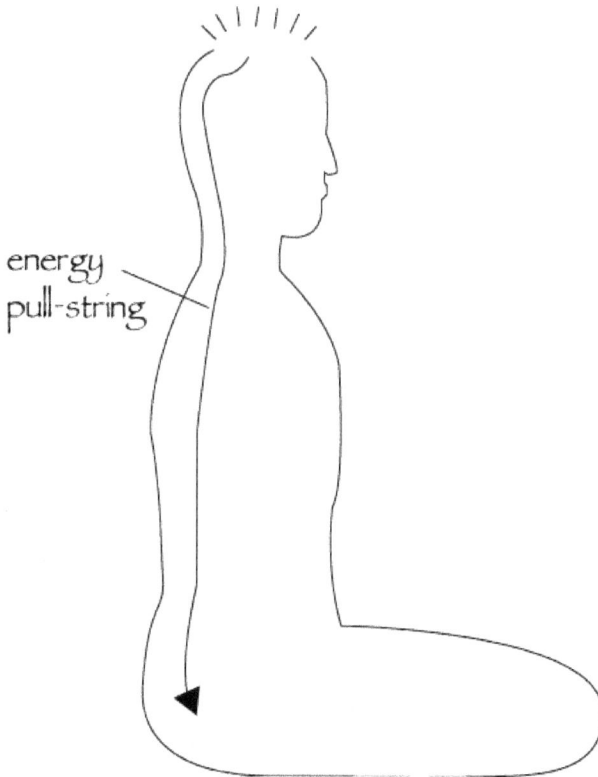

energy
pull-string

July 32, 2000

Yogeshwarananda

He showed some matching nadis. These may be sensed after a highly-energized session of breath-infusion.

July 21, 2000

Yogeshwarananda

He said, "Use the intellect. Then touch the orb. Then find the wire to the stretched nerve."

Remark:

This has to do with tracking subtle nerves which go from the intellect organ to the various parts of the subtle body. This is done while doing stretches with breath-infusion. Some yogis do not mix postures and breath-energization. They do postures first for about one hour, then they do one or two hours of pranayama. While they do pranayama, they track subtle energy. Alternately one can do postures with breath-infusion and down-draw breath, while stretching the body in various postures and applying the various locks.

August 2, 2000

Yogeshwarananda

He said, "When the subtle body is cleared, the causal form is manifested. First it shows with red, blue and greyish lights."

Remark:

These bodies are purified gradually. It does not happen all at once. Sometimes after long practice a yogi gets sudden clarity. Sometimes there is a sudden clarity after a short practice. The important thing is the log of his practice in this and in previous lives.

After so much practice one gets results. During the year of 2002 Siddha Nityananda expressed a regret to me. He said, "There was only four hours of practice for completion when he abandoned yoga. He went back to cultural life. What a waste! He was on the brink of perfection. Due to impatience, he gave it up and went away."

It is like that. One practices. After accumulating so much austerity, the results comes. If one is impatient, one may go away just before reaching the culmination. This is because of the mind's tendency for wanting full results in a short time. Under the influence of the lower nature, one may not persist to completion.

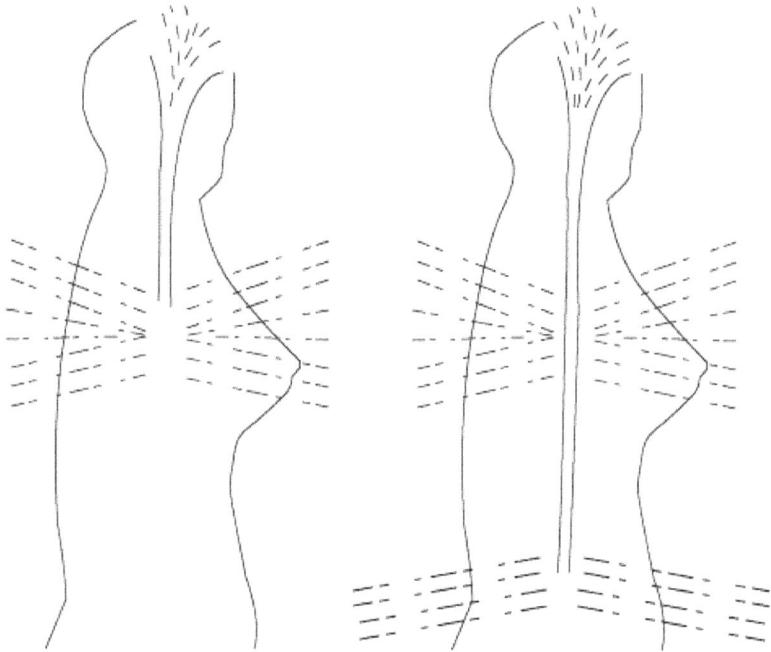

August 3, 2000

Yogeshwarananda

He said, "When the gross body dies, the subtle one becomes the basis. When the subtle one vanishes, the causal form becomes the basis. When the causal one disintegrates, the brahman spiritual energy becomes the basis. Preparations are required in each case. Do not fantasize or assume anything. Work into the next stage. Do the practice."

Shivananda

He said, "As intellect is to feelings (prana) so ahankara is to super-subtle feelings (paraprana). Get rid of the tube."

Remark:

As the intellect is an organ in the subtle body, so the ahankara sense-of-initiative to act, is an organ in the causal form. Stated differently, just as we have a physical brain, so we have a subtle brain called intellect. We have a causal organ called ahankara sense-of-initiative to act.

As the brain uses air which is absorbed by the lungs, so the intellect organ uses subtle air which is called subtle energy and the sense of initiative uses an even subtler air which is called paraprana.

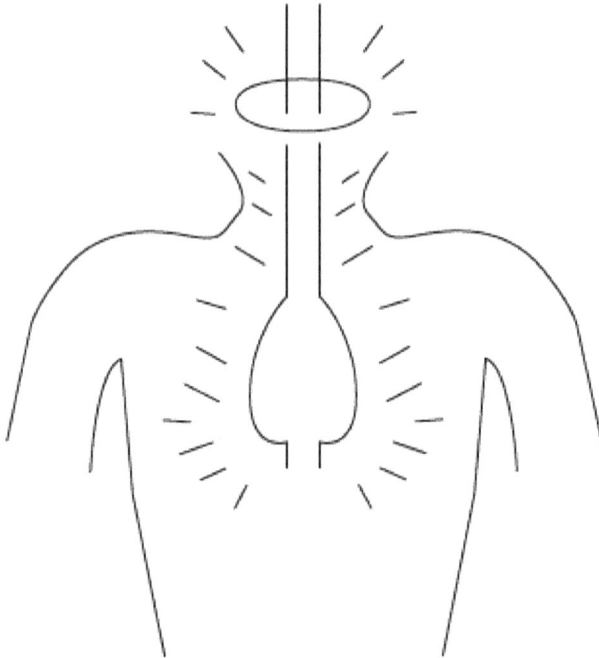

August 6, 2000

Shivananda

He showed a twisting star in the neck of the subtle body.

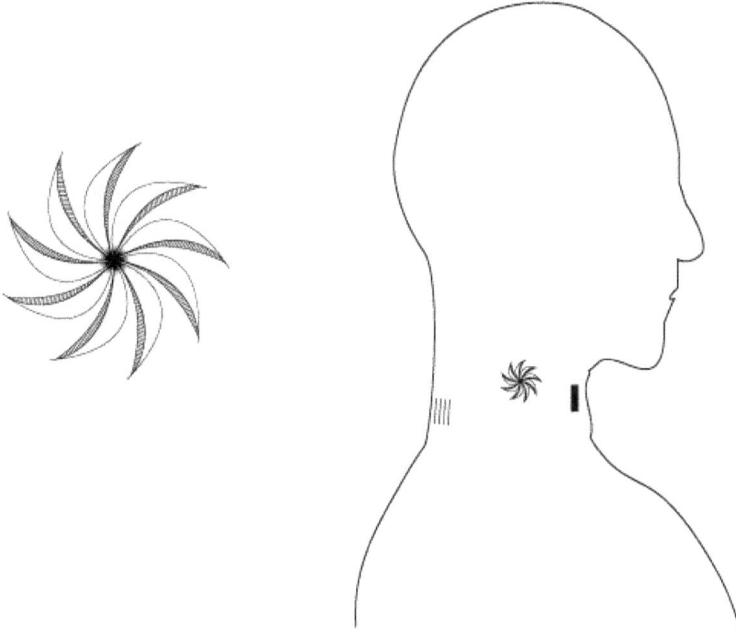

August 7, 2000

Ganesh

He said, "These are outward-going forces. Return these here."

Remark:

This was an instruction to turn-about some energy that poured out of the causal body. This energy is converted into desires in the subtle form. If it is turned about instead, it does not actuate as desires. Thus one becomes free to do yoga practice. Otherwise one becomes possessed with desires and falls under the jurisdiction of the Vishvarupa Universal Form for completion of karma yoga duties in the material world.

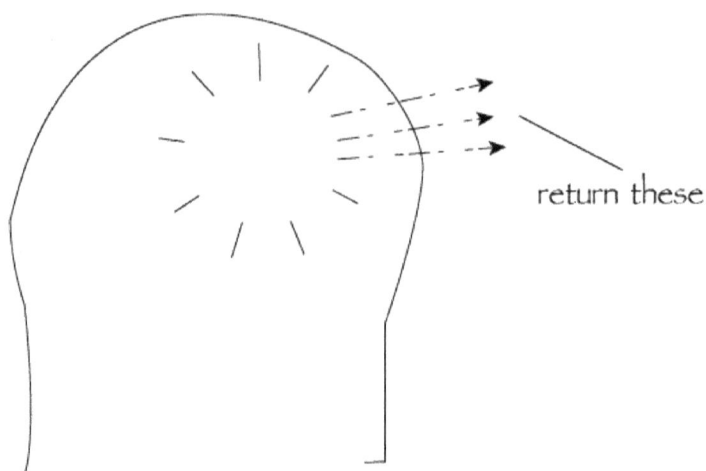

return these

August 8, 2000

Yogeshwarananda

He showed a kriya. Here is the diagram.

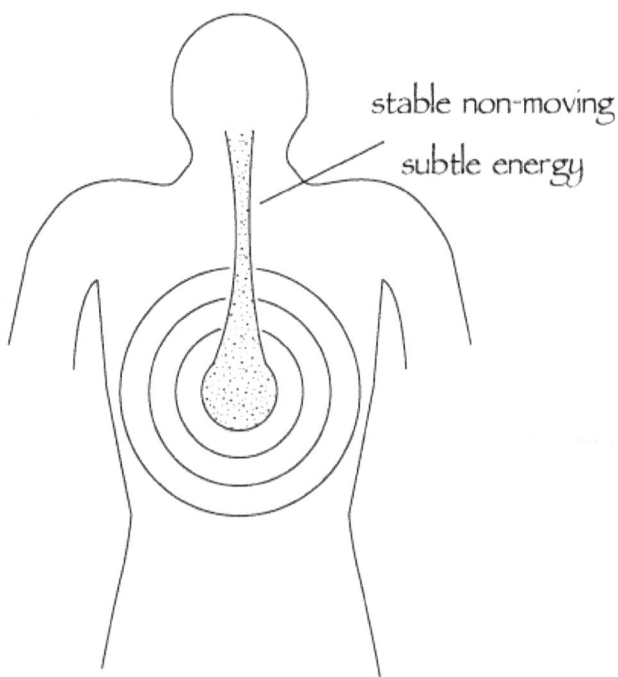

stable non-moving
subtle energy

August 9, 2000

Shivananda

At night, he showed how to collect the frontal thoughts in impulsion energy and open the brow chakra.

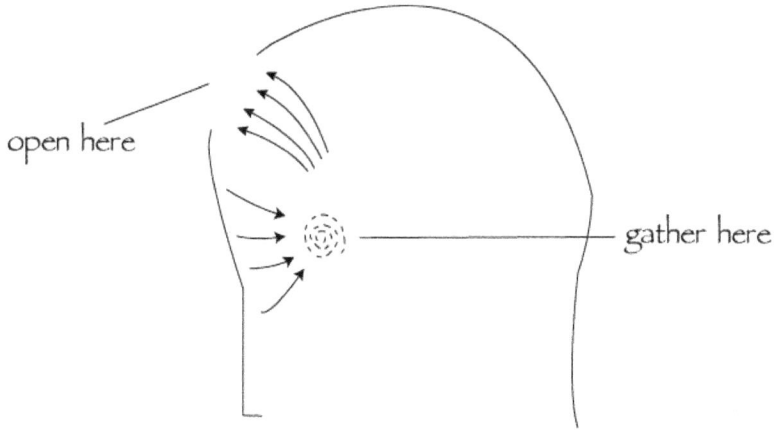

August 10, 2000

Babaji

He gave an external pull for internal reinforcement.

August 11, 2000

Lahiri Mahasaya

He said, "Use bad thoughts to increase the focus."

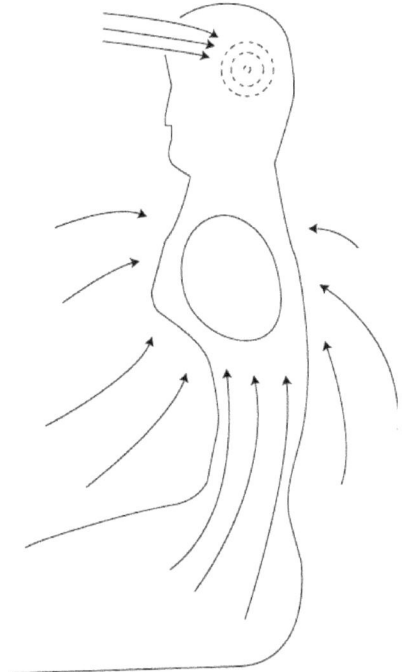

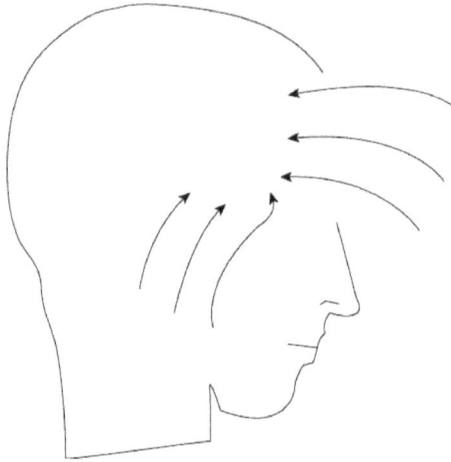

August 12, 2000

While doing exercises on this day, I realized that a certain exercise causes the strengthening of the esophagus and the trachea. This exercise may seem not to be related to the throat area but it is. It is the exercise where one squats over and bounces up and down with the thighs bouncing on the calves, while the hands are flat on the ground, being used to support the weight of the body. Postures and breath-infusion are wonderful.

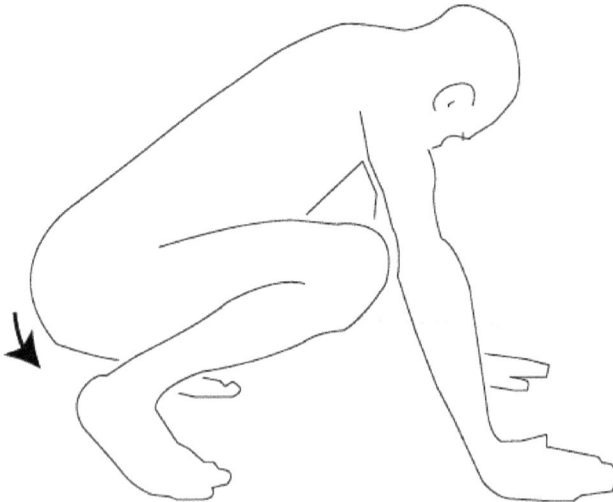

exhale as buttocks
slam down

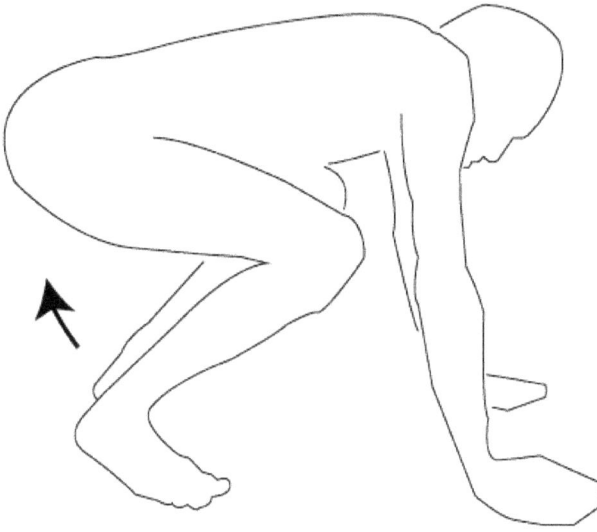

inhale as buttocks rise

April 13, 2000

I had an experience of the break down and disappearance of the entire kundalini chakra. Experiences of this sort are not permanent initially. It takes years of practice for this to take a permanent form, where the kundalini chakra actually disappears for good. In addition, if one digresses, that kundalini energy will be reformatted. Even though trees lose leaves in the winter or dry season, as soon as the spring or wet season comes, new foliage grows again. So it is. If we eliminate something, it will again become manifest under certain conditions.

It is the same with celibacy. Sexual polarity is widespread. If one perfects celibacy yoga, then if he is not careful or even if he is careful, but if the overall destiny is against him, he will find that he digresses again into sexual involvements. This happens on the subtle plane mostly with the angelic women or with the subtle bodies of physical women.

One has to be vigilant. Because the psychic apparatus has a downwards tendency which may quickly erase yoga progression, one cannot be too careful.

When I had the experience of the disappearance of the kundalini form, the lower area where that force previously resided, was saturated by a frost-white mystic energy.

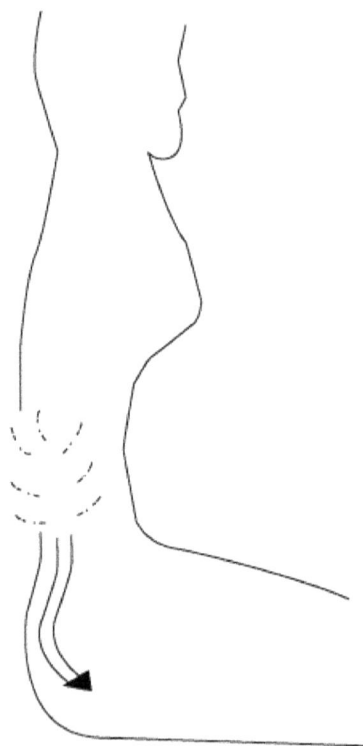

August 14, 2000

Yogeshwarananda

He said, "Stools being removed, the light is clear."

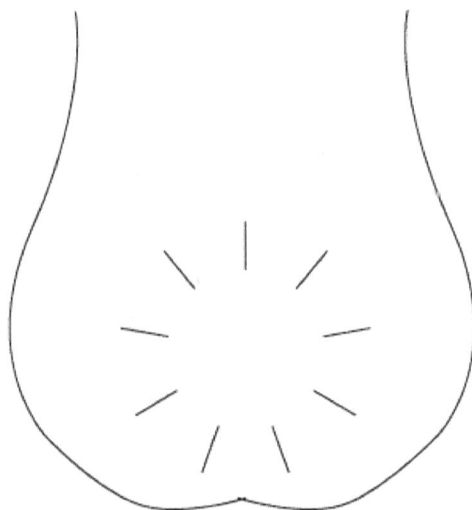

August 15, 2000

Yogeshwarananda

He said, "Work on the base. Push air down. After consistent practice, you can purify that."

August 16, 2000

Yogeshwarananda

He said, "By reducing the quantity of stools, evacuations are ordered. The minimum energy is extended. The cleaner subtle energy fills the spaces. There is more clarity below. A mystic light which is crystal clear becomes manifested."

August 17, 2000

Yogeshwarananda

He said, "With cleanliness, sushumna nadi becomes one chakra. At first, the others clear up. Then they disappear. The diversity ends."

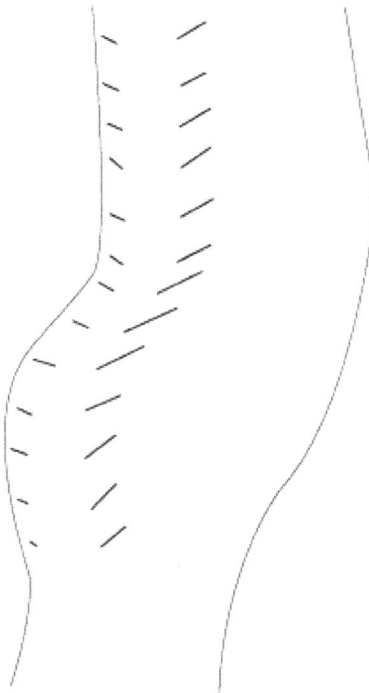

August 19, 2000

Skanda

He gave access to the Mothers, the Krittikas, in the southern sky. To them he said, *"Anumate namah."*

They poured some celibate reinforcing energy down my spine. It was a supernatural energy which has small energy beads in it.

Aug. 22, 2000

Sachidananda

He said, "Give more care to the postures and muscular locks. Your breath-infusion is doing what it should but give more form to the supportive postures. Look at this. Do this."

Remark:

He explain the use of asana postures to achieve symmetry and form. The stretching should be done carefully and accurately paying close attention within.

August 23, 2000

Sachidananda

He showed some toe-nerves subtle energy. Here is a diagram.

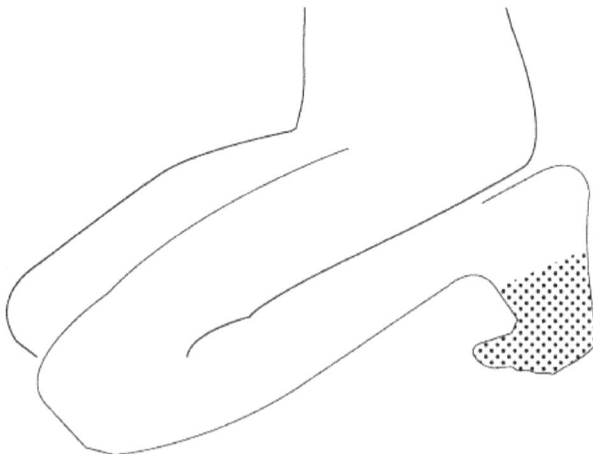

August 23, 2000

Yamaraj Devata

He is a supernatural person whose supervises the final departure of a subtle body from a gross one (death). He showed a crystal clear tube in the subtle form. It extended from the kanda sex bulb to the throat. He said to keep that tube cleared, keeping fresh subtle energy travelling through it. He suggested that I should not be attentive to the aging of the physical body but should instead observe what occurs in the subtle form. I should focus to keep the subtle energies clean and clear, flowing freely. I should be sincere and keep sensual attractions out of mind.

At the time of this discourse, I did the exercises shown below. This practice purifies the bottom portion of the lungs. One should do one side and then do the other side, kicking out the foot accordingly. When the foot is pulled in and under, one inhales and when it is kicked out one exhales.

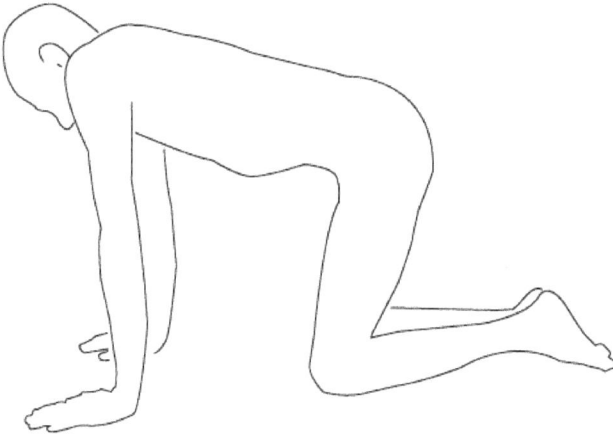

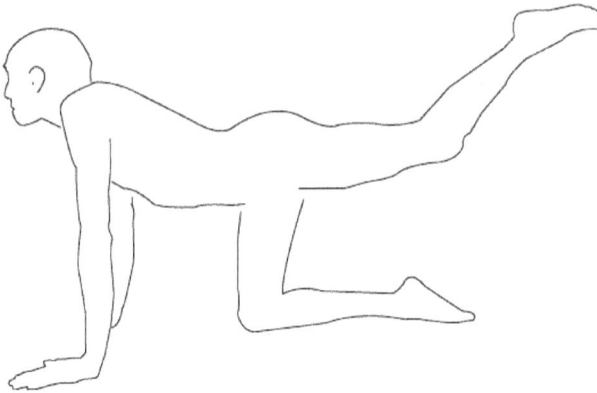

August 25, 2000

Shankara

He said, "Close down the sensual pursuits. Systematically stop the double takes."

Remark:

The double takes are when the senses, as prompted by the lifeforce, seek to reaffirm a sensual quest. Usually it is the opposite sex, a bright color seen, some exciting thoughts, some seemingly-mysterious thought or some sensual data which promises pleasure.

Shankara said, "This is a sensual energy restraint."

He showed a sensual orifice which was tightly closed. Usually that orifice expands outwards to pursue sense objects.

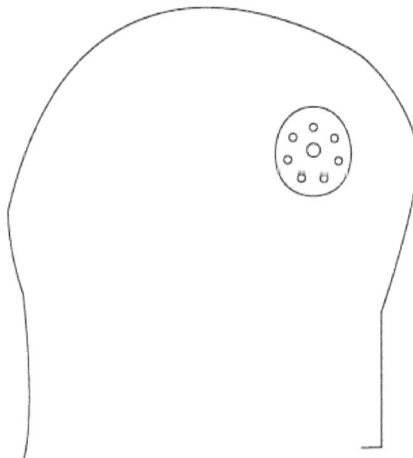

Shankara

He said, "This is another area for conservation. Stop the double checking of wasted sensual pursuits interests. Some of it is controlled by the sun, moon and air. A portion of it is due to your laxity. You can remove that portion."

Remark:

A yogi should not blame himself for influences which affect him but which come from higher persons or forces, like the sun, moon and air. He should know what he is responsible for and should be concerned with that only. Other powers which are beyond control have every right to affect him, even negatively.

Shiva

He said, "The positions changed due to shift of level and due to advancement in practice."

Remark:

This has to do with the positions of the three deities, Brahma, Vishnu and Shiva. A prayer is said to reach them, namely:

guru brahma guru vishnu guru devo mahesvara
guru shakshat parambrahma
tasmai sri gurudeva namah

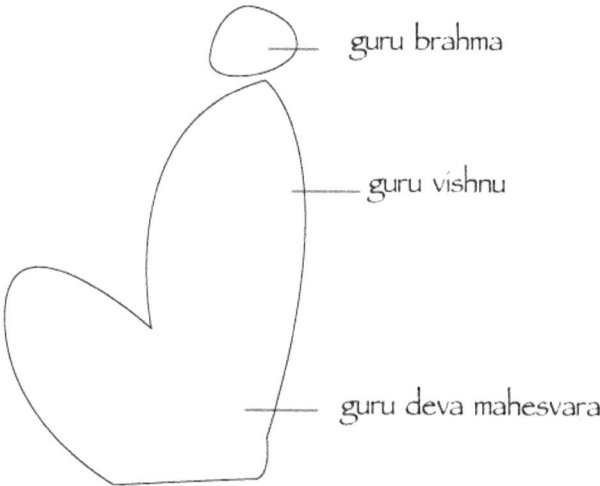

guru brahma

guru vishnu

guru deva mahesvara

When this is said in meditation while doing breath-infusion, one may be instructed to say each portion to the deity concerned. I was given an instruction to locate the deities in different parts of the subtle body.

On this day, Shiva gave this technique to practice.

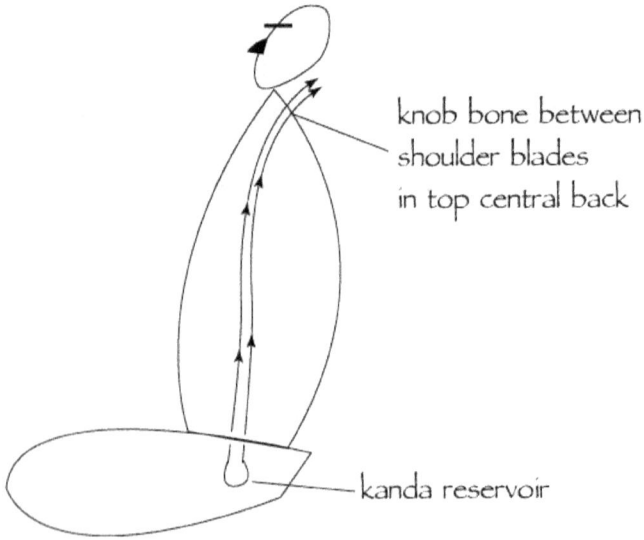

knob bone between
shoulder blades
in top central back

kanda reservoir

August 27, 2000

Shankara

He gave an advanced celibate pose.

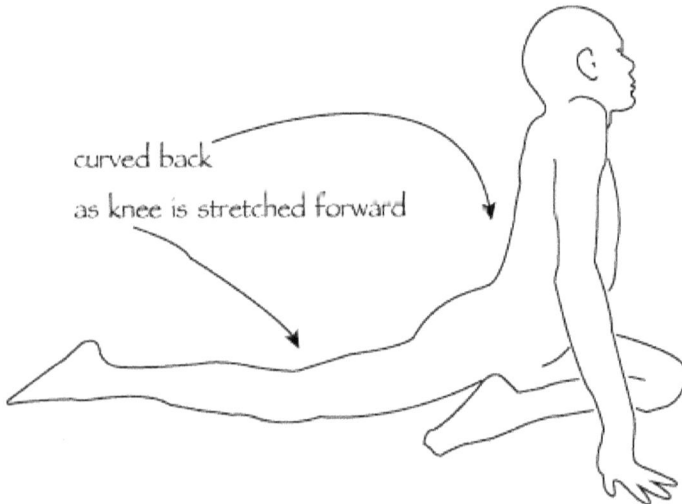

curved back
as knee is stretched forward

August 28, 2000

Shankara

He said, "The knee stretch, I showed yesterday, puts one in a youthful state, in the true sexually-neutral (brahmachari) position. This is the divine status of the organs. Reproduction development or sexual maturity is a downward trend.

Remark:

That knee stretch is shown in the posture below. One pulls the muscles and tendons from the knee upwards. One feels the stretch at the front thigh muscles. There was a girl who used to do this stretch expertly in its ideal form but she was not celibate. She did yoga since her body was in infancy. Once she questioned me in the astral world about using the stretch for celibacy.

The point is this: One may do a posture that is meant for celibate effects and not derive that benefit. It depends on the focus and intention.

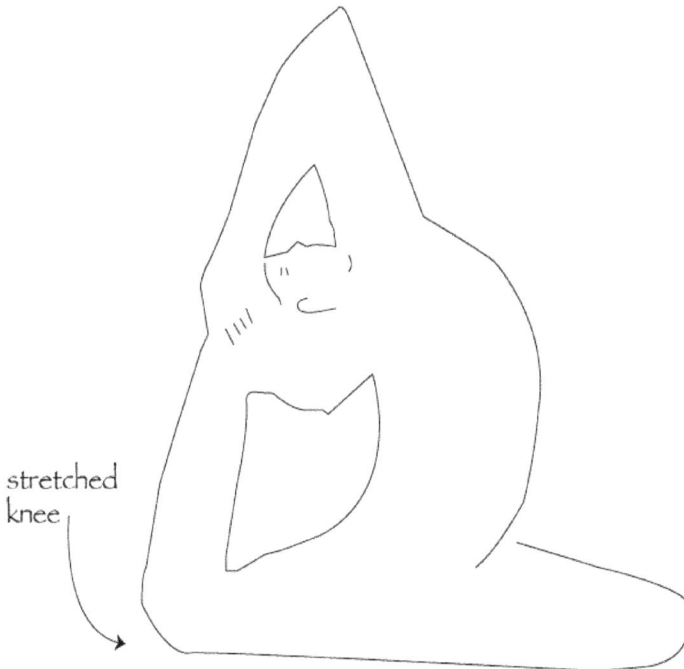

stretched knee

Part 6

Shiva

He said, "Switch Brahma to the bottom for the Skanda Creative Phase."

Remark:

This has to do with the mantra mentioned before.

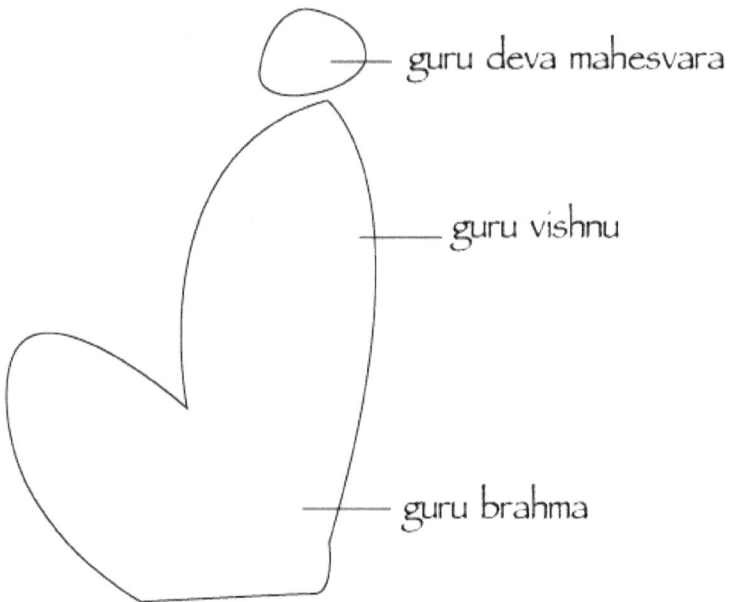

guru deva mahesvara

guru vishnu

guru brahma

Shankara

He said, "In doing that knee-thigh Skanda stretch, use the left hand as brace and right hand holding toes as the left knee is pulled up. Pay attention to what it does to your demeanor. Do other thigh stretches. Do lotus and use hands on the outside to lift the body.

Remark:

In saying prayers to the yogi gurus, one should say Shankara's name after Shivananda's. Here is a list of those names:

- *Jai Sri Ganeshaya namah*
- *Sri Sri Krishna-Balaram Namah*
- *Sri Shambuji ki namaha*
- *Sri Brahmaji ki namah*
- *Sri Narada Muni ki namah*
- *Sri Skanda Kumara brahmachari ki namah*
- *Sri Hanumanji ki namah*
- *Sri Valmiki Muni ki namah*
- *Sri Patanjali Maharshi namah*
- *Om Agastya Muni Brahmrishi Yogiraj namah Pitamaha namah*
- *Paramhansa Yogeshwarananda namah*
- *Swami Shivananda namah*
- *Sri Shankaracharya namah*

September 1, 2000

Harbhajan Singh

He showed a kundalini technique for pushing white light through the buttocks.

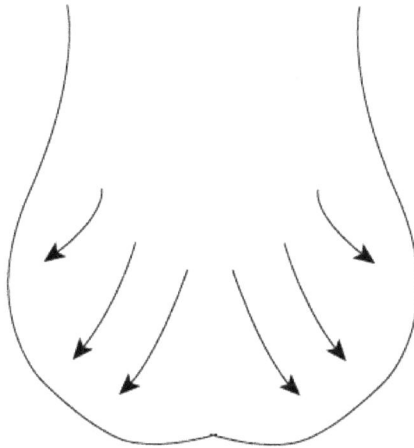

September 3, 2000

Harbhajan Singh

He showed what is called the cave-man posture. This is used for while doing breath-infusion. Air goes to the rectum in this posture.

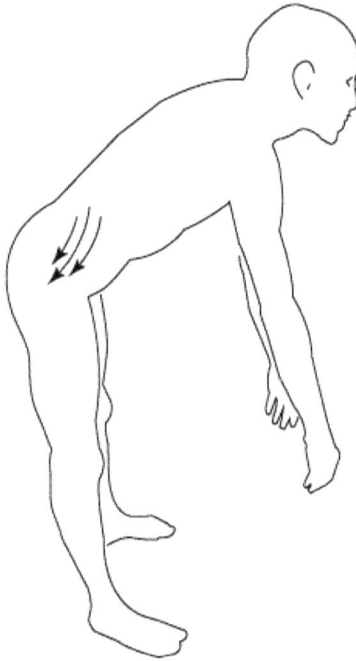

September 11, 2000

Shiva

He showed three white flames in the subtle body.

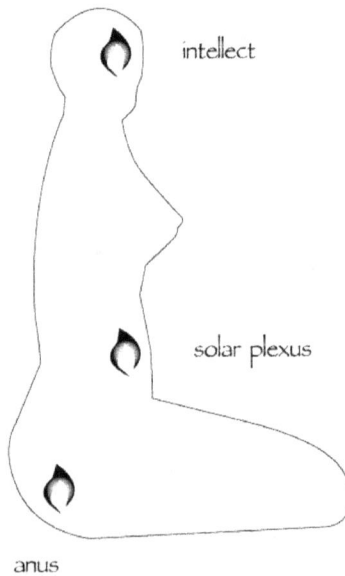

September 15, 2000

Shiva

He said, "Here is the cheesy mental energy reservoir. Conserve this. Do not let the intellect waste it by impulsive responses to haphazard thinking."

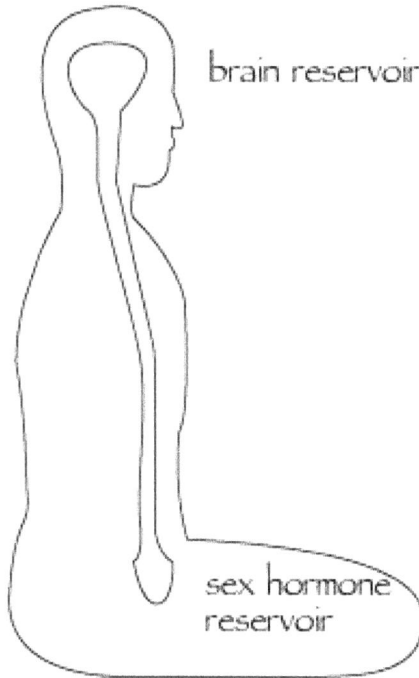

brain reservoir

sex hormone reservoir

September 18, 2000

Shiva / Babaji

They inspired a celibacy kriya. Shiva said, "If there are two holes through the knees that verifies a complete cleansing action of the sexual energy in the thigh."

Remark:

To achieve that, one should do breath-infusion, and pranavision. One should do the backward yirk-over pull with the knee and front thigh stretch. See this posture.

September 24, 2000

Shiva

He showed some coordinating points in the neck and the tubal area of the sexual organ. This particular part of the penis has to do with its thrusting power. When a male mammal, a human being or a stallion, has a sexual arousal, the arousal itself has many components. A yogi observes this and perceives the various parts.

One component of the sex urge is the power of the sexual lust which comes from the ancestors. That is actually their enthusiasm to take new bodies. This enthusiasm is experienced in a man's form as an appetite or need to see the sexually-appealing parts of a woman's body. Such parts are the thighs, buttocks, pubic area, waist, breasts, lips, eyes and hair. In the Mahabharata, it is described that Queen Draupadi, the wife of the Pandavas, that blessed and· powerful woman, had thighs like plantain / banana trees. If one removes the dry leaves from a plantain tree, one will see a very shapely form. Duryodhana, the villain of the Mahabharata, used to like to see Draupadi. Once he wanted his brother to remove her clothing. This desire was conducted by the enthusiasm of ancestors, who needed bodies and who wanted Draupadi to be their mother.

Usually children like to be with women who have a sexually-appealing form. After one loses the material body, one is transferred to the astral world as a needy ghost. In that position, one goes here and there looking for another mother. One sees various subtle bodies of women. One desires to be near the most sexually-appealing one. Once one gets a body however, one continues the search for sexually-appealing forms. This tendency leads to sexual intercourse and related fetishes. It is the quest for material bodies.

Once when I lived in the northern part of the United States, in a place called Roosevelt, Minnesota, I kept dairy goats. One nanny-goat had a very sexually-appealing form. She was buxom. She used to twist her body so that she could grab her teats and suck the milk of her udders. When it was feed time, she became vicious and would ram any other goat who came near the feed trough. This is the same ancestral force. It meant that her body was possessed by many departed spirits who wanted to take birth from her sexually-appealing form. They gave her the energy to dominate the herd. By sucking her own teats, she appeased their need for nourishment.

There is an interesting parallel in the activities of Goddess Chinnamasta, a supernatural person who is a parallel to Goddess Durga. In the Pranatoshini-tantra, she is said to have cut off her head to feed her attendants named Dakini and Varuni. After they begged for food, she decapitated her head, held it in her left palm and along with them, drank the blood that flowed in the three streams from her neck.

Apart from the power of sexual lust which comes from the ancestors there is another component in the sexual urge, which is the driving force. It is the power that is functional in a male body as the chauvinistic force. This power enters into his sexual organ when it is aroused. This power operates on its own. A boy who reaches puberty and who does not remember anything about sex from his past life, will all of a sudden without training, engage in a sexual intercourse and move his torso back and forth in reference to a female sexual organ, to expel semen.

Another component is the heat force. When the sexual organ is aroused, it generates heat. This heat causes the semen to be drawn out of the body. This heat is also in the female organ. Besides these components there are other parts of the composite sex force. In celibacy yoga, one sees these components distinctly. One develops the ability to transcend them.

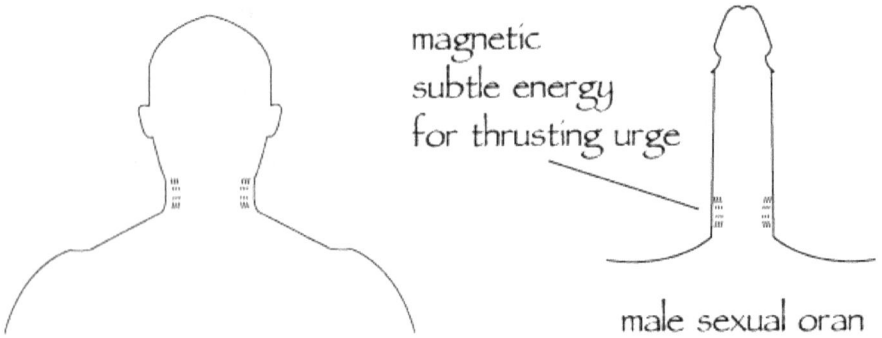

magnetic subtle energy for thrusting urge

male sexual oran

September 26, 2000

Babaji

He said, "Shankara mastered this. It was originally taught by Skanda. As assisted by contributions from the Krtikka yoginis, he took this out of the nature of Shiva."

Remark

This referred to a complete thigh clean out, after which a male yogin finds the feminine form inside the subtle thigh. He cherishes and embraces it, thus weaning his mind away from external feminine bodies.

Notation:

This happens in the advanced stage of celibacy when one does self-tantric yoga. At that stage by the grace of Ma Devi, Mother Durga, the yogi finds a feminine nature within his psyche. This is such that he no longer requires external female companionship. He finds that when he does postures and breath-infusion, this feminine form appears. It fulfills all longings. Muktananda went through a stage of practice where he was assailed by this form. At first he mistook it for a temptation but later on a great yogin alerted him that she was Kundalini Ma.

September 28, 2000

Babaji

He gave a technique for blowing through the pubic funnel in the subtle body. This can be used after one stopped taking solid food later in the day. One should eat in the early morning before sunrise or just at sunrise. One should not take solid food thereafter.

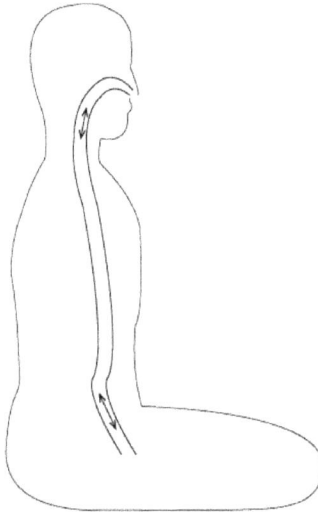

September 30, 2000

Shankara

Ha said, "Stretch the thigh thoroughly first, then transfer the released energy to the back-stretched front trunk and back-stretched chest."

Remark:

This instruction is used when doing this posture.

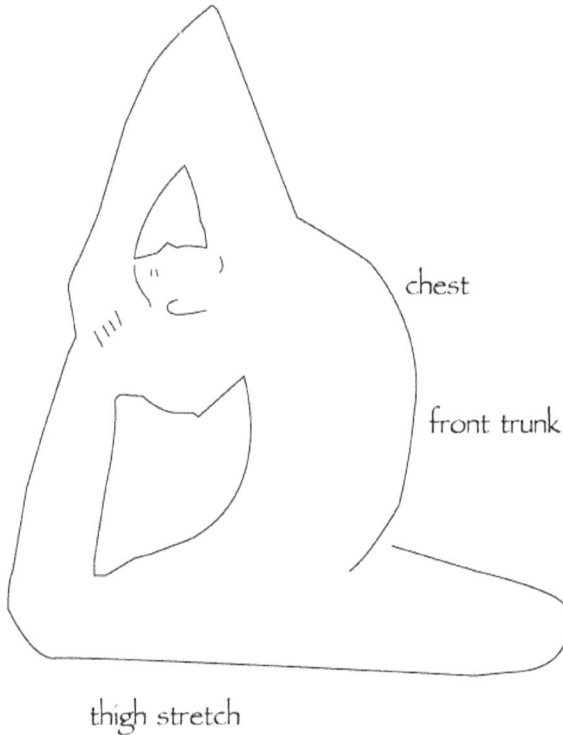

chest

front trunk

thigh stretch

September 30, 2000

Babaji

He listed these components.
- breath
- mental clarity
- Shankara's leg release
- loss-of-interest in sexual forms

- down-light technique where the intellect is focused into the subtle form
- curtailment of double checking of sensual objects by the intellect or the kundalini-goaded intellect

He stressed, "Do not try for results. Try for practice. The energy which hunts for results, should be used to motivate and increase practice."

October 7, 2000

Babaji

He said, "Do a tight lotus that is mostly one side with one knee raised off the ground and body balanced on the other thigh. Do a foot pull-up to the forehead with the astral body only, as the gross body stays in that tight lotus. Do astral yoga which is dictated by subtle energy, even if the physical body is not capable of doing every astral posture.

On this day Gambhiranath, a great Nath yogin, came. He showed some tridents he threw in the corner. These, he said, caused inner misery. He indicated that I should follow in his footsteps to throw off responsibilities.

Remark:

At a certain stage a yogin begins to realize that he is not needed socially. This place will go on just as well or even better without him. He can throw the piercing tridents of responsibility. When one throws off irresponsible living, one should take up responsible social interaction, in turn. This responsible lifestyle cuts in three ways, just as a trident cuts sharply at three points of contact.

October 9, 2000

Harbhajan Singh

He instructed, "A lack of attention brings little results. Pay attention within. Do not depend on physical revelation. Open the subtle eyes within by paying full attention. Do a tight lotus daily. Sit in it and focus. Be fearless."

October 12, 2000

Babaji

He said, "Eliminate more bad association. Take steps to see more in the afternoon."

In a vision in the astral world, a finger of mine, went to steal some food from a house. I realized it and squeezed that finger to stop it.

At the time, Ganesh came. He said,

"Stop the theft to increase conservation of energy."

Later I saw a supernatural person leaving my subtle body. It was the person who sponsored the theft energy. Ganesh then said, "These cause a pain by opening sensitivity to the nerves. It is better to buy what you want than to take from others. If you cannot purchase by a fair means overlook the desire."

When I saw the supernatural person leaving, I invited him to stay He responded, "I cannot. Once I am seen by a yogin, I can no longer stay in his body."

I told him, "No, you can stay. You are not an enemy. You are a friend. Stay, let us work together to get out of this world. Do not hang your head in shame. Many like you are in my psyche. Why not let one escape from this plane? Stay and help by reminding me to purchase what I need. By such cooperation, both of us will enhance ourselves and the creation."

Hearing this and by the power of my words, he reluctantly went back into my body.

October 22, 2000

Babaji

He showed a technique for feeding oneself from the subtle body. This happens as one develops the bubble subtle energy body. That subtle energy form has only one orifice in it. It has a sky-blue color.

October 22, 2000

Babaji

He taught me how to do lotus posture, sitting on the buttocks alone, not relying on bracing the

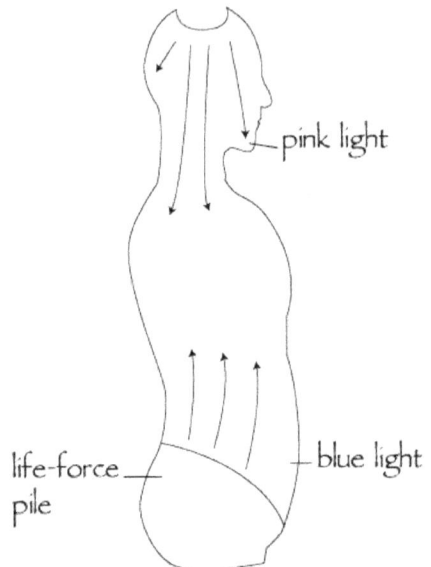
pink light

life-force pile

blue light

body on the thighs for balance. One should do the two poses shown below regularly.

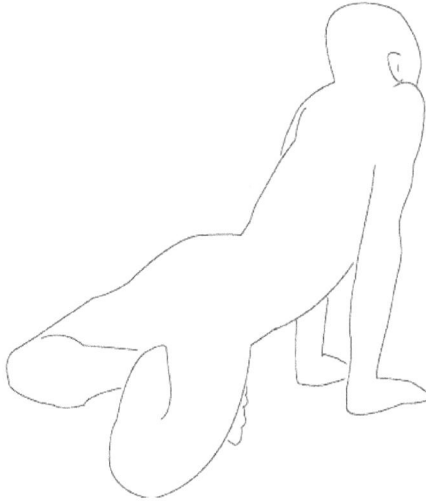

October 23, 2000

Babaji

He said, "Turn resentments into bliss."

Remarks

This is an instruction that tallies with what Krishna told Arjuna in the Bhagavad Gita about working with a free spirit without wanting results. There are many resentment energies. These always was and always will be.

Someone likes peace and hates war. Someone likes war and hates peace. Like this there are resentments. These remain bottled in the nature of the living beings, waiting to be vented in the future.

A yogin should work with a free spirit. Please study the Bhagavad Gita and pick up the freedom-to-work-for-nothing mood from Krishna.

October 24, 2000

Babaji

He advised, "A psychological changing force must be expressed. Direct it into the psyche. Leave others to earn salvation and solve complications.

Babaji assisted me in doing the posture below. He placed his hand on my back as shown.

fingers hold toes

October 26, 2000

Babaji

He said, "See the sensitiveness of the inner feelings-energy. The slightest movement, slightest thought or any mental impressions produces reactions within. The psyche should be quieted."

Remark:

For advancing into transcendental states, one has to bring on a complete quietude In the psyche.

October 28, 2000

Babaji

He said, "Thanks to your sensual energy withdrawal practice."

Remark:

Babaji referred to the advancement I made in the 5th stage of yoga. I cleaned the psyche. As soon as the intellect organ stops its external critiquing, it turns inward and gradually, the light of it on the inside of the psyche, increases. From the bottom of the trunk of the subtle body, the light from kundalini chakra increases when one stops eating so much food and increases postures and breath-infusion.

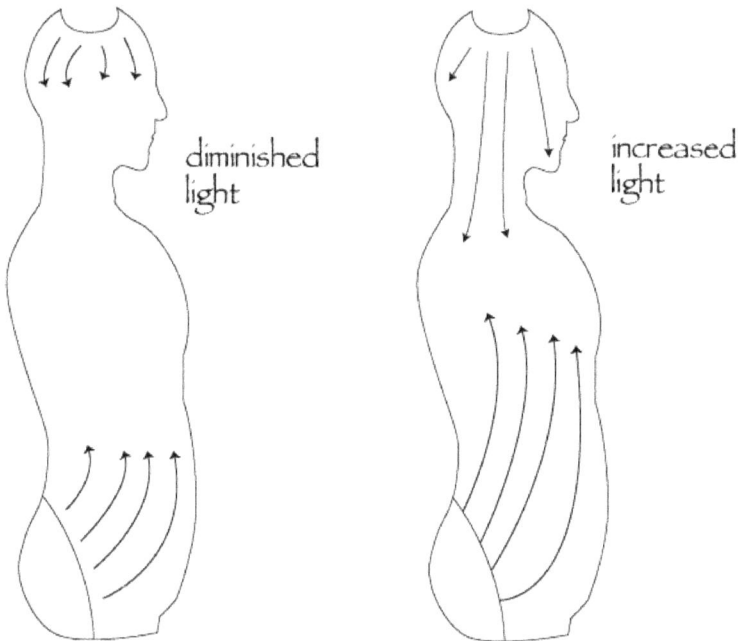

diminished light

increased light

October 22, 2000

The theft devata left my body on this date. Apparently, he got disgusted because I developed a resistance to the urge to taking things from here or there. However I took help from Jesus Christ, Ganesh and other supernatural beings. Some theft tendency remains but it is not as forceful as before. It is easy to reject.

October 23, 2000

Babaji

He showed a technique for getting spike eyes.

Remark:

These are eyes in the intellect organ which come into vision when energy shoots up from kundalini chakras at a slanted angle.

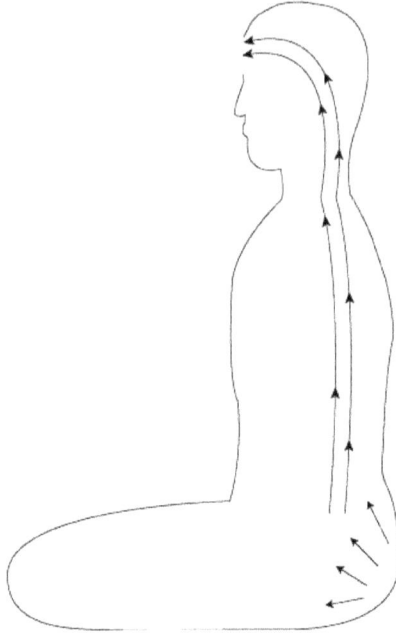

November 1, 2000

Babaji

He showed that when breath-infusion is done, the energy in the subtle body gets firm. It does not lay in a corner of the body lazily. It points upward. He showed this kriya.

November 1, 2000

On this date I had some consideration about people who do meditation in order to push on the course of their material existence. Many people who take to meditation do just that. It is what we do when we are in the womb of a mother's body. At the time, by the force of nature, one's consciousness becomes absorbed in taking nutrients to develop as an embryo.

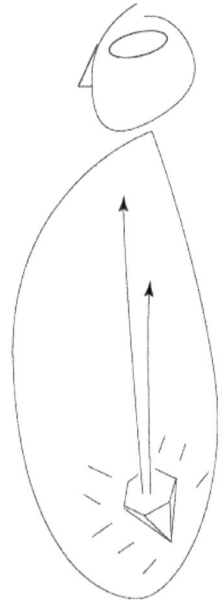

Babaji

He gave stretches for preparation of using a firm and tight lotus posture.

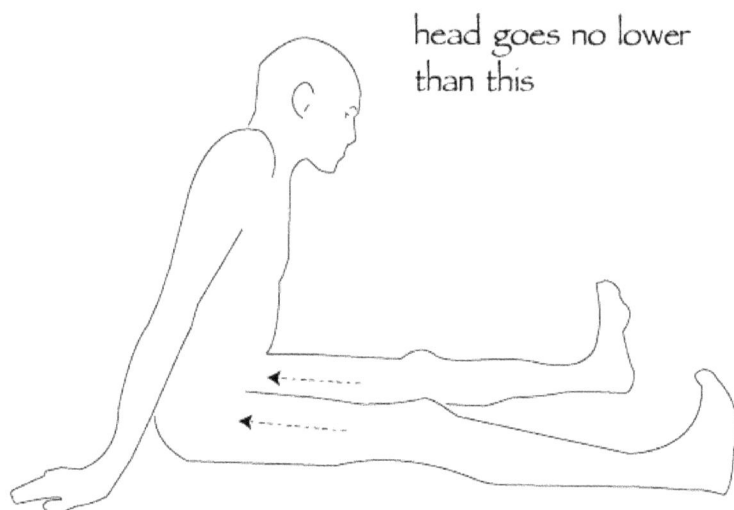

head goes no lower
than this

lean over each thigh
pull muscles and tendons
in direction of arrow

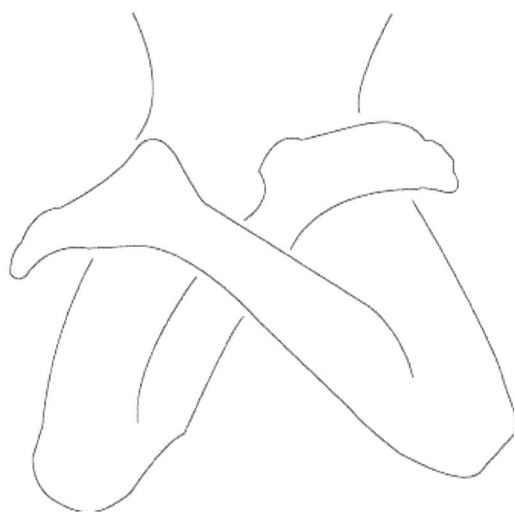

Eye exercises

These are not done for improving physical vision. The motive is to remove polluted energy which linger in the subtle tube around the subtle optic nerves. If these are done to improve physical vision, one will not derive the subtle benefit.

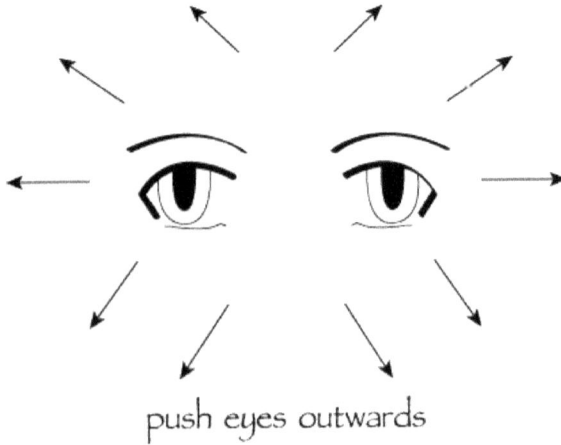

push eyes outwards

move eyes in various directions

November 3, 2000

Babaji

He said, "Do head stand. Test the weight of the body."

Remark:

This refers to the subtle form and the development of kaya siddhi. I noticed that the subtle form was weightless in the lower part of it. Much of the heavy subtle energy was gone due to improved celibacy, leg stretches, back stretches and pollution removal. It was also due to taking solid food only in the morning.

On this day Babaji made a stipulation that I should resume the afternoon session of exercises. He said it would increase siddha-sangah, the association with great yogins.

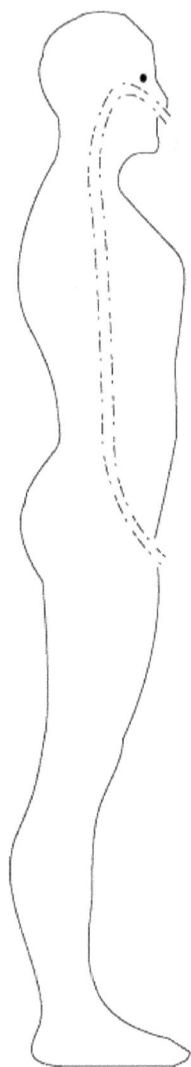

Babaji

<u>Moving the intellect near to base chakra</u>

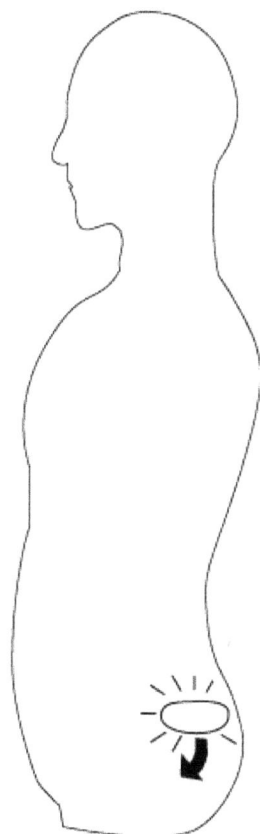

November 5, 2000

Hanuman

He expressed happiness because I progressed and had a desire for siddha-sangah. He gave this technique.

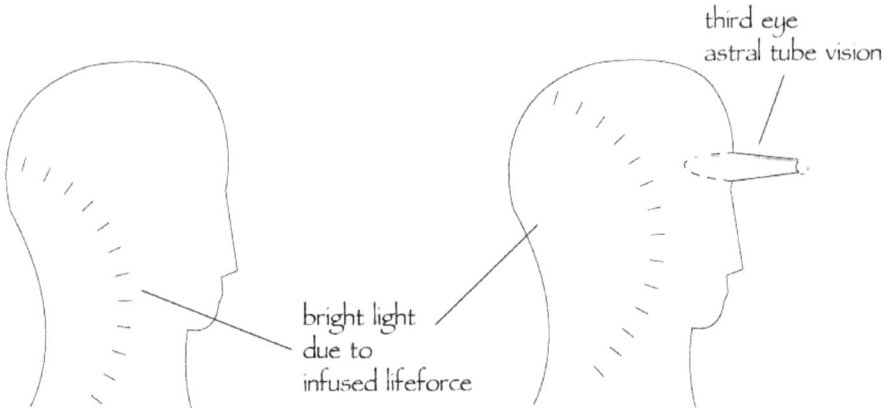

third eye
astral tube vision

bright light
due to
infused lifeforce

November 6, 2000

Babaji

He said, "Sit between legs on the floor. The fingers should be in the groin area on each side with thumbs in the back. Infuse air down the center, down the abdomen to the floor on either side. Keep the form symmetrical, even if the postures are difficult. Do long stretches with legs and thighs. Begin with foot out until the knee goes back. Pay attention within. Bring the intellect to all pain points and nerve sensitive areas."

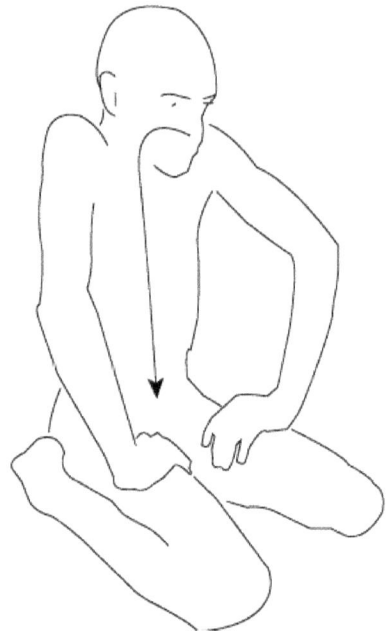

November 7, 2000

Shiva

By his grace, I had an encounter with one of the authorities in the Shankara monastic order. This was in the astral world. I was in a hallway which led to a small courtyard. Seeing a monk sitting there, I approached respectfully. He blessed two disciples who were to his right and left. I went forward, bowed and then sat on the floor. He leaned forward and said that he heard of and appreciated my family activities. He placed his hand on my head to bless me, except that I was not clean shaven as his disciples and himself. This monk was featured in an article in *Hinduism Today* magazine, which described his walks through India. He walked for thousands of miles during his life. He never used conveyances.

The monk said to me, "Change the gold and silver on your altar each day. I heard of your Archana deity worship. It is great."

After this a lady came to my right side and begged. I gave her a bright gold coin I had meant to use for my altar. She took it and left. After a short while she returned as if she was going to get something from someone else.

The lady then went to my wife, who appeared to my left. Somehow the woman could not bring herself to ask my wife for anything. It was because the gold coin I contributed covered the liabilities including the ones which involved my wife. The lady thought of asking the monks and his disciples. They began to wonder if she would approach them. They all disappeared since by rules monastic, they were not supposed to be approached by women.

After this I realized that one lady as was Jara, the person of infirmity and old age. Because they were monks who never used their material bodies for sexual indulgence, she could not approach them. They had the power to vanish. I had to deal with her because I was sexually-involved. However I gave her the gold coin willingly by a favorable instinct for doing the right thing.

If one has sexual intercourse he is automatically obliged to old age, social seniority and cultural improvements. There is no point in trying to escape when old age comes. One should pay up and be done with it.

Later on that day Shiva said this, "Their appearance with Rudra tilak marks is not important. Are they siddhas or not. Can you trust these religious leaders?"

Remark:

Shiva brought it to my attention that even though the monk appreciated me, because someone told him about my family activities, it does not mean that he is a siddha, a perfected yogin. He may not be. This is because leaders of the monastic orders in India, got bogged down by fame. Swami Rama, for instance, left that aside when he realized that the fame he acquired absorbed his attention so much as to greatly curtail his yoga practice.

However we should note that the monks, just by their non-involvement with women, had the power to disappear from Jara, the supernatural person who enforces old age for those who are sexually-involved.

November 10, 2000

Shiva

He said, "From time to time, restrain the form from eating, and drinking when you sense that there is no need and that it is just habit. Let the form live on nutrients that are stored in the blood stream and in cell pockets. Try to take a rich food every three days."

November 11, 2000

Babaji

He taught an obeisance posture.

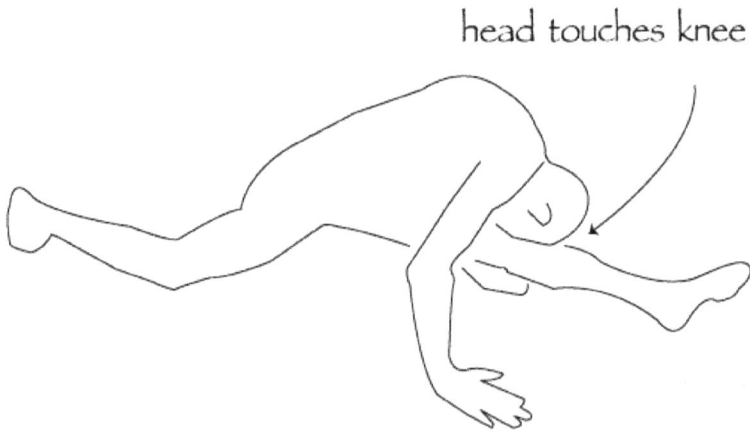

head touches knee

Shiva

He said, "Some deities are externally focused. You will not get their attention within. Do not bother them. Stay within. Be confident of the internal practice. You will locate other deities within."

November 14, 2000

Babaji

He said, "See Yogesh. He developed that fully while using a material form."

Remark:

This pertains to becoming aware of the causal body.
Here are diagrams.

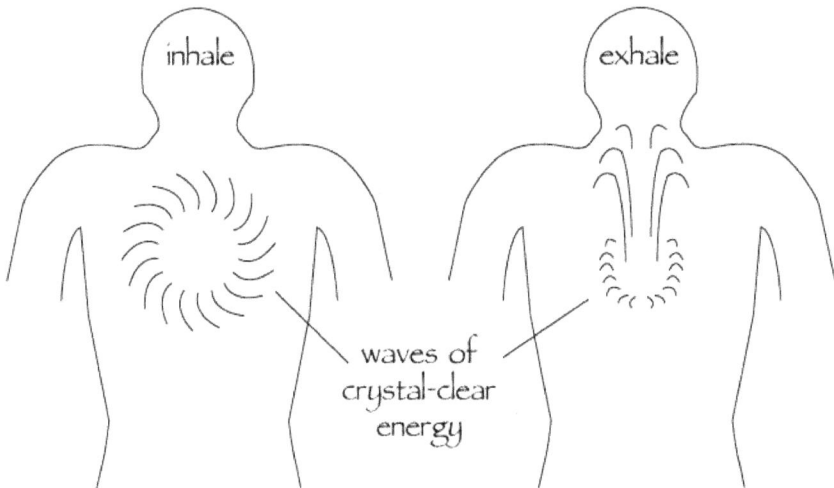

November 15, 2000

Babaji / Yogeshwarananda / Skanda

Under their combined influence I worked on pushing subtle energy to the base chakra. When doing this, one should do many sessions of pranayama breath-infusion. One pumps the air down into the abdomen. As one does breath-infusion more and more, one develops a sense for this. After the navel is cleared of pollution, one can work on the sexual area and then the anal region. It hinges on practice.

do breath-infusion
in this posture

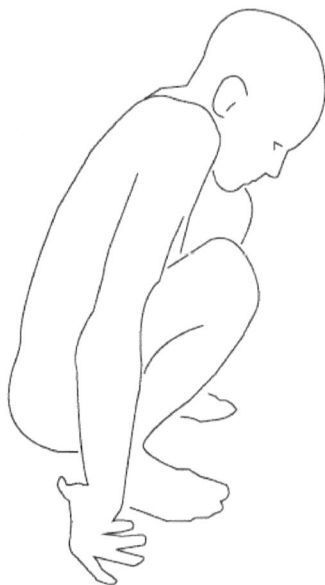

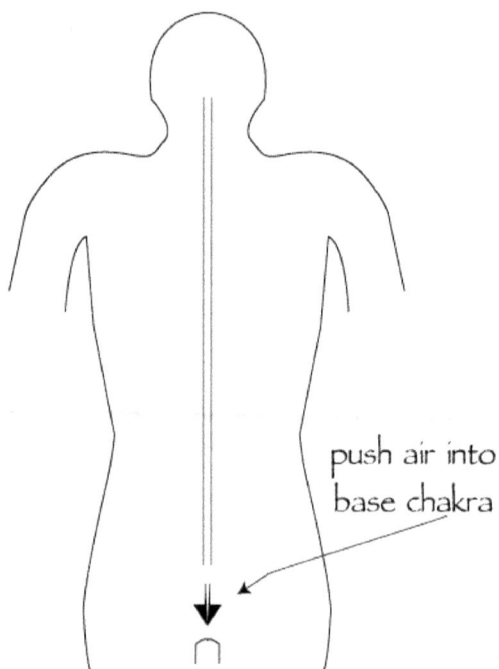

push air into
base chakra

Babaji

He said, "If it is not renounced, the visual sense ruins yoga. Take the whole sense apparatus. Use it as a whole without a specific need or focus on any of the individual senses."

Yogeshwarananda

He said, "After the navel is cleaned, push hard on the exhale to keep it cleared daily. Then go to the base. Push air through the base for some time. This eliminates kundalini eventually. In time, the causal light will be experienced. Work to brighten the causal light. While focusing on it, give it energy by doing breath-infusion. It becomes brilliant white with a blue haze."

fingers under body

November 17, 2000

Yogeshwarananda

He said, "Begin soon to eat solid food every two days. This will enable you to grab the lifeforce later at the time of death of the body. It is a course taken by great yogins.

Remark:

I am amazed that I was given this instruction and the one prior by Shiva who wanted me to eat solid food only every three days. By April 5th 2002, I did not complied with these instructions. Now I am seriously thinking that I must do this to practice the advanced transcendence.

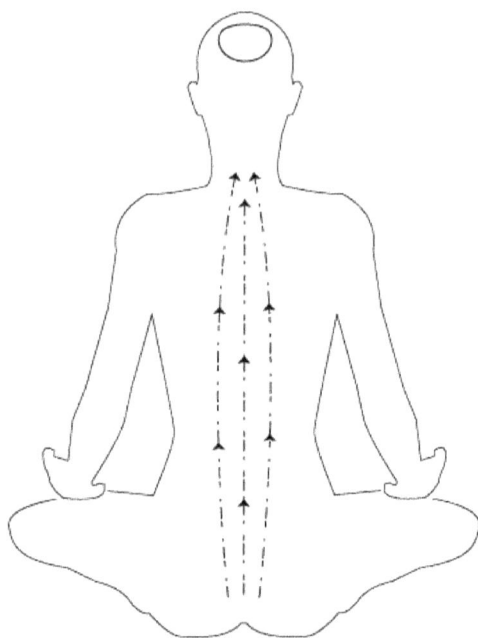

lifeforce focused on intellect

November 18, 2000

Yogi Bhajan

He gave an exhale stomach-lock kriya.

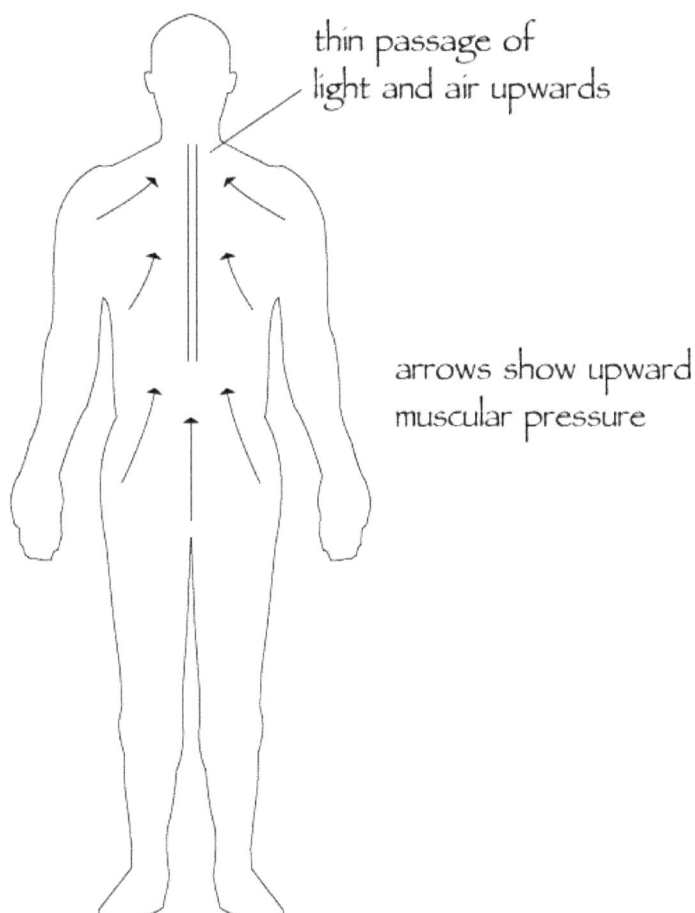

thin passage of
light and air upwards

arrows show upward
muscular pressure

He gave this spinal twist:

turn right then left

November 19, 2000

Yogi Bhajan

He said, "Work done properly, willingly and selflessly, freely, with full input, frees the yogi from former implications. It clears parts of the subtle body. Once you get such opportunities, never reject them for even Krishna, the Supreme Being, works like this. It helps yoga practice and removes impending energies which even yoga will not eradicate. Samskaras or subtle impressions and latent traces, which are formed in a particular way, are removed in particular way, layer after layer. During asanas with the gross body, pay attention to the subtle form's assumption of other postures."

physical body sitting
while subtle form
stands on one foot

November 24, 2000

Babaji

He said, "In a material body, meditation without doing postures and breath-infusion is not dynamic. The progress made in such meditation, when done with intake of drugs or with listening to music, in natural surroundings or in a building, is based on yoga practice in former lives.

"Those who endeavor in postures and breath-infusion and who concluded that with meditation, get a different experience. With breath-infusion, sensual withdrawal and transcendence focus, there comes some sharp perception of the subtle passages, and an abstract perception of the causal body."

November 26, 2000

Babaji

He said, "Postures and breath-infusion carry the focus to the subtle body, thus shifting the appreciation of consciousness to the subtle plane. Breath-infusion and sensual withdrawal where combined, make the shift to the subtle plane, a complete one, opening the doors of subtle perception, producing pranic vision, which reveals where there was no perception before.

"With breath-infusion, sensual withdrawal and transcendence focus, there comes sharp perception of the subtle passages and some abstract perception of the causal body used by the core-self. To get into the causal form, one should master spontaneous transcendence and then prolonged transcendence. It is a set system because the various bodies are interlocked. Any mechanism will require a certain amount of time, knowledge and effort to dismantle, repair, put together or create. It is not who you are but rather what time you invest, what effort you make, what knowledge you have, either by direct insight, discovery or instruction.

November 29, 2000

Babaji

He said, "Do postures, breath-infusion and sensual withdrawal more thoroughly. Review the foundation. Be able to draw all subtle apparatus through the neck into the head. Close the protrusion of the intellect organ. Before assuming lotus posture, do some lotus-preparation stretches."

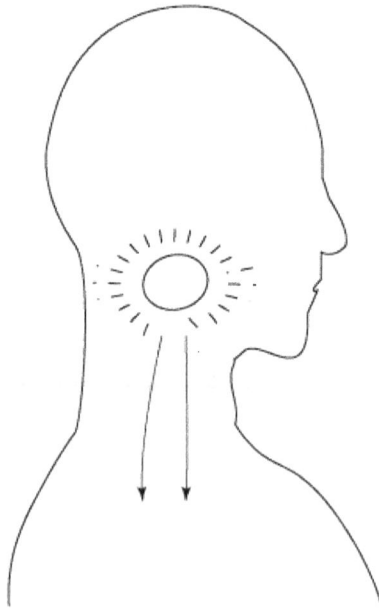

move intellect through neck

November 31, 2000

Babaji

He said, "When the nature of it changed, whereby it is no longer interested and does not display the least concern, but introverts into itself, then it is sensual energy withdrawal. It is like a horse in a circular fenced area. If the horse, even with gates open, show no interest in what is beyond the perimeter, the animal is self-controlled."

A pull into the neck technique

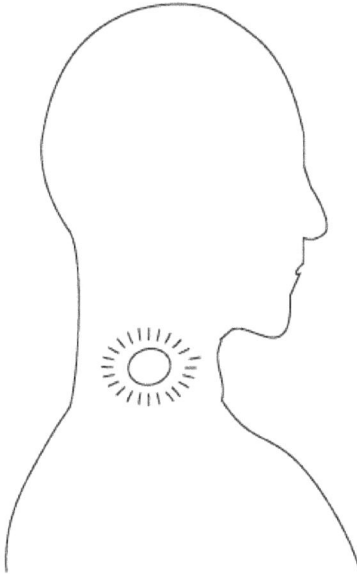

Part 7

December I, 2000

Babaji

He said, "Pull the intellect mechanism as you pull in subtle energy when doing breath-infusion. Regard the intellect as a whole organ and not as its evolved parts. This comes by a sincere need not to exploit its functions."

December 3, 2000

Babaji

He said, "The senses will appreciate and take interest in their energy source.

"By pulling the intellect into the breath intake, it will meet the solar area where the in-breath meets a crossroad from which the senses continually take energy."

December 4, 2000

Babaji

He said, "The senses are satisfied at the in-breath in-take turning point at the navel. This is preparation for transcendence absorption and mastership of internalization. Forget people or selves. Work with the subtle energy transfers."

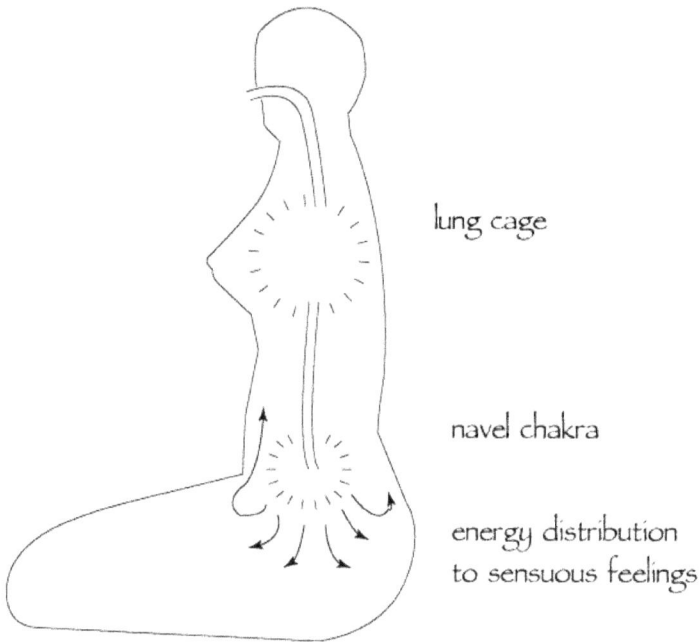

lung cage

navel chakra

energy distribution
to sensuous feelings

December 5, 2000

Babaji

He showed that if the core-self is located slightly below the intellect, that intellect would be experienced as one mechanism in a cloud form.

cloud cover surrounding intellect

intellect

core-self

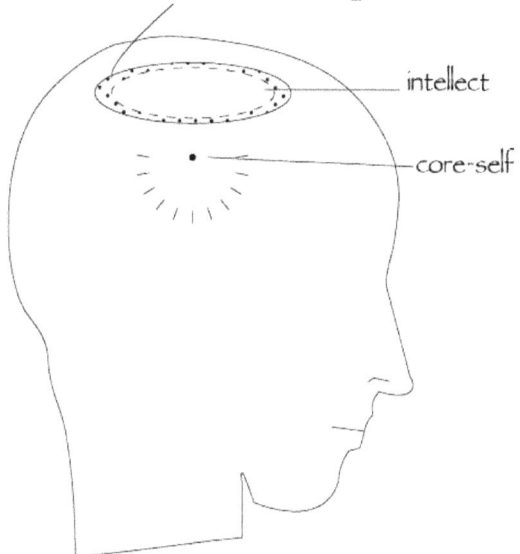

December 5, 2000

Babaji

He gave an exercise which causes earlier evacuation of stools. This is the peddle-pushing exercise, done while on the back of the body. While doing this, the bowels become active. The cells in the anus area, are exercised. This stimulates the colon.

One lays on the back and does breath-infusion with stress on one side, then on the other, as one peddle-pushes the legs and thighs.

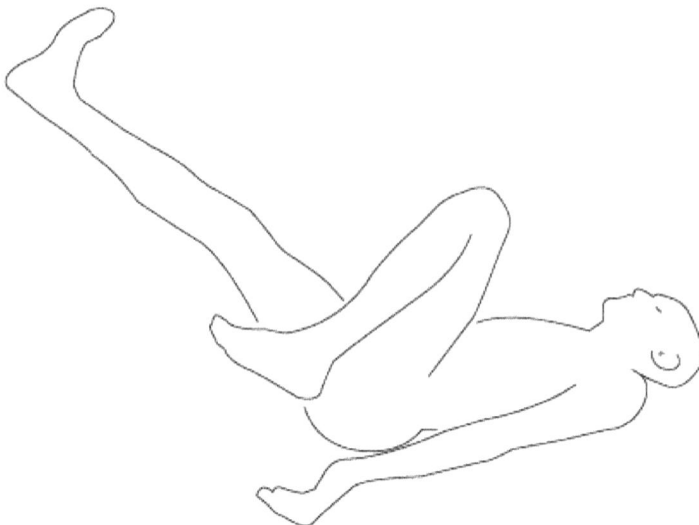

December 7, 2000

Babaji

He instructed that to further advance interest-internalization, I should stop keeping track of modern sexual trends. In other words, I was to lose interest in such aspects. There is a certain stage at which one has to be aware of those aspects of social history, so that one may recognize the source of their influence and protect oneself from it. However, as one advances, one gets out of range of being affected. One should then not track it.

Yogesh called this the stage of paravairagya which for better or worse is a complete disinterest in social interactions.

December 8, 2000

Babaji

He said, "Collapsing, folding in, shrinking of the intellect. Notice how the core-self can work without it or use its functions in a more detached, more spiritually-sane way."

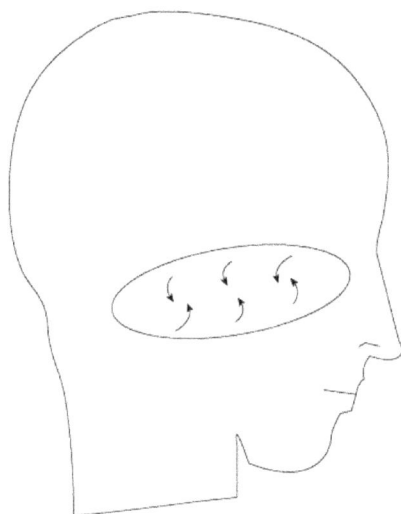

December 9, 2000

Babaji

He observed how my thigh and knees were cleansed of pollution. This is the subtle thighs and knees. These were so cleansed that one could see through them as if they were made of clear light. He told me to use a tight lotus posture with the left knee off the ground and the right foot and leg drawn up completely so that the body was balanced on the right side. I was to move the intellect down into the thigh.

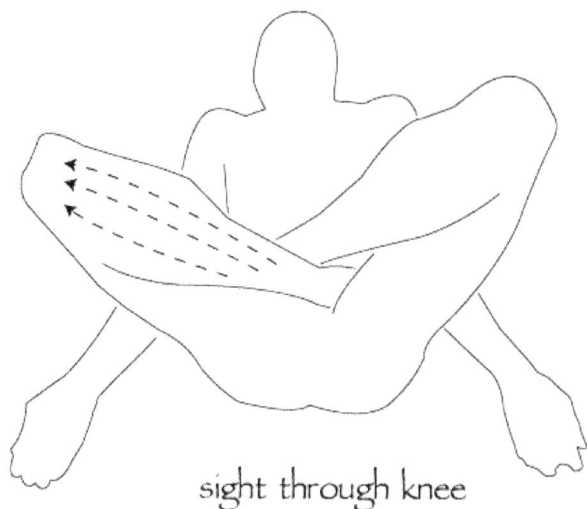

sight through knee

December 11, 2000

Babaji / Yogeshwarananda

They inspired this psychic action.

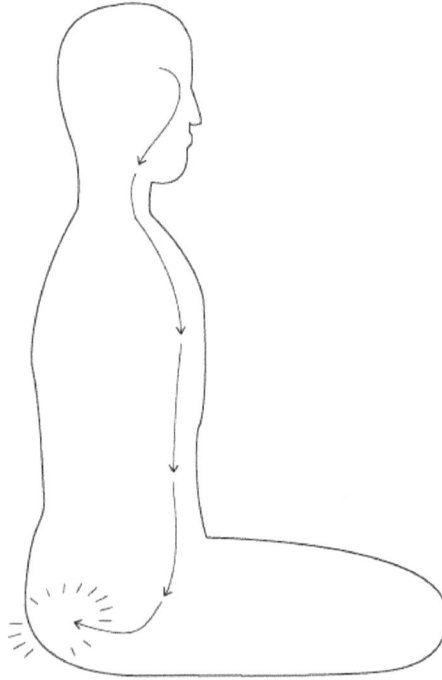

intellect travels through front of body
to base chakra

December 12, 2000

Babaji

He instructed that I clean the under-feed tube of the subtle navel. This is done by doing thigh-foot raising exercises with breath-infusion. After breathing for some time, one should hold the breath and push out where the pain in located in the abdomen area.

First one raises the head and thighs. Then one does the same thing raising only the thighs. Babaji showed a technique on this day. In that practice, a rose-shaped chakra occurs at the navel. It has 16 petals of two layers and then a set of folded petals like a partially-opened rose.

16 petal rose-chakra

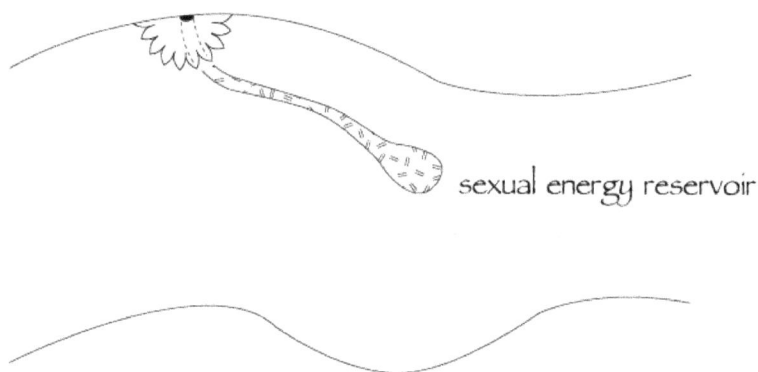

sexual energy reservoir

December 12, 2000

Babaji

By his subtle influence I was prohibited from certain actions which were impelled by the intellect and which were from certain associations which came from thought reception.

Remark:

As one advances, one must be prepared to accept more and more subtle influence from the great yogins. These are influences which nurture the student yogi. They give him the power to escape worldly associations.

December 15, 2000

Babaji

He said that a white light was required at the under-navel feed tube. This is a tube that feeds subtle fluid light from the kanda bulb to the navel.

One has to do the foot-thigh raising exercises. Then one feels a burn there. One develops the light after the burn is eliminated.

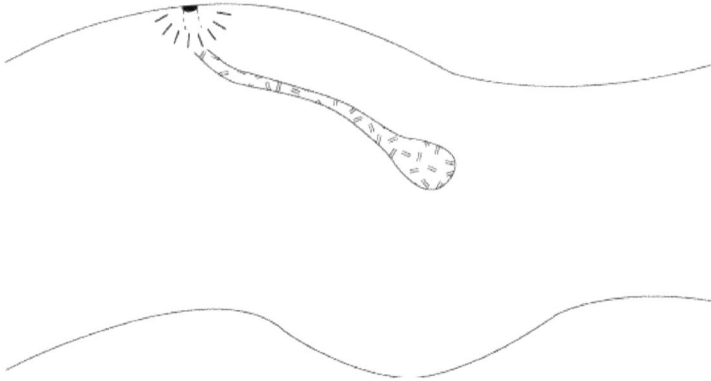

December 16, 2000

Babaji / Yogeshwarananda

Yogeshwarananda showed a tube from the bottom pubic area in the navel. He said, "A drop a second or a drop a day, accordingly, but none for a while, according to sexual expression. He also said that it needs to be sustained for proper operation.

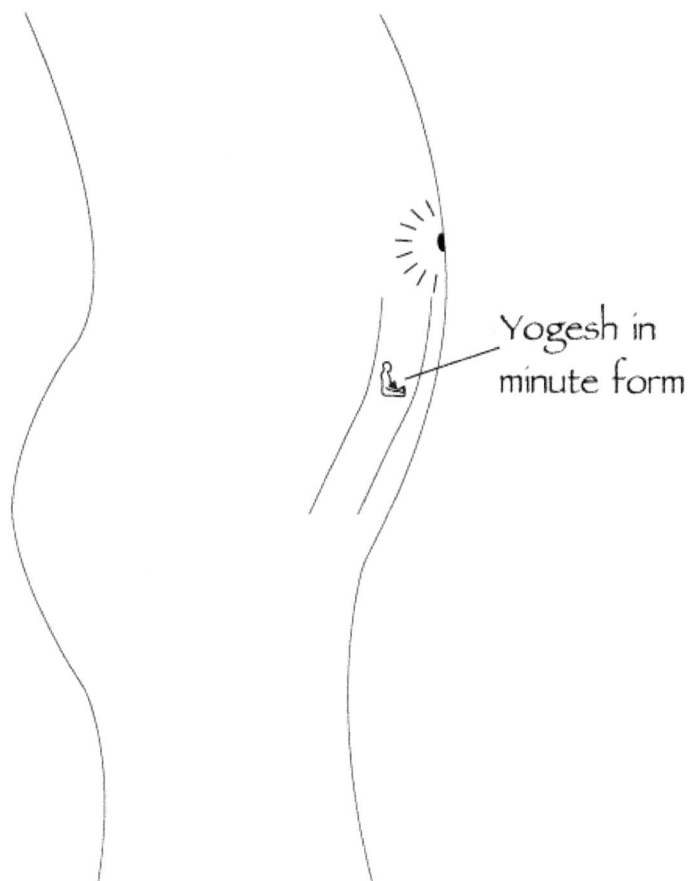

Yogesh in
minute form

Babaji

He said, "Observe this loop.

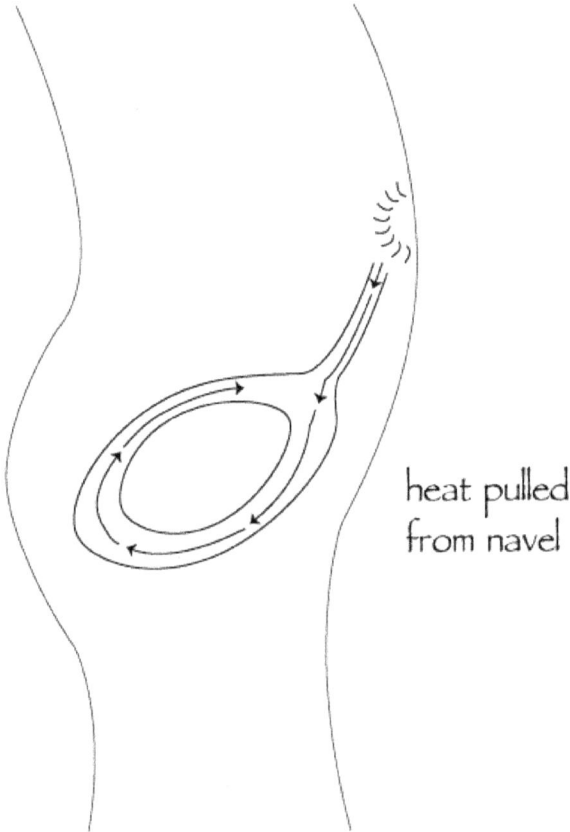

heat pulled
from navel

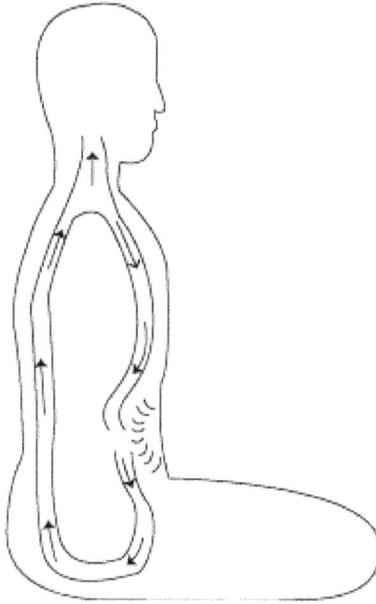

December 23, 2000

Babaji

He said, "Draw up semen from the navel under-tube. Maintain feet-thigh related exercises. After those do this with breath-infusion."

December 25, 2000

Babaji

In this communication, his voice was heard from within my psyche. He said, "Unless a path is shown before death, all should assume rebirth. Remember the uncertainty of Arjuna. Those who maintain attachment to society and family, easily take shelter in those emotions after death. Unless they are shown a path to higher locales before death, the yogis who have no social attachment will be left without birth access. What will

they do if they have no rebirth access and no path to higher realms? Those great ones like Narada and Prithu were shown higher planes beforehand."

Remark:

The verse from the Bhagavad Gita is this:

अर्जुन उवाच
अयतिः श्रद्धयोपेतो
योगाच्चलितमानसः ।
अप्राप्य योगसंसिद्धिं
कां गतिं कृष्ण गच्छति ॥ ६.३७॥

arjuna uvāca
ayatiḥ śraddhayopeto
yogāccalitamānasaḥ
aprāpya yogasaṁsiddhiṁ
kāṁ gatiṁ kṛṣṇa gacchati (6.37)

arjuna — Arjuna; uvāca — said; ayatiḥ — indisciplined person; śraddhayopeto = śraddhayopetaḥ = śraddhayā — by faith + upetaḥ — has got; yogāccalitamānasaḥ = yogāc (yogāt) — from yoga practice + calita — deviated + mānasaḥ — mind; aprāpya — not attain; yogasaṁsiddhiṁ — yoga proficiency; kāṁ — what; gatiṁ — course; kṛṣṇa — Krishna; gacchati — he goes

Arjuna said: What about the undisciplined person who has faith? Having deviated from yoga practice, having not attained yoga proficiency, what course does he take, O Krishna? (Bhagavad Gita 6.37)

December 27, 2000

Babaji

He instructed:

- Not looking for anything specific.
- Not trying to exploit.
- Preparing for samadhi.
- Relaxing the intellect.
- Training not to hunt the sense objects.

He inspired this.

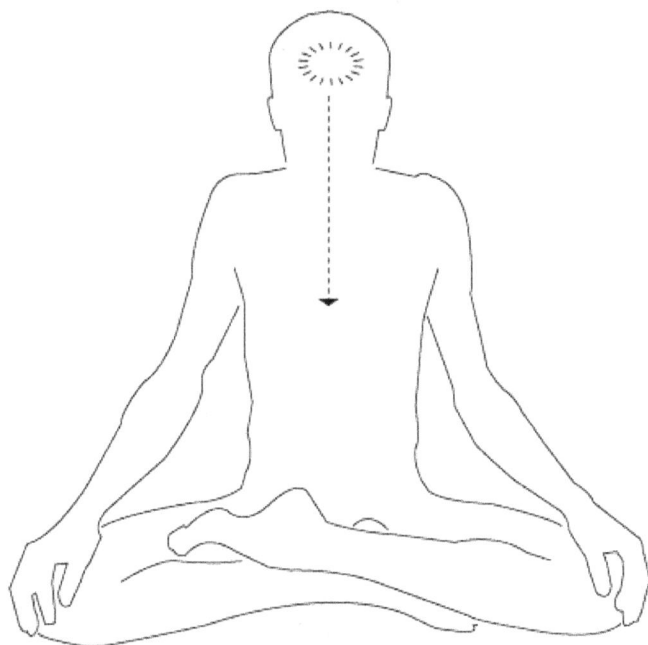

moving intellect down

December 28, 2000

Babaji

He said, "The under-abdomen tube is activated by the intellect retraction-of-interest action. The under-abdomen tube feeds the system. Do this to develop it."

He gave this technique

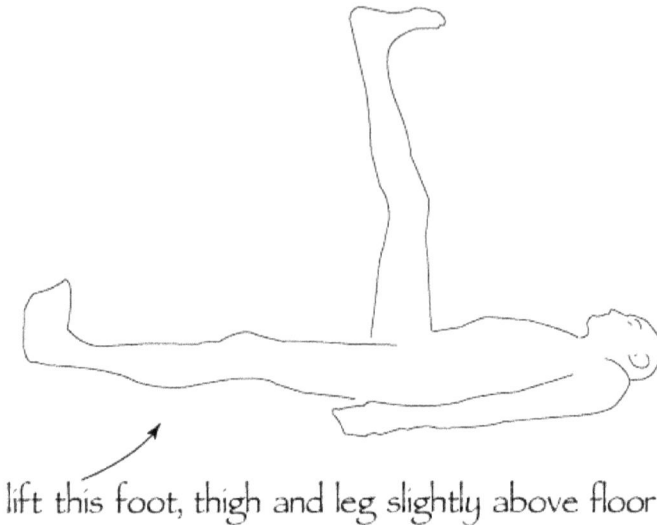

lift this foot, thigh and leg slightly above floor

Babaji said, "Always do asana postures and pranayama breath-infusion before meditating. Do not meditate on the basis of moods.

December 30, 2000

Babaji

He said, "Every incremental result is beneficial. Do not add up the increments to get a big result. Each small result during practice, is itself a result.

"Retrain the intellect and subtle energy sections to rid them of the tendency for hoping for sensational results."

January 1, 2001

Babaji

He gave a navel-to-sex function procedure. In this mystic action, one sees a tube which stretches from the navel to the sexual area. At the navel, the tube is ended into a shape like a flattened rose flower. Then the tube goes down to the pubic area where it disappears in a white light. This white light occurs when one developed a physical yoga-siddha body and is on the way to developing a subtle one.

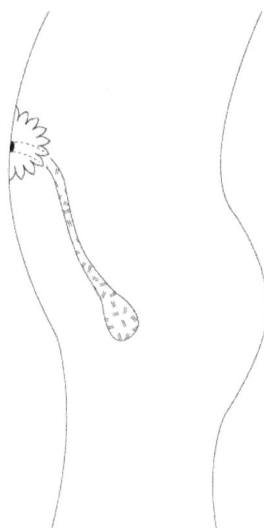

Babaji

A front-kundalini procedure

In this, which is done after an intense session of breath-infusion with asana postures, one experiences the front kundalini circuit. One's subtle hands are then put down into the stream of light which is seen and felt in the front of the body. It is crystal clear light which reaches the chin only.

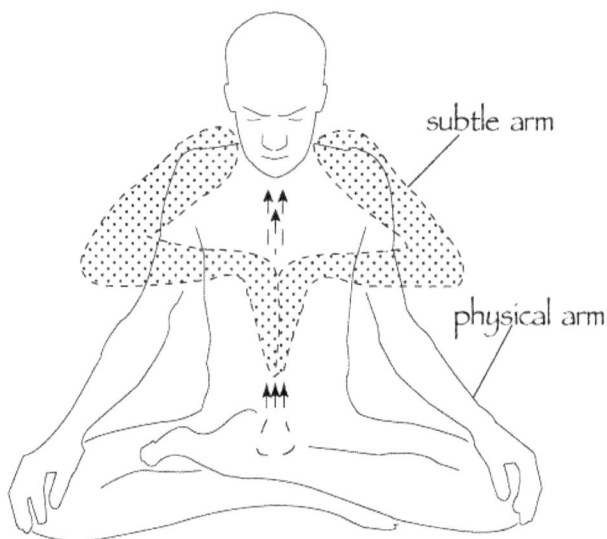

subtle arm

physical arm

January 4, 2001

Babaji

He instructed. "Do this one side crisscross. Then the other side. Then both. The astral form can do the stretches while the physical form is stationary."

Remark:

This pertains to exercises done by the astral form, while the physical body stays in another stationary posture. As one practices the asana postures and does breath-infusion, he will find, naturally, that sometimes he feels as if his astral body is moving in a way that is contrary to physical posture. He may try as a relief, to adjust the astral form so that it confirms to the physical. This also happens in dreams and in daydreaming. Sometimes, while dreaming the astral body takes an action but the physical form does not respond. One may for relief force the astral body to confirm to the physical one, or force the physical to confirm to the astral.

In the advanced stages a yogi knows exactly what his subtle body did which is contrary to the physical form. This ability comes from being conscious in dreams and knowing for sure what the subtle body is capable of. Thus when his subtle body moves, he is not confused as to whether it is a subtle movement or an imagination.

Babaji gave some actions to be completed by the subtle form only. Sometimes while doing postures and rapid breathing, one finds that the subtle body is impelled by the surcharged subtle energy to act in certain ways. As such one allows the subtle form to act in these developmental patterns. Below there is a diagram showing what my subtle body did while my physical form remained in another posture.

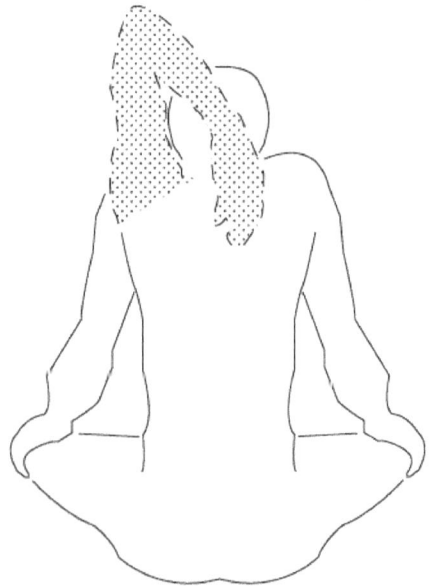

subtle left hand holds subtle spine

Babaji

Somehow I had an urge to eat ice-cream. Usually such urges come by subtle influences of either departed ancestors or embodied friends who desire that I eat with them and who are addicted to such foods. However it so happened that Babaji was with me when I felt that eating urge. He sensed it. He immediately said, "Expedite it on the subtle plane until you get out of its psychic range. Eat the urge for it on the subtle level. Swallow that urge."

Remark:

This is a mystic instruction, not a physical action.

Indradeva

He said, "Honest retraction of sensual interest yields results. See this. He showed some energies in the subtle body."

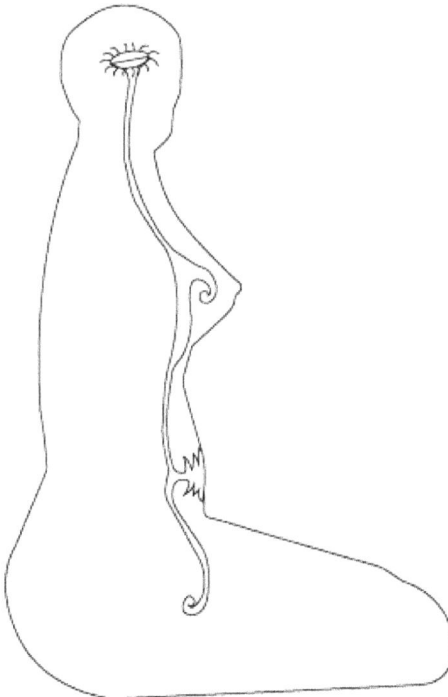

January 7, 2001

Babaji

He inspired my subtle body to display the front and back kundalini tubes at the same time. Generally one experiences either the front or the back kundalini. Neophyte yogis experience the enlivened back kundalini now and again. They can hardly stimulate the front. This is because one has to curb eating before one can do so. At first one cannot curb eating because one must first curb sexual desire before he or she can reform eating. Many persons on the spiritual path have this idea that they can curb eating without prior stress on curbing sex desire. They are inexperienced. One must first curb sex desire. Then one can work to purify the navel area. In addition a person who has not fulfilled his needs for having sex and begetting children, cannot curb the navel. He cannot do so since dormant desire in the form of hidden subtle energies, will remain as obstructions, even if he lives alone and even if he takes status as a celibate monk.

When one experiences the combined kundalini it usually happens after doing an intense session of bhastrika, then standing up, doing the down-draw pull-up breath, then doing the peacock pose and then the down-draw again, at least for twice or more times.

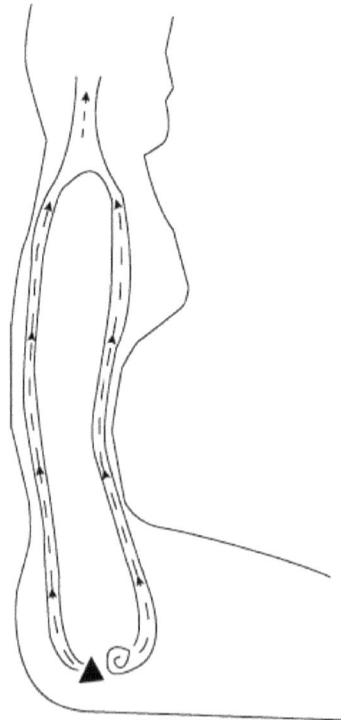

Jan 10, 2001

Shiva

He said, "Find out from him about retracting the thinking process."

Remark:

This was an instruction for me to consult Babaji about an effective way of squelching the thinking process and retracting the organ of thinking, the intellect. Unless this thinking is curbed one cannot experience the transcendence which is a necessary prerequisite for supernatural vision. Retraction of interest (pratyahar) is the process of toning down and ultimately stopping the outward-going tendency of the intellect, so that it simmers down, allowing the core-self to control it for supernatural perception.

January 11, 2001

Babaji

He said, "It is time for increasing the time spent for transcendence absorption."

Remark:

At this stage I should accelerate the yoga practice to include a session for stillness to enter transcendence at least twice per day. These would be short experiences but they would be the footing or foundation for longer periods later in the life of this body and continuing hereafter when this body passes.

January 14, 2001

Shiva

He asked, "What is lost?"

I replied, "The discrimination. That means that the core-self does not have it. The core is mostly naive by nature, conscious without rational objectivity. It is a function of reality only."

Remark:

This question of Shiva was asked to get me to think of why one loses discrimination from time to time. For instance, when one takes an infant form, discrimination is lost for a while. Then after some years it comes on with full force. When it is manifested, it may be misdirected if one is born in either a liberal or conservative cultural environment. In another instance, in an adult body with a developed discrimination, one may leave that discerning tool behind, when entering cross-worlds in other dimensions in dreams. In a cross-world, one may act in a way that is contrary to the ideals which are maintained when one uses discrimination. This indicates that as a core-self, one is basically naive. It is not that all person-cores travel without discrimination. Some spirits exhibit discrimination in just about every circumstance, while for others the discrimination is an adjunct, an addition, which they cannot carry with them everywhere, through every dimension they may enter.

For this the Upanishadic sages must be credited. They were the first ones to describe the core-self as being bare in their writings. They acknowledged the discrimination and psychological functions as adjuncts.

January 15, 2001

Shiva

He said, "Study the apparition-deities. Move away from physical representations of deities. Use the physical forms for the sake of stopping atheism and self-worship in persons who are plagued with that."

Remark:

Shiva instructed that I give more attention to deities who appear by apparitions, who appear in supernatural materials, rather than those who appear as carved or pictured forms physically. It may be said that now I prepare to transit from this body. A higher interpretation is that I advanced to the stage where I perceive the deities supernaturally. For me, the physical idols and paintings of deities do not have such a great significance. But for some others they are paramount.

January 17, 2001

Babaji

He gave a technique for moving sexual vapors up from the navel to the nose, and out of the body. This is a celibate action. In the lower stages of celibacy one is preoccupied with clearing the genital region. When one advances further, one becomes preoccupied with cleaning the navel region. With more progression, one moves the energy which rises to the navel up through the nostrils. This is the completion of celibacy practice.

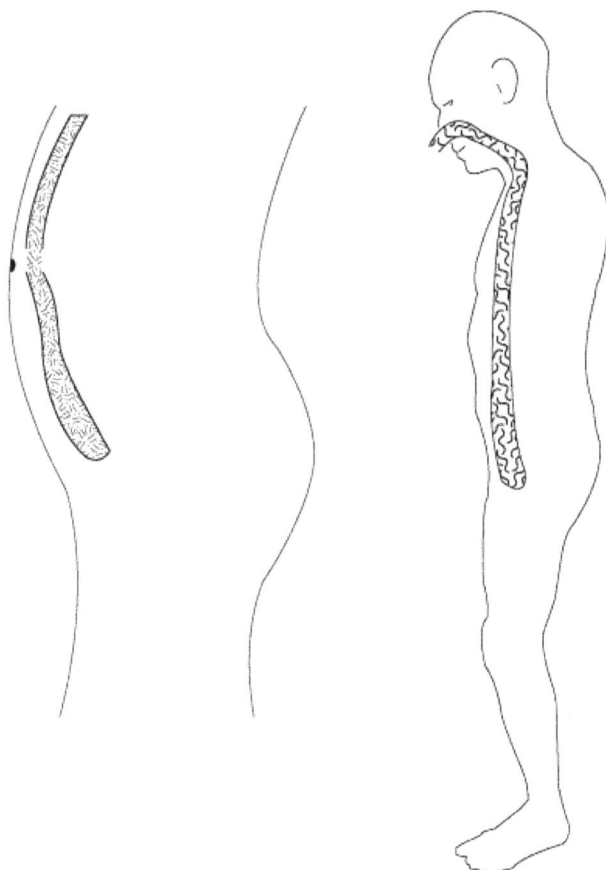

On the same day, Shiva explained to me that I should regard thoughts as subtle energy and not consider the persons who send the ideas. His view is that one should disregard the senders. One should hold no resentment against the senders but should deal with the pranic energy in a detached way.

January 19, 2001

Babaji / Shiva

Under their influence I saw a pair of capsule-like zones, being the two parts of the subtle body.

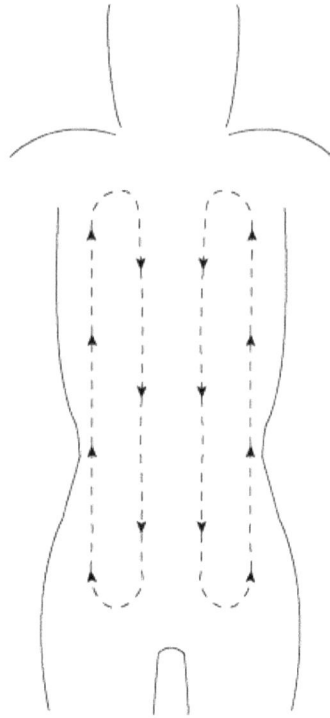

January 20, 2001

Babaji

He said, "Do the bottom-abdomen burn. This goes from the pubic area to the navel. Press out the burn to the navel, just as you did from the navel to the top channels. Use the raise-foot-thigh exercises to bring on the burn.

The bottom-abdomen burn is felt when one does breath-infusion and has impurities in the abdomen area. These are lodged between the abdomen and the pubic zones. Most humans have the impurities. At first when doing breath-infusion one will feel this burn which seems to be under the abdomen going downward to the sexual area and then going lower to the anal area, and then coming up the spine. Initially one pushes this down and it comes up the back of the spine. Some of it emits subtly through a small hole in the base of the spine in the subtle body.

Babaji supervised my practice of a higher pressure passage for the abdomen burn, where it passes up the front of the body and not through the spine. This burn may be done from a squatting, standing or lotus position. It is efficiently done also from the position shown below.

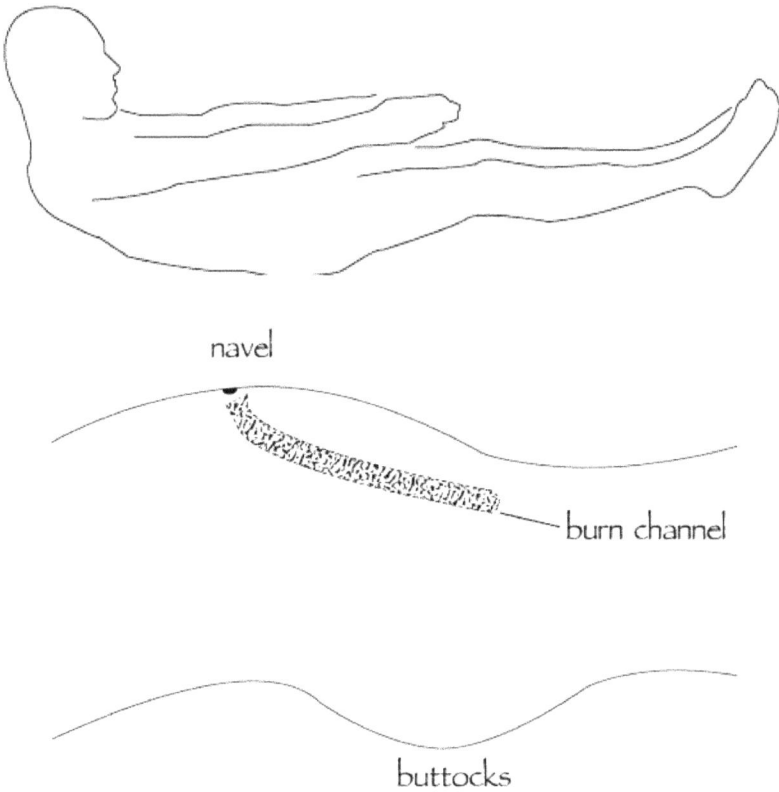

navel

burn channel

buttocks

January 25, 2001

Shiva

He showed a touch point for the under-abdomen. Such a point is sometimes used to develop mystic sensitivity. There are many such points. Usually they are revealed to the yogi as he practices. As the saying goes subtle energy (prana) itself shows the way. But in addition, the association of yogis who stay with a yogi while he exercises, also gives inspiration for one to realize touch points. In the astral world these yogins are by the side of a yogi who earnestly endeavors.

upper teeth

tongue

lower teeth

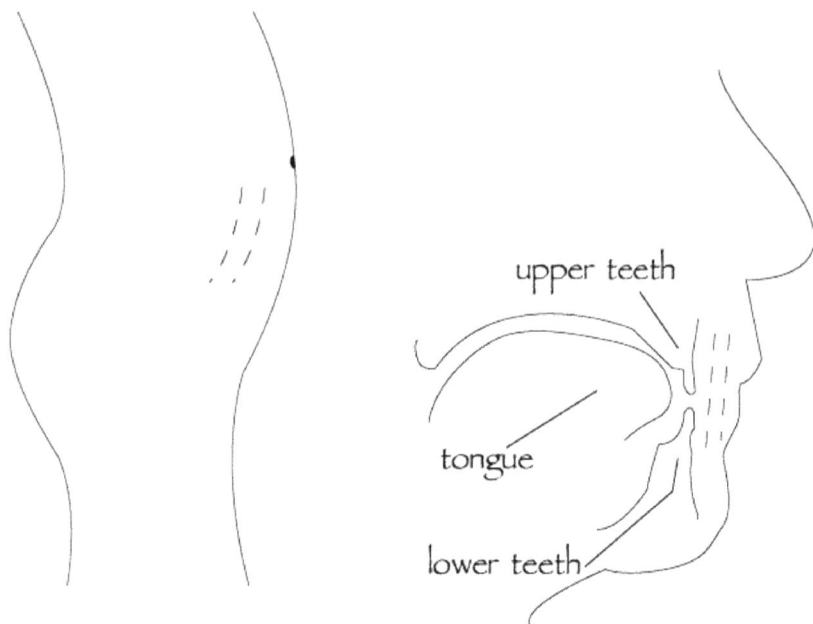

January 30, 2001

Babaji

A hands prop-up exercise

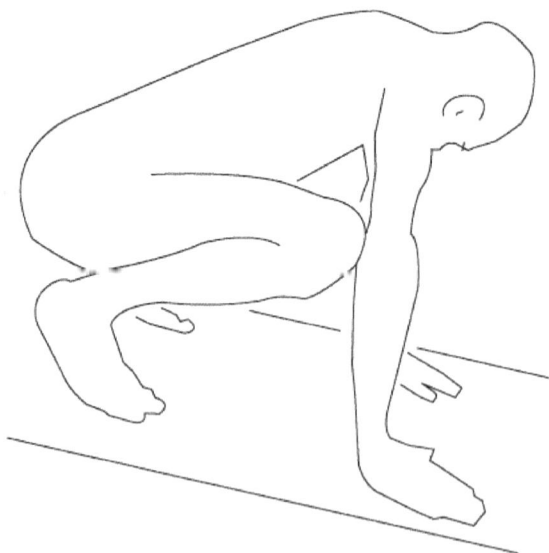

feet of ground - knees braced into elbows

Babaji gave a tongue-under-abdomen tube procedure. While this technique was revealed my subtle body was in the lotus posture. I did not take a notation of what posture by my gross body assumed.

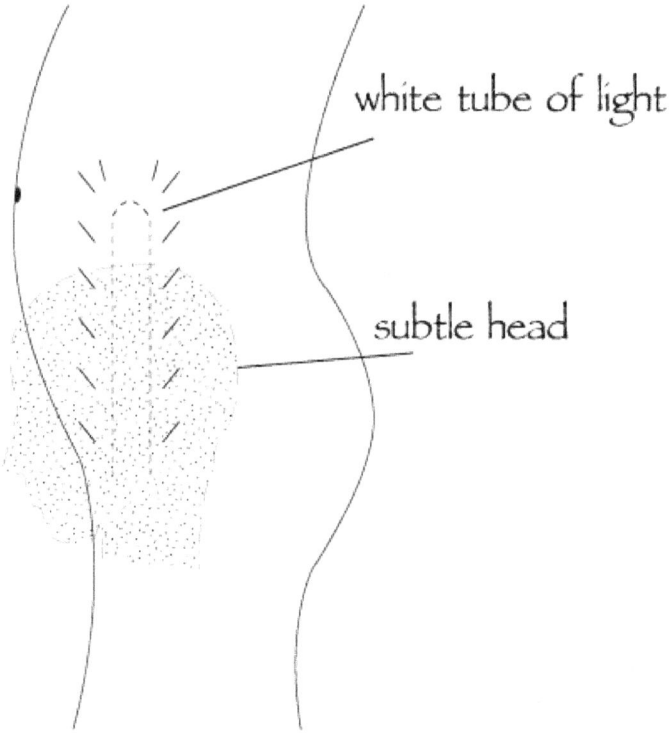

white tube of light

subtle head

physical body in lotus posture

While my subtle body was in lotus, doing this, Yogeshwarananda checked the tightness of the lotus. A loose lotus is not that good even though one may be unable to do a tight one. In the beginning. I had a tight lotus. Yogesh showed confidence in it. He checked my mind and intellect content to see if fears about doing the lotus were removed. These fears develop naturally in my psyche because I took birth in a non-yogic family.

Interestingly, the technique yogins, even though they may be from different lineages, do not bicker and fight over assisting someone. They gave assistance, and even work together to help an upcoming yogi. They agree that any disciple can have more than one teacher. They do not selfishly retain students.

Babaji

He wanted me to do the bow posture with special emphasis. This one is done by laying on the back and pushing up.

stretch here

push up here

The bow is a highly specialized posture. It may benefit one yogi in one way and another yogi in another manner, all depending on where emphasis of stretches are made. In this posture as the arrow in the diagram indicates, there was stress on the pubic area, especially the thigh-groin area. Usually this area is protected by the sex function. Thus it is very difficult to find a posture which can target this area. The body is designed in such a way as to protect this area from interference.

When doing the bow, one should be sure that the hands and feet have good traction on a non-slippery surface. If necessary one should dampen or dry the hands and feet to increase grip on the surface. When doing this or any posture, full interest should be given internally in order to get the full benefit.

February 2, 2001

Shiva

He advised that I hold no need-energies but rather release needs to the whole existence. He advised that I should see my psyche as a part of the cosmic apparatus such that any needs which become manifest, can easily pass through and not be held with attachment. He showed that the need-energies come in from the back of the causal cove chakra and pass through the front side of it into the subtle causal atmosphere.

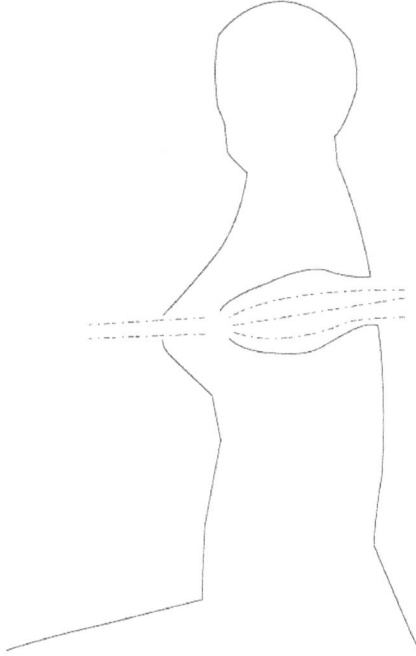

February 4, 2001

Babaji

Separation of front-kundalini channel from the navel.

This is achieved by doing thigh-foot rises with the proper diet and with a loss of sexual interest. When one masters this, one causes the front-kundalini to be separated from the navel orb. This separation indicates that one is free from food cravings.

direct channel
separated

navel Join-tube

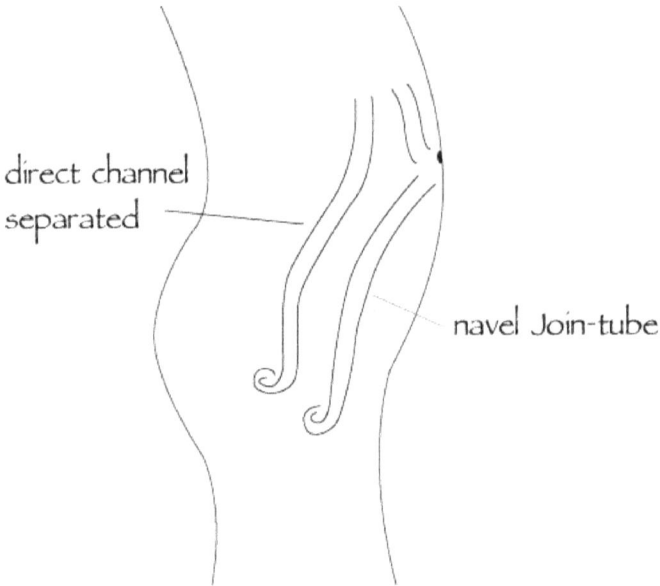

February 4, 2001

Shiva

He showed the movement of some atomic food nutrients, moving with sub-atomic food particles, moving down to the navel, then through the pubic belt. Food pranas are heavy subtle energies which one ingests when one eats physical foods. Some advanced yogis develop a siddhi or capability to live only on the subtle energy, even while using physical bodies. Their physical forms become very thin, as if it were a skeleton in a bag of skin. Their bodies stay alive because they extract gross energy from subtle food. The purpose of their doing this is to study the subtle and causal territories so that they can properly select which zones they desire to be in after their physical forms are discarded. Usually people misunderstand such yogis, feeling that they perform unusually terrible austerities with ulterior motives.

Even though in the history of yoga, there were persons with ulterior motives, still many yogins performed these horrific penances with good motives. The austerities are not terrible but they appear so to persons who are unfamiliar. Thus the misunderstandings about yoga and yogis continue.

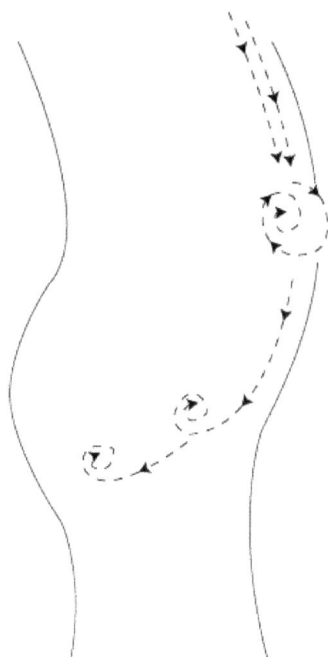

February 25, 2001

Babaji

He remarked, "By the grace of a more thorough hatha yoga, you can find this hidden place."

breathe air
into inner thighs

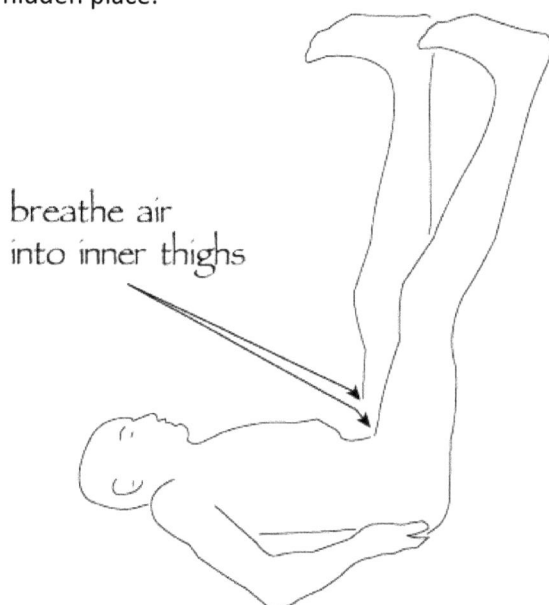

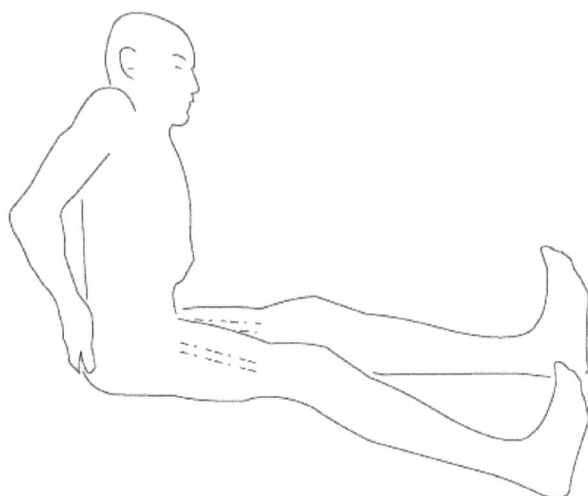

thighs subtle tubes (nadis)

February 2, 2001

Babaji

He showed a technique for blowing through holes in the energy-cleaned buttocks. The idea is a completely cleaned psyche from head to toe, especially cleaned in the navel, sexual and anal areas.

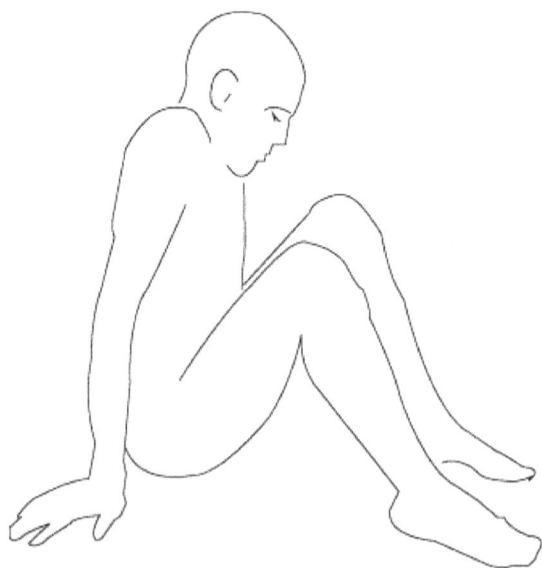

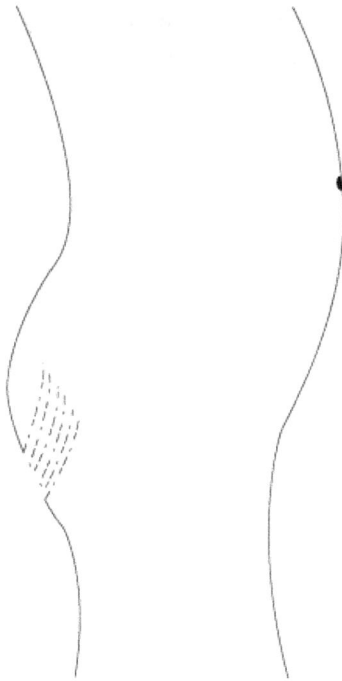

February 6, 2001

Babaji

A nerves-in-the-feet activation posture

This posture is also used to activate the nerves in the hand. Except for the brain, spine and genitals, proportionately the hands have many more subtle nerves than any other part of the body. The genital nerves are activated during sexual intercourse. They are a distraction. It is best to forego sexual involvement and the related pleasures.

The nerves in the feet are protected by the sexual impulse. Thus generally persons, even those who do yoga, do not exercise these nerves. By instinct for reproduction, one does not tamper with the nerves in the feet, legs, thighs and buttocks. But one naturally operates and stimulates the sexual nerves, since these promote sexual indulgence.

However, for success in yoga, a person should turn away from the reproduction capacity of the body. He should stimulate nerves which depress the reproductive system and bring on higher awareness. Some seekers should be involved with sexual indulgence while others should remove themselves from it. It is not that everyone who is attracted to technique yoga, must initially be celibate. It is not so. It depends on one's evolutionary development. Technique yoga does not encourage a person to avoid what is necessary for his development but it does better prepare him to face it and be responsible. No one can avoid mandatory sexual involvements and mandatory parental responsibilities, merely on the basis of doing technique yoga. A person who practices will be able to better gage errors and take courage for correction with a repentant and humble attitude.

For the complete energy cleansing of the subtle body from head to toe, Babaji encouraged the activation of the nerves in the feet. This is in preparation of full purity of the nadi tubes in the subtle body.

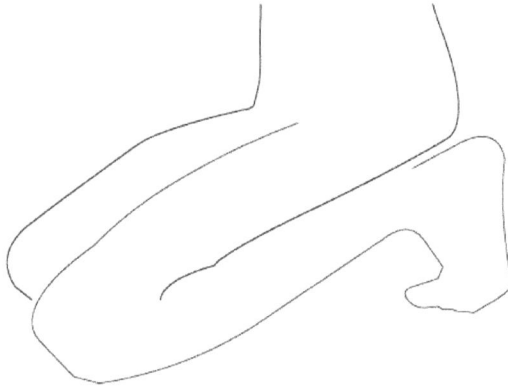

February 7, 2001

Shiva

He said, "Release that to the whole. See yourself as an errand-boy, a serf. You do not have the intelligence to figure these aspects. You are a dependent. Your expenses are serviced over your head by someone bigger. You are an infant."

Remark:

This advice is related to seeing myself as a nothing but with a servant mentality. My life is, anyway, part of the gamut of this existence, and a planned part at that, but not planned by me. Realization of this, makes my existence very easy. In technique yoga, we are required to make many adjustments for success. Most of my slow progression has to do with losing time while assisting others. If one runs with the tigers, one will stalk deer. And if one runs with the deer one will take to pastures and forests. It is like that. It hinges on association. Now that I am more in association with great yogis, I do not have time to be with humans. However out of a sense of responsibility, I record these experiences.

February 9, 2001

Babaji / Shiva

Babaji said, "The mind likes pain. It requires painful experience. Give it this pain daily and keep it functioning properly. Wean it from enjoying the pain of others. Hatha yoga is the classic way to allot its quota of pain. Do this by the stretches, otherwise by its nature, it will seek the pain of others, as a matter of routine. Then you will forego progression, and superficially and exploitatively display an interest in others."

February 11, 2001

Babaji

He said, "Begin to throw the tridents in that corner. Relieve yourself of their miseries."

He gave a foot breathing process to get rid of miseries which enter the psyche from the aura of others. Some extraneous miseries are removed by certain exercises.

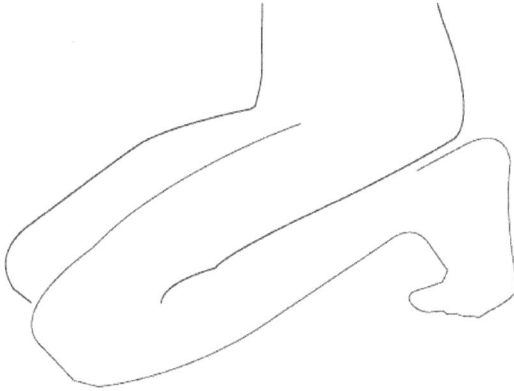

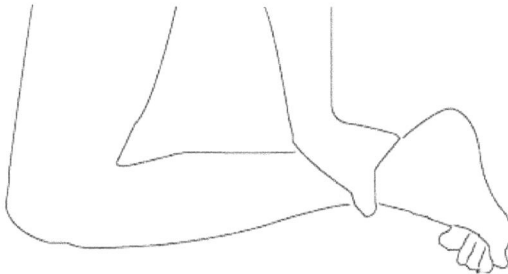

Shiva gave a complicated technique.

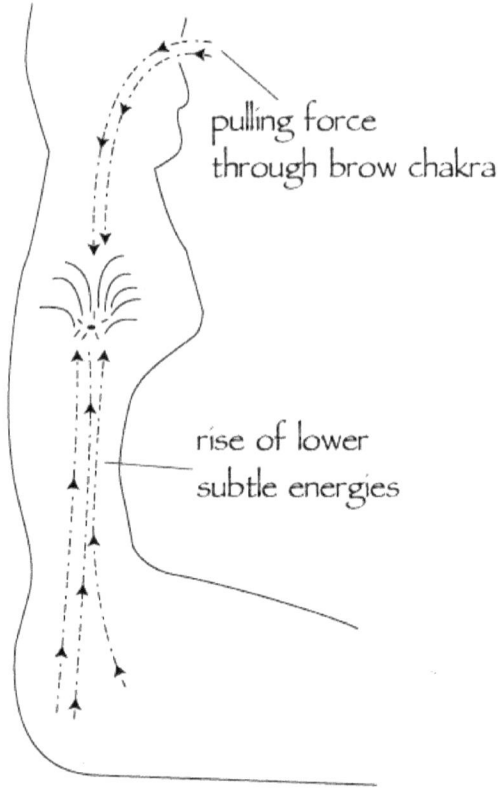

pulling force
through brow chakra

rise of lower
subtle energies

withdrawal of intellect, sense of identity
and core-self into causal cove

The process of throwing the tridents in the corner is performed at an advanced stage by those entities whose evolutionary level permits that they be excused from material existence. By advising me to discard the tridents, Babaji signaled that I should dissolve myself out of social existence. Persons like Babaji, Agastya. Vishvamitra, Skanda, Shuka, and Gambhiranath who used to be in India long ago as a foremost yogin, are persons who threw the tridents of misery. Others must keep inflicting self-misery.

When one throws all tridents in a corner. One is said to have become a Shiva, a person who is pacified and who assumed auspiciousness and exemption from liabilities.

A yogi like myself who is in the process of discarding the tridents, can just as well pick up such tridents again in this or in a future life. In fact there is no guarantee that I will not have to hold the tridents again and inflict self-injuries in the future. After all I am not in charge of this existence. However at the present time, I am relieved by the supernatural persons who are in charge.

February 13, 2001

Babaji

He showed the energies of the psyche operating without an input from the core-self. This is confirmed in the Bhagavad Gita, where Krishna explained that material nature is conducting everything in the mundane situation. This includes the subtle mundane universes as well. The cores are unable to act here. In the case of their participation, they are involved superficially, mostly due to their innate inattentiveness.

Their energies are harnessed by sensuality. The realization of this makes life easy for an advanced yogi but it does little for others. The advanced yogi's problems, his reformation and criticism of others, becomes nil once he understands that all subtle and gross operations are being conducted by material nature. This existence functions only within the potential of that nature.

On this day I asked Babaji a question because he seemed to be in a mood to answer an inquiry. I said, "Why is it that I have not seen Yogesh for some time?"

He replied, "He completed the austerities which were stopped on earth when he took disciples and spent time preaching for improved social conduct."

I remarked, "Thus only guys like you are free to stay with us continuously."

He replied, "Yes, and if you plan to complete the austerities, you too will have to isolate yourself in some hidden dimension later."

February 14, 2001

Babaji

I entered a transcendence zone in his presence. After my body was put in lotus, I lost track of it. It was as if it was not there. By Babaji's influence I began to feel a cone-shaped form which had light energy within it. From the top of it, a mystic smoke emitted.

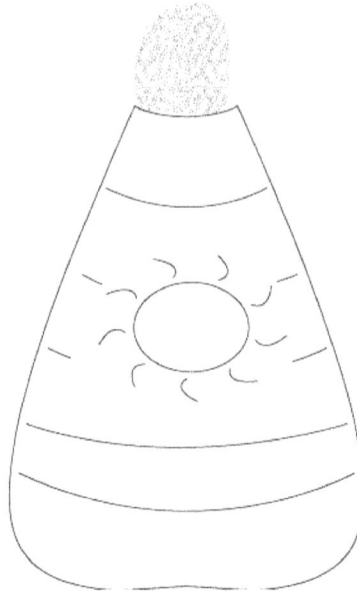

Feb 16, 2001

Shiva

He said, "To pursue the criminal behavior of others, the mind ignores its malice. Make the mind observe its faults. Then it will not have the appetite to pursue errors of others. When it errs it cancels out the feeling of wrong done by adopting a neutral attitude. This nullifies the conscience and permits the psyche to promote complications. Change this by focusing the mind on its faults."

February 16, 2001

Babaji

He taught a yoni technique.

Just as kechari psychic actions are used by males, yoni kriyas are used extensively by yoginis, female ascetics. For instance, the males try to do several exercises which are called kechari mudra, which means that they draw up semen into the spine or into the central and front kundalini passages. This is the effort to stop semen from being emitted through the penis.

In any case, some males practice female postures in order to purify the feminine capacity of their bodies. Some females practice special male postures, for the same reason.

This yoni mudra is a vaginal exercise for purifying the female sexual organ. Sometimes I get instruction from Goddess Durga about special postures and breath methods to curb the female capacity of my male body. Here is a diagram of what Babaji showed.

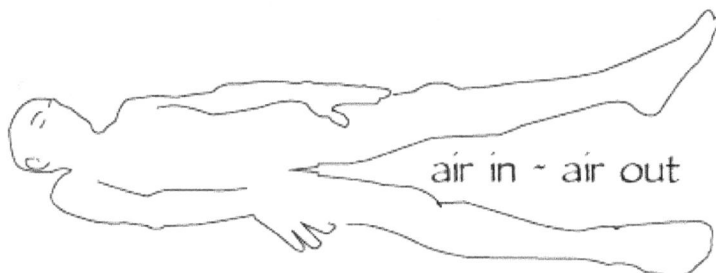

air in ~ air out

February 22, 2001

Babaji

On this day my relationship with Babaji was sealed since he freed me from having to be a figurehead yoga teacher. That is a burden I was permitted to put down. Once a few men asked me about becoming disciples, as to whether I would accept them as such. I said that being a disciple is a disciple's concern. It is not my interest.

If someone wants to be a disciple, he is welcomed, but that does not mean that I am obliged as his teacher or teacher-deity. He should form an obligation according to what he gets in my association. He should stick to whatever obligation he makes for himself. He may change or cancel the obligation at will. Kriya technique is a commitment to self-purification as authorized in the Bhagavad Gita, covered in verses 11 of chapter 5 and verse 12 of chapter 6. In essence it is a commitment to oneself.

I have little to do with disciples because I do not have the time to make myself available for honors. That lifestyle consumes time. I have sufficient time to complete my spiritual practice. If I were to stop to get honors and to make myself available so that crowds would adore, worship and formally respect me, I would hamper the development.

In any case, if anyone wants to be a disciple, the person has permission. Do all honoring, worshiping and respecting at a distance so that it does not interfere with my time. If however you need some instruction on how to perform yoga austerities, I am available. Study the books and cull information.

Babaji is the real guru, not me. Currently he uses a yoga-siddha subtle body. Such a person can be a guru in the full sense. Yogesh can be a real guru.

He lives in a subtle intellect organ and in the causal zone alternately. He does not enter into lower forms. He is worthy to be a guru.

Babaji permitted that I entrust all applicants to him. This allows me to continue as a student of the mahayogins without having to be distracted by accepting students. Still, as I said, if you feel that you want to be a disciple, create an obligation for yourself. Tell yourself that you are obliged to me in this or that way and see if you can live up to the commitment, otherwise I would help anyone who wants to learn about the austerities and about my obligations to the mahayogins at whose feet I sit as a student.

February 22, 2001

Babaji

He said, "Use the head stand for balance of energy. Use self-beneficial pain in postures to free the mind from whatever pain it needs, thus freeing it from the non-beneficial pain of others.

"Generally in small or short-duration transcendental absorptions a total balance of energies is·not required. In small absorptions, one may be located anywhere in the psyche where the pranic energies concentrate. That may be in an off-balanced position. However in larger or extended absorptions which involve a balancing of the energies of the entire psyche, there must be a resolution between the various types of subtle forces. The head stand and other postures gives one an instinctive understanding of how to balance the energies."

February 24, 2001

Babaji

He said, "Bring these together to reach the causal form."

Remark:

He referred to the brow chakra astral tubing and the subtle spine tubing (sushumna) and their related energies.

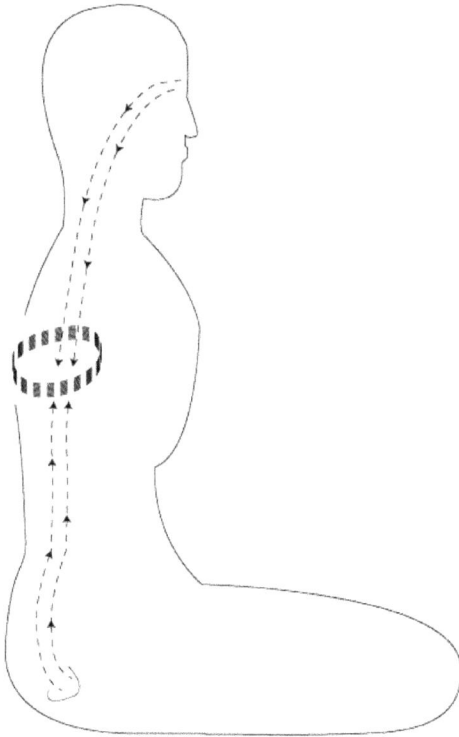

Do an intense exercise session with postures and breath-infusion combined or with postures prior to doing alternate breathing. It is essential that some breathing be done either during or immediately after postures. Old subtle energy must be cleared from the subtle body. Carbon dioxide must be cleared out of the physical system. The yogi may use any effective method. After this, one should sit in lose loose or full lotus. Loose lotus should be used by those students whose bodies are not limber. One should hold down the eyes with the fingers to visualize the brow chakra. This practice is called shanmukhi mudra.

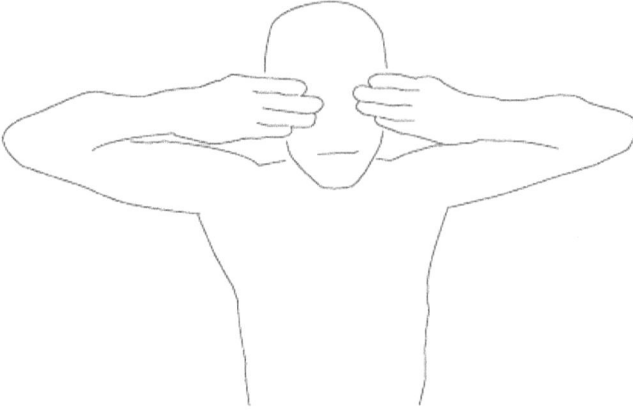

When holding down the eyes with the fingers, one should first squeeze down the eyelids then put the fingers on the squeezed eyelids as shown above. One should apply gentle pressure on the eyelids while doing this. Behind the closed eyes, one should then focus the vision in the center of tiny specks of light which are seen.

After a while, the lights should increase in brilliance becoming little specks of colored lights. After a little more time, the energy should form into circular patterns. These patterns may be intensified by focus and by doing rapid breathing.

As soon as the circular pattern is seen, one should concentrate simultaneously on the spinal energy and make an effort to move the two energies together to the causal cove area which is in the central chest region of the subtle form.

The circular pattern seen behind the closed eyes, when finger pressure is applied, is the configuration of the brow chakra. The colors of it, would change until it reaches a bright yellow color. In some circumstances of the practice, that color may disappear and a star may appear or it may just disappear and a black-blue space may appear.

February 26, 2001

Babaji

He said, "Repeatedly focus the mind on the inner pain in the stretches, to show the mind how it can find this pain in the body. This will free the mind from its desire to digest the pain of others. After some practice the mind will become habituated to finding pain within the psyche. This will develop into a sincere interest in self-development.

February 28, 2001

Yogeshwarananda

He said, "As an interest in the inner psyche, pratyahar sensual energy recognition and containment is a convergence of the various subtle energies in the psyche. The interest is shown by the intellect which is directed by the sense of identity, the ahankara, as prompted by the core-self, the atma. From this comes pranavision through a genuine effort to stop the external pursuits, particularly for nutritional and sexual forms.

"If there is cheating, there will not be full results. It means that the previous yogis who succeeded were favored by their sincere non-cheating practice. Failure is a directly related to cheating on the process."

Remark:

This instruction of Yogeshwarananda may be used by any yogi at any time.

February 29, 2001

Babaji

Sexual memory elimination procedure.

On this day he gave a sexual memory technique for getting rid of the constant tendency of the mind and intellect to invoke sexual thoughts and pictures. This is important for freedom from excitement. In the more advanced stages one must eliminate sexual memory circuits which occur involuntarily and which disturb the development of deep meditation and piercing supernatural vision.

One uses the lotus posture to do this. There are touch points in the mouth and brain but Babaji did not mention these. Thus it was sufficient for me to meditate on the area shown in the diagram.

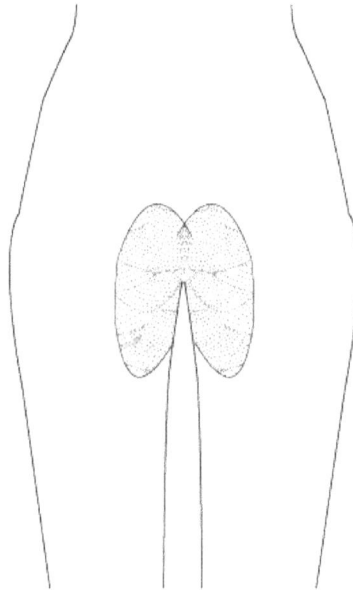

back of body

February 29, 2001

On this day by the grace of Shiva, there was a realization that one area is covered by the other. When an area becomes transparent, locations below it may be seen but seen though several transparencies of the previously cleared sectors. It is like seeing though several clear lenses or passing through several defogged zones.

There is a method of penetrating through each area and going to the level desired but that is attained by high mystic penetration. Usually one penetrates each layer just like a needle passing through several layers of cloth. All this can be visualized by pure reason but that is not yoga. This yoga is based on seeing by direct mystic perception though developed supernatural and spiritual vision. It is not based on believing or imagining.

One is required to perform the proper penance to develop the required means of perception. One must activate the siddhi perceptive abilities of the subtle body.

March 4, 2001

Yogeshwarananda

On this day, by his grace, because of his proximity and interest in my development and because at the time, he entered the brahmrandra of my subtle body, I got up early and began meditating.

This rising early before doing exercises and meditation, even before leaving the bed area, was an advice given to me by Shivananda some years ago. His idea is that when one gets a first wake-up urge, one should rise in bed, do only one or two spinal stretches and then sit up in lotus or half lotus to meditate. The spinal stretches should be one or two stretches which exercise the neck area under the brain. This opens up channels in the head and eliminates drowsiness. In the astral world, Shivananda mentioned this on three occasions. He swore by it as something that makes for a certain rapid advancement.

What happens is this: One gets a first wake-up urge but one usually disregards it and gets up about half hour or one hour later. Shivananda said that the first wake-up urge is important and that an hour or half of an hour of meditation at that time would contribute to advancement.

According to what he explained, a yogi should observe how consciousness increases in the body upon rising and how the intellect is activated in the body. He said that this is part of transcendence absorption preparation practice.

In any case, in my experience, this cannot be followed consistently if one does not rest early and also if one is not freed from personal or imposed anxieties.

On this morning Yogesh was present. I did the first-call meditation, as recommended by Shivananda. Subsequently I felt the intellect become stabilized. It pointed downward completely, down into the body, on the causal-cove.

Later in the year 2001, Yogesh gave some psychic actions as a practice for internalizing the intellect energies and for reaching the cosmic intellect.

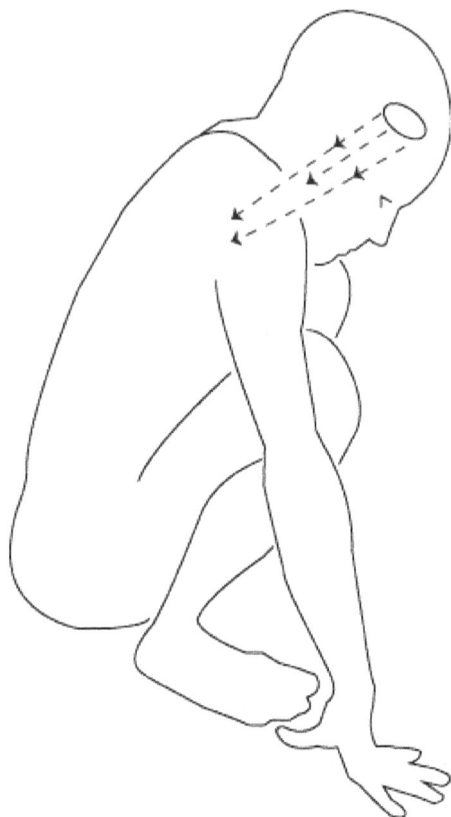

March 4, 2001

Babaji

On this day by his influence, I understood in practice (not in mental theoretical analysis), that one must be sincere to somehow stop the senses from sensual pursuits. In the long term, all interest in material existence eventually leads to a sexual attraction.

I tracked some lost subtle energy to a woman and her daughter whom I had to deal with on a job. The woman affected subtle energy in the back of my body. Her daughter affected subtle force in my testes. Neither one did this deliberately. It was done by the bio-emotional force in our bodies. By applying the sex lock, I stopped the energy leakage. The portion from the back stopped of its own accord.

In the case of the daughter however, due to the energy which was activated in the testes, there was a slight arousal or sexual enthusiasm in my body. An ancestor who lived in the girl's form, wanted her to be a mother. Since the girl's parents used contraceptives and did not want to beget children, the ancestor motivate the girl to encourage me to petition for a sexual intercourse.

In such cases, a man may have intercourse with a woman and then later the same day, or days after, the female may have intercourse with another man or with the husband. From the first intercourse a pregnancy may develop. The husband may assume that the child was derived from his semen, while in fact, it came from the fluids of another man.

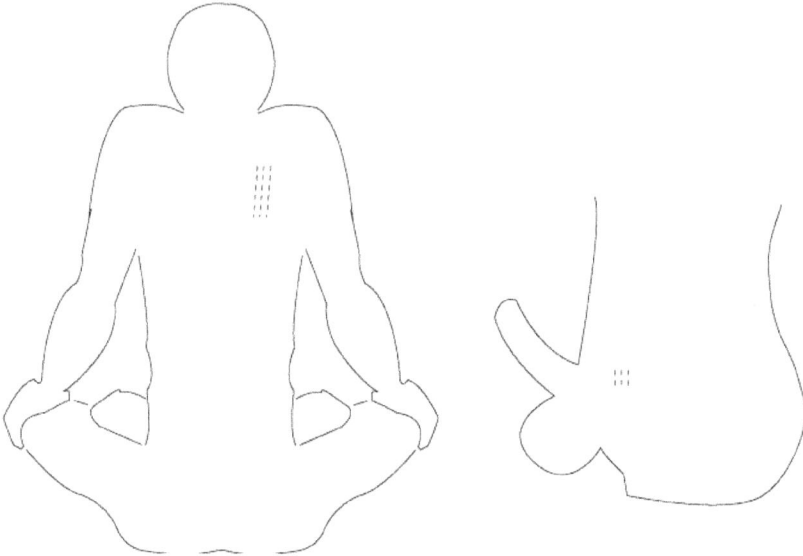

March 4, 2001

Babaji

He said, "Use that for the inner focus. It will be a great help."

Remark:

This remark was made while I worked on a wall for a man. The man hire me with intentions of working side by side with me. He did not have the expertise but he knew enough to be a helper. He hired me to supervise the work with himself as a worker.

After we began his wife, a young attractive woman with a figure like a gun trigger, came there in a tight sleeve-less sweater, and very short pants. Her sweater was so tight that her breasts were bulging out of it. Her pants were so short and tight that her buttocks were peeling through the bottom of it. She was all smiles and enjoying as she moved in and out between myself and her husband. She was having a good time. She was very sexual about it.

At the time, Babaji was in the atmosphere nearby. I do not think that he was there just to protect me but on some days, for one reason or the other, a great yogin may stay with me. On this day he made a remark which meant that I was not to consider the woman's sexuality as an annoyance but as an advantage to use technique focus. What Babaji meant was this: The presence of the sexually-excited woman would stimulate my intellect organ in certain areas of it that correspond to sexual arousal. I would then focus on those areas within the intellect.

In that way I would maintain some small absorptions and some pratyahar sensual withdrawal. This would be added to my practice. This way, the woman's sexually charged body would not be an impediment but would actually add to my practice. This would turn a harmful encounter into a positive celibate effort.

March 6, 2001

Yogeshwarananda

He said, "Whenever there is a blare intellect, it would externalize. Take it and direct it downwards into the body. Make it soothing. Then it will develop the proper interest as pratyahar sensual withdrawal.

"Increase meditation time. Develop steady posture."

Remark:

This was said while Yogesh was in my body in the top brahmrandra crown chakra. He advised that I re-read one of the books he published while he used his last human body. That book is titled, *Science of the Soul.*

The blare intellect is the intellect organ in the mood of seeing outward to be stimulated by subtle or gross items in the external world. This mood of the intellect destroys yoga practice but it sponsors cultural interactions in the material world.

March 6, 2001

Yogeshwarananda

He said, "You acted correctly by abandoning the quest to help others. Even I went around, feeling that I could assist nearly everyone. Most people used what is given for cultural advantage. Or they reject it half-heartedly. Your action is correct because they are powerless when compared to the acquired habits of the subtle body.

"The more you attend them, the less you attend your lessons, thus the result is your retardation. To see the potential of each student's subtle body and to figure the probability of the person's success in relation to the subtle form, and then to decide as to whether to assist or not, is the proper way to gage a person's eligibility for these techniques."

Remark:

Yogesh encouraged me in the decision to stop assisting so many persons who may approach for instructions in spiritual life. Instead of merely responding to the person's call for assistance, his idea is to assess their capacity to follow technique yoga in terms of the resistant tendencies which are in the subtle body.

I used to be interested also in teaching many of the other religious systems in so far as I was familiar with and had practiced any of them. However by the instruction of Shiva and Balarama, I stopped, except that now and again, as beckoned by providence, under dire pressure of time, I may explain and advise someone. Once when he saw me writing a commentary and explanation of Srimad Bhagavatam, Balarama objected and told me not to write in that particular tone, since He said that the system and authority under which I wrote was in deviance from the original way of the Bhagavatam austerities.

In the Srimad Bhagavatam, persons like Vyasa, attained perfection by yoga practice as the foundational austerity, but the system of authority under which I wrote at the time, disbanded and condemned the same yoga and in translations and commentary converted those austerities into devotional service or bhakti, which is also in the Bhagavatam process. Thus Balarama stopped me from the commentaries and explanations I did at the time. I had a bulk of writings which were to be published. Seeing his dislike I destroyed that commentary.

Later, Shiva called me aside and told me to stay very close to him and not to go following any wishy washy devotee of Krishna. Thus I was restricted in whom I could associate with. On the other hand my yoga practice became firm and my heart-felt desires for personal perfection became consistently realized, since I was told to sit at Shiva's lotus feet and be with the mahayogins who reside there. That assisted me, for there was no need for me to go to India, the Himalayas or anywhere else looking for advanced yoga teachers. From anywhere, any physical place, I could by mystic capability, see and talk to yogis on the subtle plane.

I used to want to associate with Krishna and Balarama, because of attraction to them but I usually found that somehow when I would approach Them, I would be located by Balarama. I would be near him for some time. Taking notice of me, He would always say, "Go to Mahadeva. Render service there. You are not of much use here."

Then I would find myself in the association of Shiva. This Shiva is known as Bhava. There is more than one Shiva. One has to know which one is which. In any case, due to this, I came to the lotus feet of Shiva, being placed here by Balarama.

There are many types of incentive religions. A person should see them for what they are, or he will remain in the neophyte phase hearing what he desires to hear and reading into scriptures what he desires to acquire from them. When one is beyond hypocrisy one can discover the path of definite advancement. One will become purified to the extent that one no longer fantasizes about an easy path.

People cannot be assisted easily. They are bound to the whole scan of mundane existence by actual and potential innate tendencies of the subtle body. Thus there are many false hopes given by teachers and embraced by disciples.

Index

Y, Z

About the Author

Michael Beloved (Yogi *Madhvāchārya)* took his current body in 1951 in Guyana. In 1965, while living in Trinidad, he instinctively began doing yoga postures and tried to make sense of the supernatural side of life.

Later in 1970, in the Philippines, he approached a Martial Arts Master named Arthur Beverford. He explained to the teacher that he was seeking a yoga instructor. Mr. Beverford identified himself as an advanced disciple of *Śrī* Rishi Singh Gherwal, an Ashtanga Yoga master.

Beverford taught the traditional Ashtanga Yoga with stress on postures, attentive breathing and brow chakra centering meditation. In 1972, Michael entered the Denver, Colorado Ashram of *kundalini* yoga Master *Śrī* Harbhajan Singh. There he took instruction in bhastrika pranayama and its application to yoga postures. He was supervised mostly by Yogi Bhajan's disciple named Prem Kaur.

In 1979 Michael formally entered the disciplic succession of the Brahmā - Madhava-Gaudiya Sampradaya through *Swāmī* Kirtanananda, who was a prominent sannyasi disciple of the Great Vaishnava Authority *Śrī Swāmī* Bhaktivedanta Prabhupada, the exponent of devotion to Sri Krishna.

However, yoga has a mystic side to it, thus Michael took training and teaching empowerment from several spiritual masters of different aspects of spiritual development. This is consistent with *Śrī* Krishna's advice to Arjuna in the *Bhagavad Gītā*:

Most of the instructions Michael received were given in the astral world. On that side of existence, his most prominent teachers were *Śrī Swāmī* Shivananda of Rishikesh, Yogiraj *Swāmī* Vishnudevananda, *Śrī Bābāji Mahasaya* - the master of the masters of *Kriyā* Yoga, *Śrīla* Yogeshwarananda of Gangotri - the master of the masters of *Rāj* Yoga (spiritual clarity), and Siddha *Swāmī* Nityananda the Brahmā Yoga authority.

The course for kundalini yoga using pranayama breath-infusion was detailed by Michael in the book *Kundalini Hatha Yoga Pradipika*. This current book was composed from meditation and breath-infusion notes which were originally shared in staple bound booklets as Yoga Journals.

Michael's preliminary books relating to this topic are *Meditation Pictorial*, *Meditation Expertise*, and *Meditation ~ Sense Faculty* (co-author). Every technique (kriya) mentioned was tested by him during pranayama breath-infusion and samyama deep meditation practice.

This is a result of over forty years of meditation practice with astute subtle observations intending to share the methods and experiences. The information is published freely with no intention of forming an institution or hogtying anyone as a disciple.

Publications

English Series

Bhagavad Gita English

Anu Gita English

Markandeya Samasya English

Yoga Sutras English

Hatha Yoga Pradipika English

Uddhava Gita English

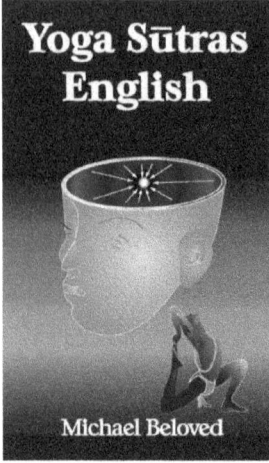

Yoga Sūtras English — Michael Beloved

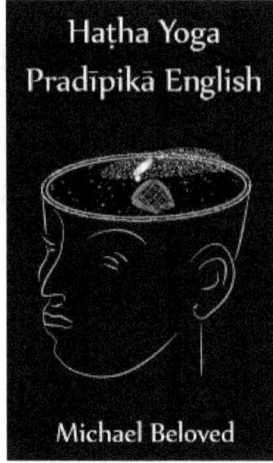

Haṭha Yoga Pradīpikā English — Michael Beloved

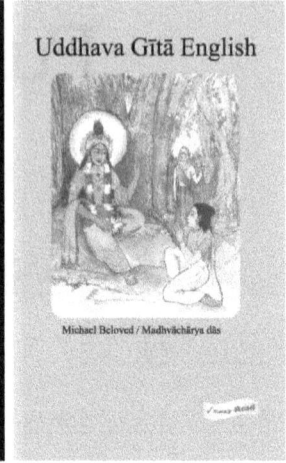

Uddhava Gītā English — Michael Beloved / Madhvāchārya dās

These are in 21st Century English, very precise and exacting. Many Sanskrit words which were considered untranslatable into a Western language are rendered in precise, expressive and modern English.

Three of these books are instructions from Krishna. **In Bhagavad Gita English** and **Anu Gita English**, the instructions were for Arjuna. In the **Uddhava Gita English,** it was for Uddhava. Bhagavad Gita and Anu Gita are extracted from the Mahabharata. Uddhava Gita was extracted from the 11th Canto of the Srimad Bhagavatam (Bhagavata Purana). One of these books, the **Markandeya Samasya English** is about Krishna, as described by Yogi Markandeya, who survived the cosmic collapse and reached a divine child in whose transcendental body, the collapsed world was existing.

Two of this series are the syllabus about yoga practice. The Yoga Sutras of Patanjali is elaboration about ashtanga yoga. Hatha Yoga Pradipika English, is the detailed information about asana postures, pranayama breath- infusion, energy compression, naad sound resonance and advanced meditation. The Sanskrit author is Swatmarama Mahayogin.

My suggestion is that you read **Bhagavad Gita English**, the **Anu Gita English**, the **Markandeya Samasya English**, the **Yoga Sutras English**, the **Hatha Yoga Pradipika** and lastly the **Uddhava Gita English**, which is complicated and detailed.

For each of these books we have at least one commentary, which is published separately. Thus your particular interest can be researched further in the commentaries.

The smallest of these commentaries and perhaps the simplest is the one for the Anu Gita. We published its commentary as the _Anu Gita Explained_. The

Bhagavad Gita explanations were published in three distinct targeted commentaries. The first is <u>Bhagavad Gita Explained</u>, which sheds lights on how people in the time of Krishna and Arjuna regarded the information and applied it. Bhagavad Gita is an exposition of the application of yoga practice to cultural activities, which is known in the Sanskrit language as karma yoga.

Interestingly, Bhagavad Gita was spoken on a battlefield just before one of the greatest battles in the ancient world. A warrior, Arjuna, lost his wits and had no idea that he could apply his training in yoga to political dealings. Krishna, his charioteer, lectured on the spur of the moment to give Arjuna the skill of using yoga proficiency in cultural dealings including how to deal with corrupt officials on a battlefield.

The second Gita commentary is the <u>Kriya Yoga Bhagavad Gita</u>. This clears the air about Krishna's information on the science of kriya yoga, showing that its techniques are clearly described for anyone who takes the time to read Bhagavad Gita. Kriya yoga concerns the battlefield which is the psyche of the living being. The internal war and the mental and emotional forces which are hostile to self-realization are dealt with in the kriya yoga practice.

The third commentary is the <u>Brahma Yoga Bhagavad Gita</u>. This shows what Krishna had to say outright and what he hinted about which concerns the brahma yoga practice, a mystic process for those who mastered kriya yoga.

*There is one commentary for the **Markandeya Samasya English**. The title of that publication is <u>Krishna Cosmic Body</u>.*

There are two commentaries to the Yoga Sutras. One is the <u>Yoga Sutras of Patanjali</u> and the other is the <u>Meditation Expertise</u>. These give detailed explanations of ashtanga Yoga.

The commentary of Hatha Yoga Pradipika is titled <u>Kundalini Hatha Yoga Pradipika</u>.

For the Uddhava Gita, we published the <u>Uddhava Gita Explained</u>. This is a large book and requires concentration and study for integration of the information. Of the books which deal with transcendental topics, my opinion is that the discourse between Krishna and Uddhava has the complete information about the realities in existence. This book is the one which removes massive existential ignorance.

Meditation Series

Meditation Pictorial

Meditation Expertise

Core-Self Discovery

Meditation Sense Faculty

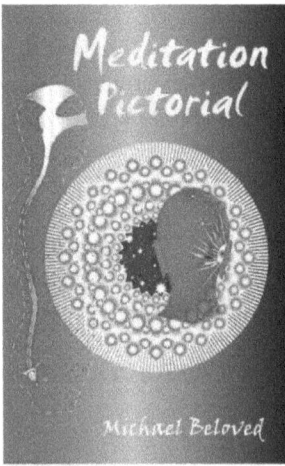

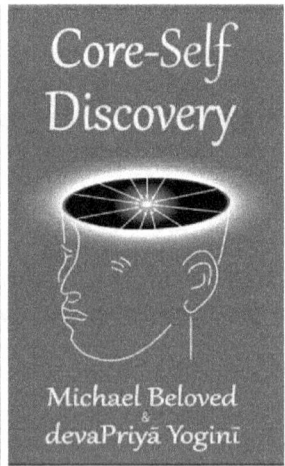

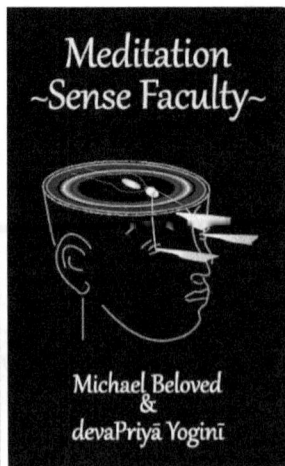

The specialty of these books is the mind diagrams which profusely illustrate what is written. This shows exactly what one has to do mentally to develop and then sustain a meditation practice.

In the **Meditation Pictorial**, one is shown how to develop psychic insight, a feature without which meditation is imagination and visualization, without any mystic experience per se.

In the **Meditation Expertise**, one is shown how to corral one's practice to bring it in line with the classic syllabus of yoga which Patanjali lays out as the ashtanga yoga eight-staged practice.

In **Core-Self Discovery**, (co-authored with devaPriya Yogini) one is taken though the course of pratyahar sensual energy withdrawal which is the 5th stage of yoga in the Patanjali ashtanga eight-process complete system of yoga practice. These events lead to the discovery of a core-self which is surrounded by psychic organs in the head of the subtle body. This product has a DVD component.

Meditation ~ Sense Faculty (co-authored with devaPriya Yogini) is a detailed tutorial with profuse diagrams showing what actions to take in the subtle body to investigate the senses faculties. The meditator must first establish the location and function of the observing self. That self must be screened from the thoughts and ideas which usually hypnotize it.

These books are profusely illustrated with mind diagrams showing the components of psychic consciousness and the inner design of the subtle body.

Explained Series

Bhagavad Gita Explained

Uddhava Gita Explained

Anu Gita Explained

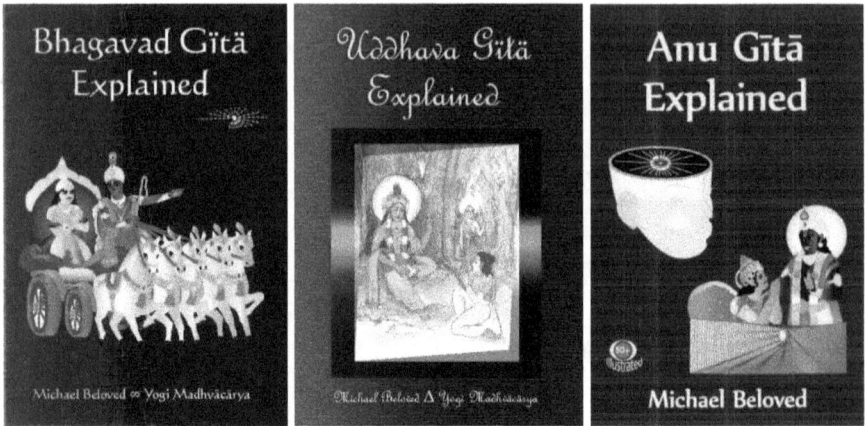

Bhagavad Gītā Explained — Michael Beloved ∞ Yogi Madhvācārya

Uddhava Gītā Explained — Michael Beloved ∆ Yogi Madhvācārya

Anu Gītā Explained — Michael Beloved

The specialty of these books is that they are free of missionary intentions, cult tactics and philosophical distortion. Instead of using these books to add credence to a philosophy, meditation process, belief or plea for followers, I spread the information out so that a reader can look through this literature and freely take or leave anything as desired.

When Krishna stressed himself as God, I stated that. When Krishna laid no claims for supremacy, I showed that. The reader is left to form an independent opinion about the validity of the information and the credibility of Krishna.

There is a difference in the discourse with Arjuna in the Bhagavad Gita and the one with Uddhava in the Uddhava Gita. In fact these two books may appear to contradict each other. In the Bhagavad Gita, Krishna pressured Arjuna to complete social duties. In the Uddhava Gita, Krishna insisted that Uddhava should abandon the same.

The Anu Gita is not as popular as the Bhagavad Gita but it is the conclusion of that text. Anu means what is to follow, what proceeds. In this discourse, an anxious Arjuna request that Krishna should repeat the Bhagavad Gita and again show His supernatural and divine forms.

However Krishna refuses to do so and chastises Arjuna for being a disappointment in forgetting what was revealed. Krishna then cited a celestial yogi, a near-perfected being, who explained the process of transmigration in vivid detail.

Commentaries

Yoga Sutras of Patanjali

Meditation Expertise

Krishna Cosmic Body

Anu Gita Explained

Bhagavad Gita Explained

Kriya Yoga Bhagavad Gita

Brahma Yoga Bhagavad Gita

Uddhava Gita Explained

Kundalini Hatha Yoga Pradipika

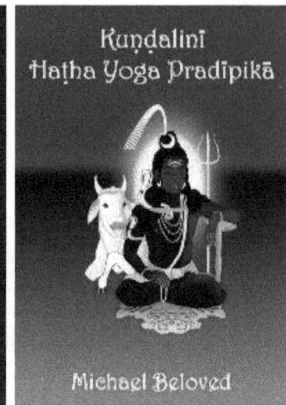

Yoga Sutras of Patanjali is the globally acclaimed text book of yoga. This has detailed expositions of yoga techniques. Many kriya techniques are vividly described in the commentary.

Meditation Expertise is an analysis and application of the Yoga Sutras. This book is loaded with illustrations and has detailed explanations of secretive advanced meditation techniques which are called kriyas in the Sanskrit language.

Krishna Cosmic Body is a narrative commentary on the Markandeya Samasya portion of the Aranyaka Parva of the Mahabharata. This is the detailed description of the dissolution of the world, as experienced by the great yogin Markandeya who transcended the cosmic deity, Brahma, and reached Brahma's source who is the divine infant, Krishna.

Anu Gita Explained is a detailed explanation of how we endure many material bodies in the course of transmigrating through various life-forms. This is a discourse between Krishna and Arjuna. Arjuna requested of Krishna a display of the Universal Form and a repeat narration of the Bhagavad Gita but Krishna declined and explained what a siddha perfected being told the Yadu family about the sequence of existences one endures and the systematic flow of those lives at the convenience of material nature.

Bhagavad Gita Explained shows what was said in the Gita without religious overtones and sectarian biases.

Kriya Yoga Bhagavad Gita shows the instructions for those who are doing kriya yoga.

Brahma Yoga Bhagavad Gita shows the instructions for those who are doing brahma yoga.

Uddhava Gita Explained shows the instructions to Uddhava which are more advanced than the ones given to Arjuna.

Bhagavad Gita is an instruction for applying the expertise of yoga in the cultural field. This is why the process taught to Arjuna is called karma yoga which means karma + yoga or cultural activities done with yogic insight.

Uddhava Gita is an instruction for apply the expertise of yoga to attaining spiritual status. This is why it is explains jnana yoga and bhakti yoga in detail. Jnana yoga is using mystic skill for knowing the spiritual part of existence. Bhakti yoga is for developing affectionate relationships with divine beings.

Karma yoga is for negotiating the social concerns in the material world. It is inferior to bhakti yoga which concerns negotiating the social concerns in the spiritual world.

This world has a social environment. The spiritual world has one too.

Currently, Uddhava Gita is the most advanced and informative spiritual book on the planet. There is nothing anywhere which is superior to it or which goes into so much detail as it. It verified that historically Krishna is the most advanced human being to ever have left literary instructions on this planet. Even Patanjali Yoga Sutras which I translated and gave an application for in my book, **Meditation Expertise**, does not go as far as the Uddhava Gita.

Some of the information of these two books is identical but while the Yoga Sutras are concerned with the personal spiritual emancipation (kaivalyam) of the individual spirits, the Uddhava Gita explains that and also explains the situations in the spiritual universes.

Bhagavad Gita is from the Mahabharata *which is the history of the Pandavas. Arjuna, the student of the Gita, is one of the Pandavas brothers. He was in a social hassle and did not know how to apply yoga expertise to solve it. On the battlefield, Krishna gave him a crash-course on yogic social interactions.*

Uddhava Gita is from the Srimad Bhagavatam (Bhagavata Purana), *which is a history of the incarnations of Krishna. Uddhava was a relative of Krishna. He was concerned about the situation of the deaths of many of his relatives but Krishna diverted Uddhava's attention to the practice of yoga for the purpose of successfully migrating to the spiritual environment.*

***Kundalini Hatha Yoga Pradipika** is the commentary for the Hatha Yoga Pradipika of Swatmarama Mahayogin. This is the detailed process about asana posture, pranayama breath-infusion, complex compressions of energy, naad sound resonance intonement and advanced meditation practice.*

This is the singular book with all the techniques of how to reform and redesign the subtle body so that it does not have the tendency for physical life forms and for it to attain the status of a siddha.

These books are based on the author's experiences in meditation, yoga practice and participation in spiritual groups:

Specialty

Spiritual Master

sex you!

Sleep Paralysis

Astral Projection

Masturbation Psychic Details

Spiritual Master

sex you!

Sleep Paralysis

Michael Beloved

michael beloved

Michael Beloved

Astral Projection

Masturbation Psychic Details

Michael Beloved

Michael Beloved

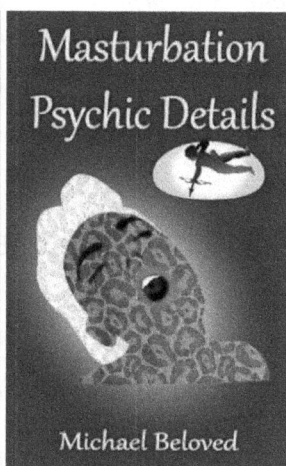

In **Spiritual Master**, Michael draws from experience with gurus or with their senior students. His contact with astral gurus is rated. He walks you through the avenue of gurus showing what you should do and what you should not do, so as to gain proficiency in whatever area of spirituality the guru has proficiency.

sex you! is a masterpiece about the adventures of an individual spirit's passage through the parents' psyches. The conversion of a departed soul into a sexual urge is described. The transit from the afterlife to residency in the emotions of the parents is detailed. This is about sex and you. Learn about how much of you comprises the romantic energy of your would-be parents!

Sleep Paralysis clears misconceptions so that one can see what sleep paralysis is and what frightening astral experience occurs while the paralysis is being experienced. This disempowerment has great value in giving you confidence that you can and do exist even if you are unable to operate the physical body. The implication is that one can exist apart from and will survive the loss of the material form.

Astral Projection details experiences Michael had even in childhood, where he assumed incorrectly that everyone was astrally conversant. He discusses the life force psychic mechanism which operates the sleep-wake cycle of the physical form, and which budgets energy into the separated astral form which determines if the individual will have dream recall or no objective awareness during the projections. Astral travel happens on every occasion when the physical body sleeps. What is missing in awareness is the observer status while the astral body is separated.

Masturbation Psychic Details is a surprise presentation which relates what happens on the psychic plane during a masturbation event. This does not tackle moral issues or even addictions but shows the involvement of memory and the sure but hidden subconscious mind which operates many features of the psyche irrespective of the desire or approval of the self-conscious personality.

inVision Series

Yoga inVision 1

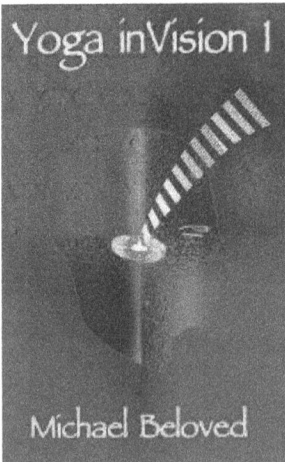

Yoga inVision 1, the first in this series, describes the breath infusion and meditation practices during the years of 1998 and 1999. There are unique, once in a lifetime as well as recurring insights which are elaborated. inFocus during breath infusion and the meditation which follows is an adventure for any yogi. This gives what happened to this particular ascetic.

Online Resources

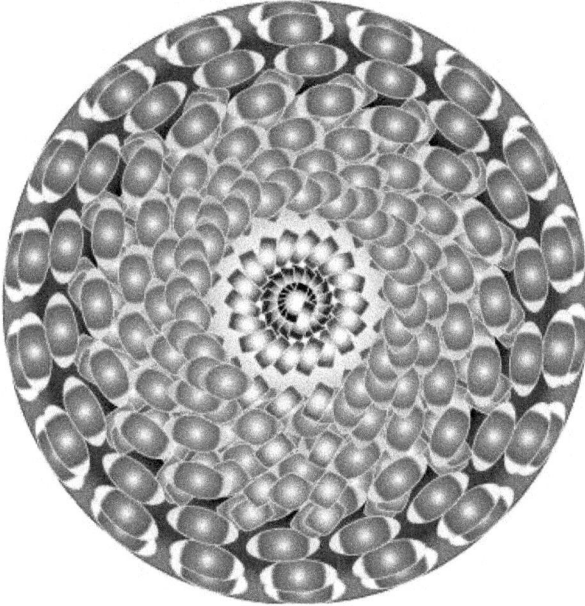

Email:	**michaelbelovedbooks@gmail.com**
	axisnexus@gmail.com
Website:	michaelbeloved.com
Forum:	inselfyoga.com
Posters:	zazzle.com/inself

www.ingramcontent.com/pod-product-compliance
Lightning Source LLC
Chambersburg PA
CBHW070039110426
42741CB00036B/2866